150+ Crochet Borders

Edgings & Decorative Finishes for Every Project

Bernadette Baldelli

Quarto.com

First Published in 2026 by Quarry Books, an imprint of The Quarto Group,
100 Cummings Center, Suite 265-D, Beverly, MA 01915, USA.
T (978) 282-9590 F (978) 283-2742

This translation of *Bordures au crochet* first published in France is published in arrangement with Cat on a Book Agency, France.

EEA Representation, WTS Tax d.o.o.,
Žanova ulica 3, 4000 Kranj, Slovenia.
www.wts-tax.si

Quarry Books titles are also available at discount for retail, wholesale, promotional, and bulk purchase. For details, contact the Special Sales Manager by email at specialsales@quarto.com or by mail at The Quarto Group, Attn: Special Sales Manager, 100 Cummings Center, Suite 265-D, Beverly, MA 01915, USA.

10 9 8 7 6 5 4 3 2 1

ISBN: 978-0-7603-9976-7

Digital edition published in 2026
eISBN: 978-0-7603-9977-4

Page Layout: John Hall Design Group

Printed in Guangdong, China TT092025

CONTENTS

BORDERS INSPIRED BY

ABBREVIATIONS

ch(s)	chain(s)	*hdc*	half double crochet	*sl st(s)*	slip stitch(es)
col	color	*pic*	ch-3 picot	*st(s)*	stitch(es)
dc	double crochet	*rnd*	round	*tr*	treble crochet
dtr	double treble crochet	*sc*	single crochet		

BEGINNING A ROW

To begin the work, make a slip knot on the hook followed by the number of chains indicated.

After the initial starting chain, the first stitch of each row is replaced by a specific number of chains; these chains replace the first stitch to obtain the required stitch height.

It is common to work an additional chain when these starting chains become part of multiple treble crochets or double treble crochets worked in the same space.

WORKING BACK AND FORTH IN ROWS

Crochet is generally worked back and forth in rows. Rows are crocheted from right to left. At the end of the row the work is turned, and the next row is crocheted from right to left. Diagrams, however, are read from right to left and left to right. Odd number rows are usually read from right to left and even number rows from left to right unless otherwise specified.

Certain borders in this book are crocheted with the right side always (or almost always) facing, and this will be reflected in the instructions. On the diagrams, you will find a marker to indicate the beginning of each row, in the color to be used. In these cases, the diagram will be read from right to left for all rows.

WORKING IN THE ROUND

Make a starting chain of as many chains as instructed and close it with a slip stitch in the first chain. In the resulting ring, make the number of chains required to obtain the height needed for the stitch used (this will be specified). End the round with a slip stitch in the indicated starting chain.

If the work consists of double crochets, you will make 3 chains to start (these starting chains replace the first double crochet and bring the work to their height), and you will end the round with a slip stitch in the third starting chain.

HOW TO CHANGE COLORS

Color changes generally occur at the end of the row but can also occur within the row: Make the last yarn over of the last stitch (single crochet, half double crochet, double crochet, or treble crochet) with the next color. The loop on the hook is in the new color.

THE IMPORTANCE OF A GAUGE SWATCH

Before you begin, it is recommended that you make a gauge swatch with the yarn and hook you want to use. Making a swatch or sample length of edging allows you to calculate the length of your border based on your actual gauge (stitch and row length).

ASTERISKS * AND PARENTHESES ( )

These symbols indicate a repeat. Instructions for the motif are written between the * and must be repeated across the row. The ( ) indicate a number of stitches to be crocheted, often in the same stitch, or a repetition of stitches to be crocheted as many times as indicated.

WORKING IN MULTIPLE PARTS

Some borders consist of two or more parts. Motifs are crocheted one after the other and assembled with a slip stitch or attached to the border in the starting chain of the support strip. When you do this, make sure each motif is positioned with its right side facing. The progression of the work is explained in the instructions, with steps identified on the diagram.

HIDING THE YARN

When you begin a row with a new color, or if you change color within a row, hide the yarn ends in the work over 1 inch (2.5 cm) by working your stitches over them. When alternating between two colors in a row and to avoid cutting the yarn each time, carry the yarn on the previous row and work your stitches over it.

CROCHET JACQUARD

Change color at the last yarn over of the stitch that precedes the color change and drop the yarn behind the work to be picked back up when needed.

WEAVING ENDS IN

Using a tapestry needle and with the wrong side facing, hide yarn ends inside the stitches.

HOW TO USE THIS BOOK

In this book you'll discover a world of inspiration from different cities around the globe. From the lively colors of New Orleans to the intricate elegance of Paris, these designs are bursting with personality and cultural flair. Whether you're drawn to bold geometrics, delicate lacework, or playful picot trims, each border invites you to travel through texture and color without ever leaving the comfort of your favorite crafting chair. Patterns are grouped by city, making it easy to find the right vibe for your project. With clear instructions and stitch diagrams, you'll be inspired to mix, match, and make your crochet projects truly unforgettable.

Borders can be created independently and then sewn onto garments, home decor, or other accessories. For more advanced makers, you can adapt these borders to be worked as edges directly into existing patterns. Add a bit of whimsy to the hem of your next crocheted sweater or a playful trim to a crocheted baby blanket. There are 150+ borders here to inspire you!

BORDER 1

DIFFICULTY *

COLORS: (A) Olive Green; (B) Light Green; (C) Brown

STITCHES USED: Slip stitch (sl st) • chain (ch) • single crochet (sc) • ch-3 picot (pic)

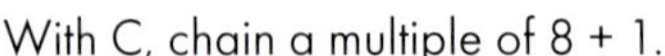

With C, chain a multiple of 8 + 1.

Row 1: Ch 1, sl st across. Ch 1 to turn.

Row 2: *(Sc, ch 3, sc) in next st, ch 3, skip 3, (sc, ch 6, sc) in next, ch 3, skip 3*. Repeat from * to *. End with (sc, ch 3, sc) in last. Fasten off.

Row 3 (A): Insert hook in last ch-3 space of previous row, *(sc, ch 6, sc, ch 3) in ch-3 space, (sc, ch 3, sc, ch 3) in ch-6 space*. Repeat from * to *. End with (sc, ch 6, sc) in last ch-3 space. Fasten off.

Row 4 (B): Insert hook in first ch-6 space of previous row, *(sc, ch 3, sc, ch 3) in ch-6 space, (sc, ch 6, sc, ch 3) in ch-3 space*. Repeat from * to *. End with (sc, ch 3, sc) in last ch-6 space. Fasten off.

Row 5 (C): Repeat Row 3. Fasten off.

Row 6 (A): Repeat Row 4. Fasten off.

Row 7 (B): Repeat Row 3. Fasten off.

Row 8 (C): Insert hook in first ch-6 space from previous row, *(sc, ch 3, sc, ch 3) in ch-6 space, (sc, pic, sc, ch 3) in ch-3 space*. Repeat from * to *. End with (sc, ch 3, sc) in last ch-6 space. Fasten off.

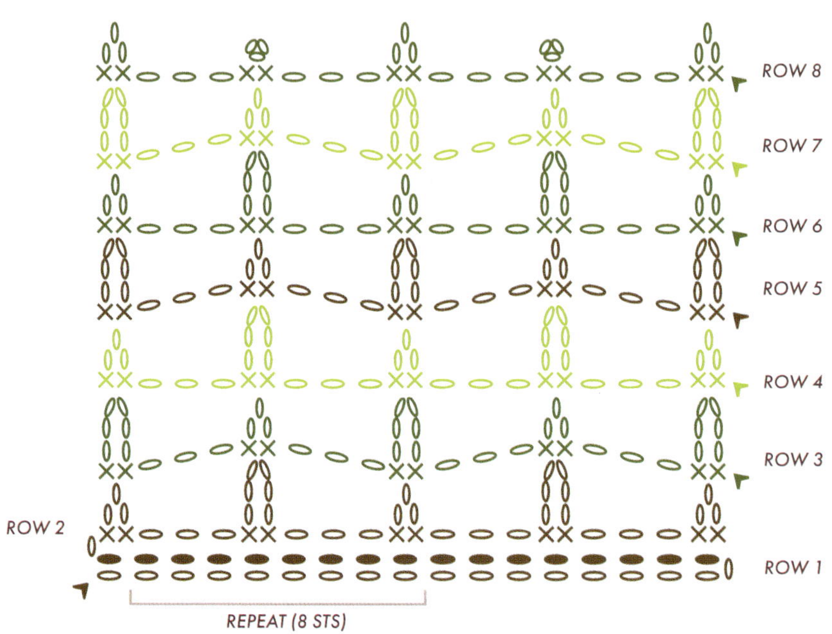

BORDER 2

DIFFICULTY *

COLORS: (A) Olive Green; (B) Light Green; (C) Brown

STITCHES USED: Slip stitch (sl st) • chain (ch) • single crochet (sc) • ch-3 picot (pic)

Worked with right side always facing.

With A, chain a multiple of 4 + 1 turning chain.

Row 1: Sc across. Fasten off.

Row 2 (C): Sl st across. Fasten off.

Row 3 (B): Sl st across. Fasten off.

Row 4 (C): Sl st across. Fasten off.

Row 5 (A): Sl st in first, *(sc, pic) in next, sl st in next—changing to B, (sc, pic) in next, sl st in next—changing to next col*. Repeat from * to *. Fasten off.

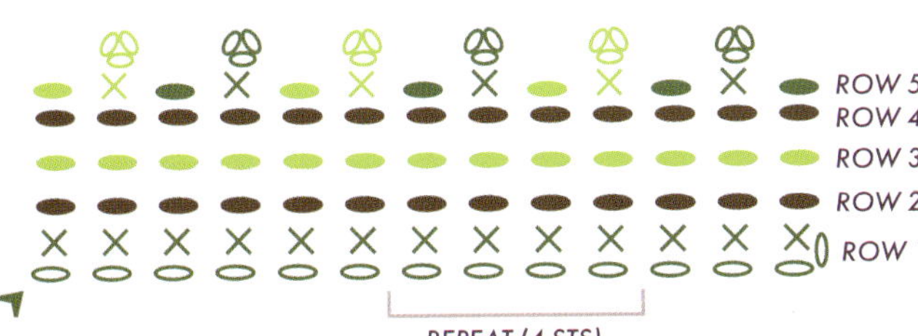

BORDER 3

DIFFICULTY *

COLORS: (A) Light Green; (B) Brown

STITCHES USED: Slip stitch (sl st) • chain (ch) • single crochet (sc) • ch-3 picot (pic)

Worked with right side always facing.

With B, chain a multiple of 6 + 1.

Row 1: Ch 1, sl st across. Fasten off.

Row 2 (A): In first st make *(sc, pic), ch 2, ch 5, sl st in first of 5 chs, ch 2, skip 5 sts*. Repeat from * to *. End with (sc, pic) in last. Fasten off.

BORDER 4

DIFFICULTY **

COLORS: (A) Olive Green; (B) Brown; (C) Red; (D) Grey

STITCHES USED: Chain (ch) • single crochet (sc) • half double crochet (hdc) • double crochet (dc) • treble crochet (tr) • ch-3 picot (pic)

With C, chain a multiple of 6 + 1.

Row 1: Ch 1, sc across. Fasten off.

Row 2 (D): Insert hook in first st, *sc, ch 3, skip 2, 2 hdc closed together in next st, ch 3, skip 2*. Repeat from * to *. End with sc in last. Fasten off.

Row 3 (A): Insert hook in first st, ch 5 (to replace tr), 2 tr closed together in top of hdc-group, pic, *ch 5, 2 unfinished tr in same hdc-group, skip 3 chs, unfinished tr in next sc, skip 3 chs, 2 unfinished tr in next hdc-group, close these 5 tr together, pic*. Repeat from * to *. End with ch 5, 2 unfinished tr in same hdc-group, skip 3 chs, unfinished tr in last sc, close these 3 tr together, pic. Fasten off.

Row 4 (B): Insert hook behind first pic and pull up a loop, sc in same st, *ch 2, skip 2 chs, 3 dc in next ch, ch 2, skip 2 chs, sc behind next pic*. Repeat from * to *. Fasten off.

Row 5 (C): Insert hook in first pic of Row 3 and pull up a loop, *sc in pic, ch 3, (sc, ch 2, sc, ch 3) in central dc of next dc-group*. Repeat from * to *. End with sc in last Row 3 pic. Fasten off.

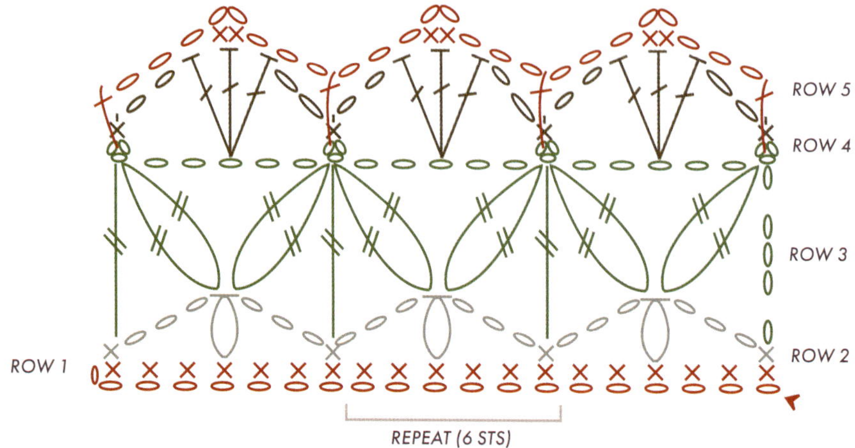

BORDER 5

DIFFICULTY ***

COLORS: (A) Olive Green; (B) Light Green; (C) Brown; (D) Red

STITCHES USED: Chain (ch) • single crochet (sc) • half double crochet (hdc) • double crochet (dc) • back post treble crochet (BPtr) • ch-3 picot (pic)

Worked with right side always facing.

With B, chain a multiple of 6 + 1.

Row 1: Ch 1, sc across. Fasten off.

Row 2 (B): Pivot work to crochet on opposite side of starting chain, ch 3 (to replace dc), *ch 2, skip 2 chs, dc in next ch*. Repeat from * to *. Fasten off.

Row 3 (C): Insert hook right after the starting ch-3 from previous row and pull up a loop, ch 3, pic, then hdc in front of ch-3 just made, *ch 2, skip 2 chs, sc in next dc, ch 2, skip 2 chs, hdc after next dc, pic, hdc before same dc*. Repeat from * to *. Fasten off.

Row 4 (D): Turn edging to work with right side of Row 1 facing; insert hook in first st and pull up a loop, sc in same st, *ch 3, skip 2 sc, BPtr around dc from Row 2, ch 3, skip 2 sc, sc in next sc*. Repeat from * to *. Fasten off.

Row 5 (A): Insert hook in first st and pull up a loop, sc in same st, *ch 3, skip 3 chs, 2 crossed sc separated by a pic around tr, ch 3, skip 3 chs, 2 crossed sc around next sc*. Repeat from * to *. Fasten off.

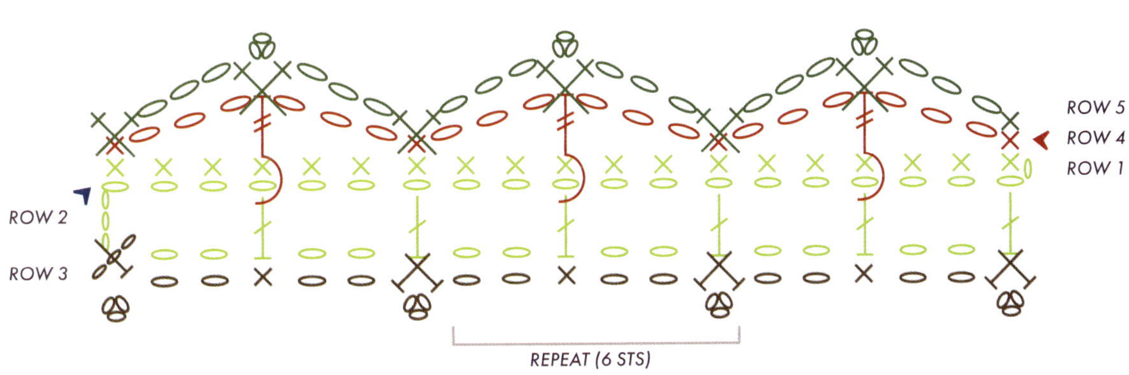

BORDER 6

DIFFICULTY ***

COLORS: (A) Olive Green; (B) Light Green; (C) Brown; (D) Red; (E) Grey

STITCHES USED: Slip stitch (sl st) • chain (ch) • single crochet (sc) • half double crochet (hdc) • double crochet (dc) • treble crochet (tr) • ch-3 picot (pic)

Worked with right side always facing.

With E, chain a multiple of 6 + 1 turning chain.

Row 1: Sc in next 2, *(sc, ch 10, sc) in next, sc in next 5*. Repeat from * to *. End with sc in last 3. Fasten off.

Row 2 (D): Insert hook in turning ch, ch 3 (to replace first dc), 2 dc closed together in first st, *ch 3, skip 2 sc, sc in next ch-10 space, ch 3, skip 2 sc, 3 dc closed together in next sc*. Repeat from * to *. Fasten off.

Row 3 (B): Sc in top of dc-group, *ch 3, skip 3 chs, 2 hdc closed together in sc, ch 3, skip 3 chs, sc in next dc-group*. Repeat from * to *. Fasten off.

Row 4 (A): Insert hook in first st, ch 3, long tr in ch-10 space from Row 1, *ch 3, 3 dc closed together in top of hdc-group, ch 3, long tr in same ch-10 space from Row 1, ch 1, long tr in next ch-10 space from Row 1*. Repeat from * to *. End with tr in last sc. Fasten off.

Row 5 (E): Insert hook in first st, ch 3, pic, dc in same space as starting chs, skip 3 chs, *sl st in top of next dc-group, skip 3 chs, (dc, pic) 3x in next ch, dc in same ch*. Repeat from * to *. End with (dc, pic, dc) in last st. Fasten off.

Row 6 (A): Now working on opposite side of starting ch with right side facing; insert hook in first st and pull up a loop, sc in same st, *ch 3, skip 2 chs, 2 dc closed together in next ch, ch 3, skip 2 chs, sc in next ch*. Repeat from * to *. Fasten off.

Row 7 (C): Insert hook in first st and pull up a loop, (sc, pic) in same st, *2 sc in next ch-3 space, pic in top of next dc-group, 2 sc in next ch-3 space, pic in next sc*. Repeat from * to *. End with (sc, pic) in last. Fasten off.

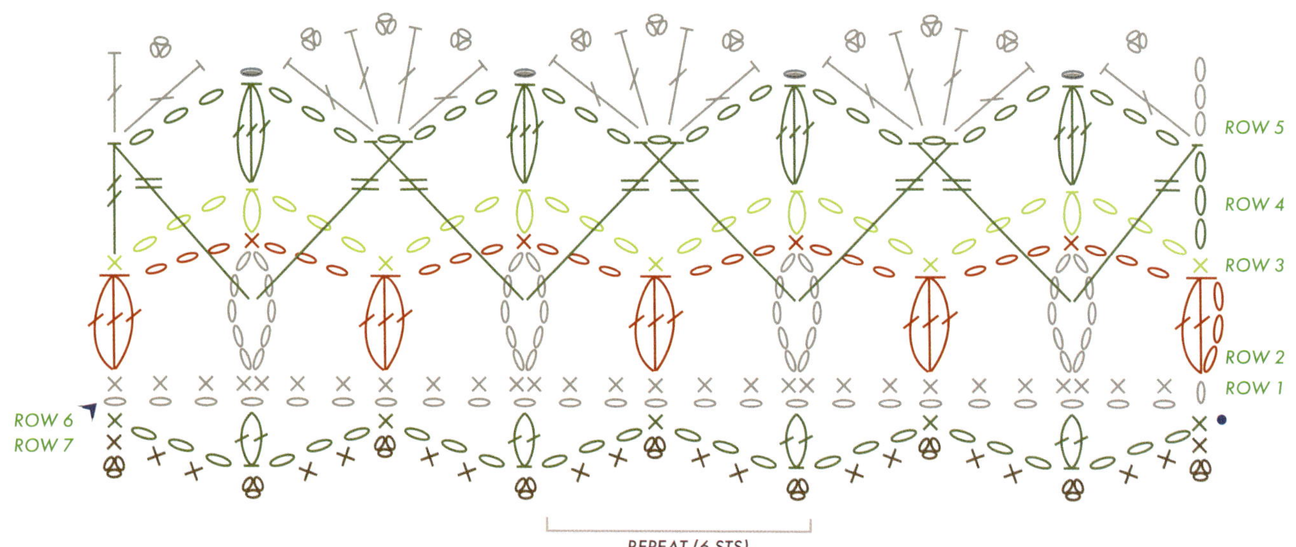

BORDER 7

DIFFICULTY **

COLORS: (A) Pink; (B) Yellow

STITCHES USED: Slip stitch (sl st) • chain (ch) • single crochet (sc) • half double crochet (hdc) • double crochet (dc) • treble crochet (tr) • ch-3 picot (pic)

With B, chain a multiple of 8 + 1.

Row 1: Ch 1, (sc, hdc) in each ch across. Fasten off.

Row 2 (A): With right side facing, (hdc, sc) in each hdc across. Fasten off.

Row 3 (B): With right side facing, (sc, hdc) in each hdc across. Fasten off.

Now work the fans separately, starting each one by working into Row 3.

Row 4 (B): Insert hook in tenth stitch and pull up a loop, *ch 3 (to replace first dc), 4 dc in same space, turn.

Row 5: Ch 3 (to replace first dc), dc in first st, dc in next, 5 dc in next, dc in next, 2 dc in last, turn.

Row 6: Ch 1, sc in first dc, skip next dc, 5 dc in next, sc in central dc of next dc-group, skip 2 dc, 5 dc in next dc, sc in last dc, turn.

Row 7: Sl st in first 3 dc, ch 1, 5 dc in next sc, ch 1, sl st in last 3 dc. Fasten off.*

Skip 16 sts and, starting from Row 4, repeat from * to *.

Row 8 (A): With right side facing, insert hook in first st and pull up a loop, ch 4 (to replace first tr), *2 tr closed together in same st, sl st in first sl st from previous row, [sl st in next, pic, sl st in next] twice, sl st in next, [sl st in next, pic, sl st in next] 3x, sl st in next, skip 8 sts from Row 3*, repeat from * to * beginning with 3 tr closed together. End with 3 tr closed together in last. Fasten off.

BORDER 8

DIFFICULTY ***

COLOR: Pink

STITCHES USED: Slip stitch (sl st) • chain (ch) • single crochet (sc) • crab stitch (single crochet worked from left to right)

Crocheted progressively to desired length with the right side always facing.

Step 1: Ch 3, ch 5, sl st in sixth ch from hook.

Step 2: 12 sc in ring just made, sl st to close. Repeat from the beginning. End with 2 chs. Fasten off.

Finish with one row of crab stitch across. Fasten off.

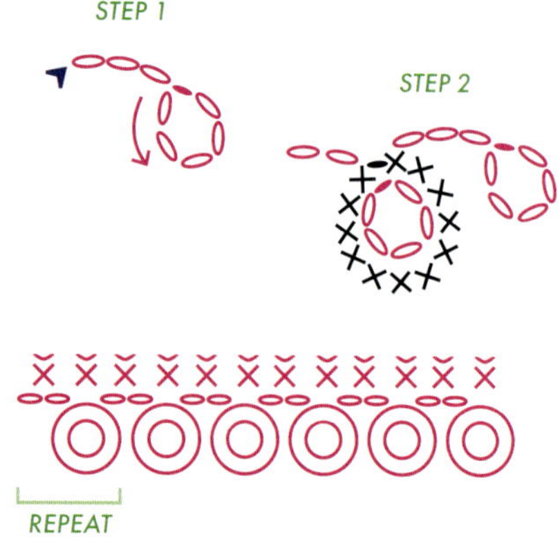

BORDER 9

DIFFICULTY **

COLORS: (A) Pink; (B) Turquoise Blue; (C) Yellow; (D) Ochre

STITCHES USED: Slip stitch (sl st) • chain (ch) • single crochet (sc) • double crochet (dc) • treble crochet (tr) • ch-3 picot (pic)

Worked in the round with right side always facing.

Crocheted progressively to desired length, with Rnd 1 as the base.

Crochet the motifs following the instructions below, alternating between A and C for the center of the motif.

With A or C, ch 5.

Rnd 1: Ch 3 (to replace first dc), 3 dc in fourth ch from hook, dc in next 3, 7 dc in next; continue working around the starting chain: dc in next 3, 3 dc in next, sl st in 3rd starting ch to close the rnd. (20 dc, counting starting ch-3). Fasten off.

Rnd 2 (D): Insert hook under sl st and pull up a loop, sc in each dc of Rnd 1. End with a sl st to close the rnd. Fasten off.

Rnd 3 (B): Insert hook in first sc and pull up a loop, ch 4 (to replace first tr), ch 1, (tr, ch 1, tr) in same sc, ch 1, (tr, ch 1, tr) in next sc, [ch 1, tr in next st, ch 1 (tr, ch 1, tr) in next st] 4x, (ch 1, tr) 3x in next st, ch 1, (tr, ch 1, tr) in next st, [ch 1, tr in next st, ch 1, (tr, ch 1, tr) in next st] 4x, ch 1, sl st in fourth starting ch to close the rnd. Fasten off.

Rnd 4 (D): Insert hook under sl st and pull up a loop, sc in first ch, pic, *sc in next tr, sc in next ch, pic*. Repeat from * to *. End with sl st in first st. Fasten off.

Attach motifs over 4 outer pics by making a sl st in the previous motif's pic (see diagram) to replace the pic's second chain. There are 13 free pics at the top and bottom of the motif, between each connection.

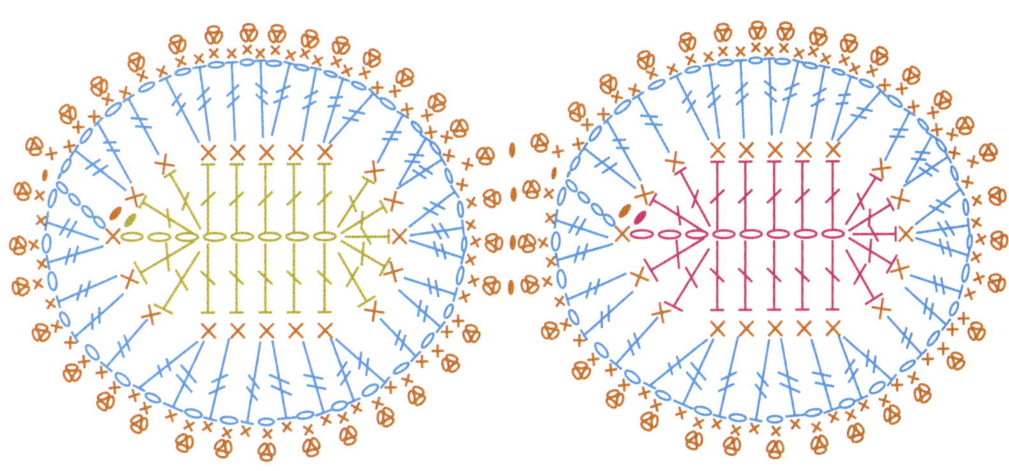

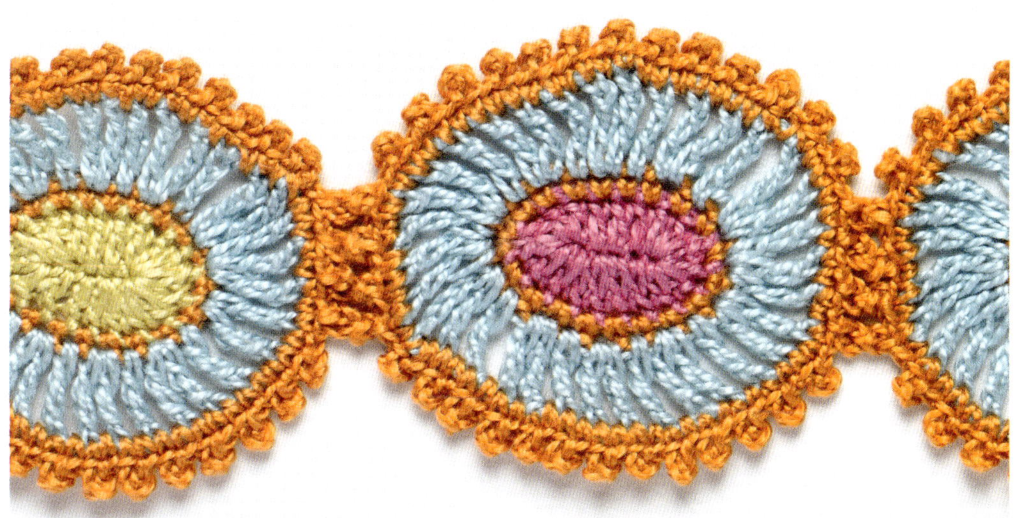

BORDER 10

DIFFICULTY ****

COLORS: (A) Pink; (B) Turquoise Blue; (C) Yellow

STITCHES USED: Slip stitch (sl st) • chain (ch) • single crochet (sc) • double crochet (dc) • treble crochet (tr) • ch-3 picot (pic)

Worked with right side always facing. Crocheted progressively to desired length, with Row 1 as the base.

With B, crochet as many motifs as required for desired length.

Row 1: *Ch 5, 5 tr closed together in first ch, tassel (ch 12, 2 tr closed together in fifth ch from hook), ch 5, sl st in next 6 chs, sc in last ch*. Repeat from * to *. End with ch 5, 5 tr closed together in fifth ch from hook. Fasten off.

Row 2 (C): Insert hook at base of first st of Row 1 and pull up a loop, ch 3, *ch 3, sl st in center of last tr of tr-group from Row 1, ch 2, 5 tr closed together in first of 3 chs, ch 2*. Repeat from * to *, progressively connecting the motifs (tr-groups) across. End with dc at the end of Row 1. Fasten off.

Row 3 (C): Insert hook at base of first st of Row 2 and pull up a loop, ch 5 (to replace first tr), 2 tr closed together in same space, *ch 2, dc in center of last tr of tr-group from Row 2, ch 2, 5 tr closed together in ch-2 space*. Repeat from * to *. End with 3 tr closed together in last dc. Fasten off.

Row 4 (A): Insert hook in first tr-group of Row 3 and pull up a loop, sc in same space, *ch 3, dc in ch before and dc in ch after next dc, closing these 2 dc together, pic, ch 3, sc in next tr-group*. Repeat from * to *. Fasten off.

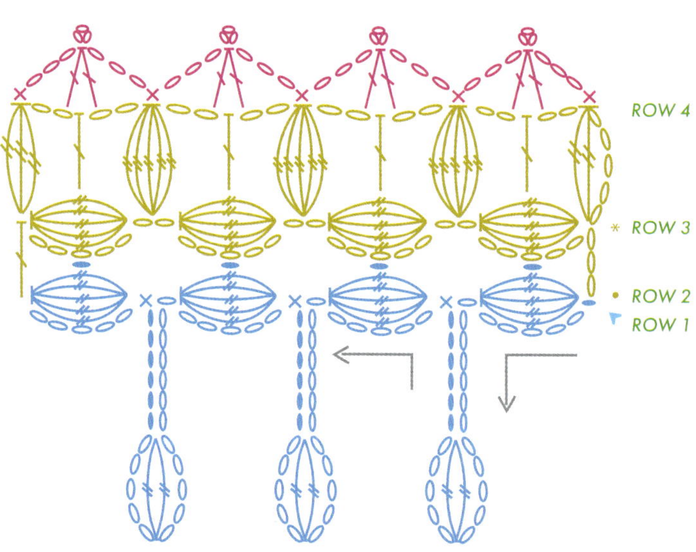

BORDER 11

DIFFICULTY **

COLORS: (A) Pink; (B) Turquoise Blue; (C) Ochre

STITCHES USED: Slip stitch (sl st) • chain (ch) • single crochet (sc) • double crochet (dc) • treble crochet (tr) • double treble crochet (dtr) • pic A (ch 3, sl st in first ch) • pic B (ch 5, sl st in first ch)

With B, chain a multiple of 6 + 1.

Row 1: Ch 1, sc in each ch across. Turn.

Row 2: Insert hook in first st, ch 3 (to replace first dc), 2 dc closed together in same st, pic A, *ch 2, skip 2, dc in next, ch 2, skip 2, 3 dc closed together in next, pic A*. Repeat from * to *. Fasten off.

Row 3 (A): Working on opposite side of starting chain, under last group of dc closed together, *ch 5, begin 2 tr in same space as chs, skip 5, begin 2 tr in next, close all 4 tr together, pic A, ch 5, sl st in same st as last 2 tr*. Repeat from * to *. Fasten off.

Row 4 (A): Insert hook in same st as first tr-group of Row 3 and pull up a loop, ch 6, in first pic A close 2 tr together, ch 5, sl st in same pic A, *ch 5, begin 2 tr in same pic A, begin 2 tr in next pic, close all 4 tr together, ch 5, sl st in same pic A as last 2 tr*. Repeat from * to *. End with ch 5, 2 tr closed together in same pic A, dtr in last st. Fasten off.

Row 5 (C): Insert hook in first st, sc in same st, *ch 2, pic A, ch 2, pic B, ch 2, pic A, ch 2, sc between next 2 petals*. Repeat from * to *. End with sc in last. Fasten off.

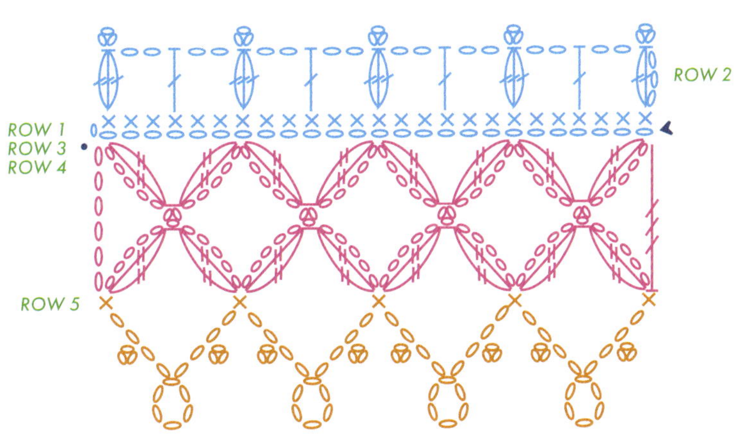

BORDER 12

DIFFICULTY ****

COLORS: (A) Pink; (B) Turquoise Blue; (C) Yellow; (D) Ochre

STITCHES USED: Slip stitch (sl st) • chain (ch) • single crochet (sc) • half double crochet (hdc) • double crochet (dc) • treble (tr) • ch-3 picot (pic)

Worked with right side always facing.

Step 1: To begin the support strip with D, chain a multiple of 6 + 1.

Row 1: *Ch 1, sc, ch 5, sl st in sc just made, sc in next 5*. Repeat from * to *. End with sc, ch 5, sl st in sc just made. Fasten off.

Row 2 (B): Now working on opposite side of starting chain, insert hook in first st and pull up a loop, *sc, pic, sc in next 2*. Repeat from * to *. End with sc, pic in last. Fasten off.

Step 2: Make the motifs separately and attach them to the edging. With A or C, ch 5, sl st to close ring. Fasten off.

Rnd 1: Insert hook in last st from previous rnd and pull up a loop, ch 2 (to replace first hdc) then, working in ring, 3 hdc, 3 dc, 3 tr, 3 dc, 3 hdc. End with sl st in top of starting ch. Fasten off.

Rnd 2 (D): Insert hook in last st from previous rnd and pull up a loop, [sc in next 2, 2 sc in next] 5x. End with sc in last, sl st in first st.

Rnd 3: Insert hook in last st from previous rnd and pull up a loop, ch 3 (to replace first dc), join motif to Row 2 with sl st in second ch-5 space (subsequent motifs will be joined in every other ch-5 space), dc in same space, (dc, hdc) in next, hdc in next 2, ch 1, [hdc in next, ch 1] twice, [dc in next, ch 1) 7x, skip 1, dc in next, ch 1, [hdc, ch 1] twice, hdc in next 2, (hdc, dc) in next. End with sl st in top of starting chain.

Step 3: Attach motif to edging with sc in third ch of ch-5 space from Row 1, being careful to attach motifs with their right side facing.

Row 4 (B): Insert hook in first ch-5 ring and pull up a loop, sc in third ch of ring, pic, *ch 5, working in motif edge, sc in ninth st, [sc in next ch, pic in next dc] 8x, sc in next 2, ch 5, sc in third ch of next ring, pic*. Repeat from * to *. Fasten off.

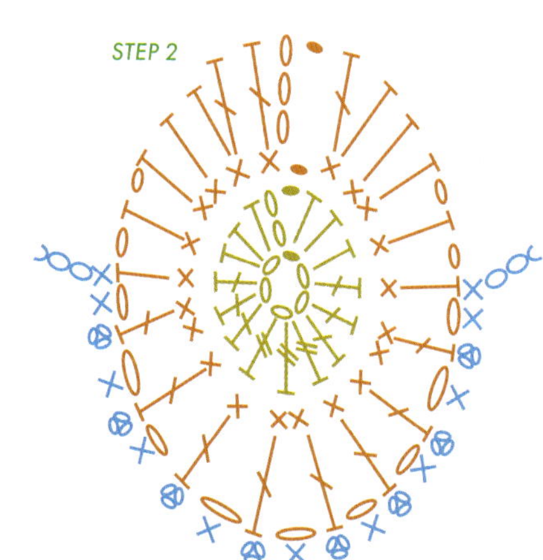

BORDER 13

DIFFICULTY **

COLORS: (A) Deep Purple; (B) Wisteria; (C) Powder Pink

STITCHES USED: Slip stitch (sl st) • chain (ch) • treble crochet (tr)

Worked with right side always facing.

This edging consists of a central motif and two lateral motifs.

Row 1 (A): Ch 1, *ch 5, 2 tr closed together in first of 5 chs, ch 1*. Repeat from * to * to desired length. Fasten off.

Row 2 (B): Insert hook in last st from Row 1 and pull up a loop, *ch 5, 2 tr closed together in first ch from Row 1, 2 sl sts in top of next tr, sl st in first ch made between motifs*. Repeat from * to *. Fasten off.

Row 3 (C): Insert hook in first st from Row 1, work as per Row 2. Fasten off.

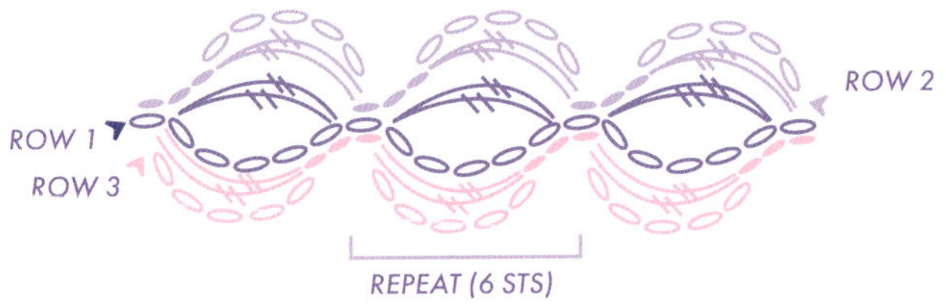

BORDER 14

DIFFICULTY *

COLORS: (A) Deep Purple; (B) Wisteria; (C) Powder Pink; (D) Off-White

STITCHES USED: Slip stitch (sl st) • chain (ch) • single crochet (sc) • half double crochet (hdc) • double crochet (dc)

This edging consists of a string of small rings in different colors.

With D, ch 8, sl st to form a ring.

Sc, 2 hdc, 3 dc, 2 hdc, in ring changing to next col at the last yarn over of the last hdc, alternating between D, C, B, A; make a new 8-ch ring and turn it after having made the sl st. Repeat from * to * throughout.

Additional information on the positioning of motifs already completed as you work: from the second motif, work in the ring from right to left (with the ring's wrong side facing) and place yarn behind the work (the previous motif's wrong side is facing, the sc, hdc and dc are at the bottom). Continue like this to desired length.

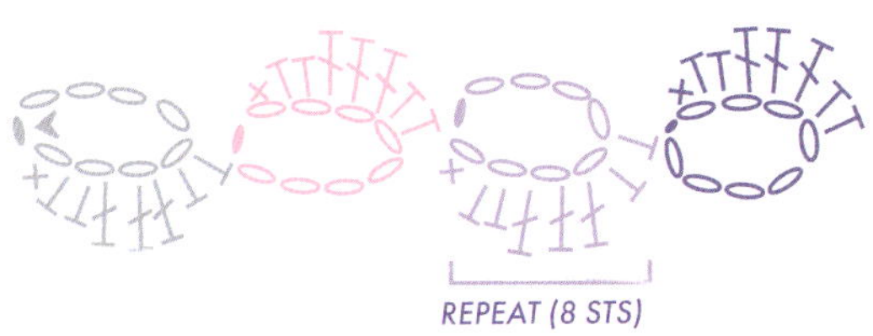

BORDER 15

DIFFICULTY ****

COLORS: (A) Deep Purple; (B) Wisteria; (C) Powder Pink; (D) Off-White

STITCHES USED: Slip stitch (sl st) • chain (ch) • single crochet (sc) • double crochet (dc) • ch-3 picot (pic)

For the support strip, repeat is worked over 5 rings + 1. Determine how many rings are needed for desired length and add 1 ring to that number.

With A, ch 12, sl st to form a ring.

Rnd 1: 16 sc in ring, sl st to close. Fasten off.

Repeat the same operation, linking the rings together with a sl st after the fourth sc into the fourth sc before the end of the rnd of the previous ring (between each sl st, there are 7 sc on each ring).

Now working around the ring band with B, chain a multiple of 5 + 1 turning chain.

Match the rings to the starting chain, positioning the beginning of Rnd 1 of each ring outwards.

Row 1: Ch 1 to turn, *sc in next 5, sl st in central st at bottom of ring to join*. Repeat from * to *. End with sc in next 6, ch 3, sc in side of last ring, ch 3 (with these chs you are moving to work across the top of the rings).

Row 2: Working across the top of the rings, ch 4, sc in 3 sc at the top of the first ring, *ch 2, sc in 3 sc at the top of the next ring*. Repeat from * to *. End with 4 chs, (move down the other side of the band of rings), ch 3, sc in side of last ring, ch 3, sl st in first sc from Row 1. Fasten off.

Row 3: Now starting in first ch from Row 2, sc across. Fasten off.

Row 4 (C): Insert hook in first st and pull up a loop, ch 3 (to replace first dc), dc in first st, *ch 2, skip 2 sc, 2 dc closed together in next*. Repeat from * to *. Fasten off.

Row 5 (B): Insert hook in first st and pull up a loop, sc across. Fasten off.

Row 6 (D): Insert hook in first st and pull up a loop, sl st in first st, *sl st in next, pic, sl st in next 2*. Repeat from * to *. Fasten off.

Make the flowers following the diagram and color changes; with A, ch 5, sl st to form a ring.

Rnd 1: 10 sc in ring, sl st to close the rnd. Fasten off.

Rnd 2 (B, C or D): Insert hook in first st and pull up a loop, *ch 3, 2 dc closed together in next, ch 3, sc in next*. Repeat from * to *. End with sc in first st. Fasten off.

Make a second flower, assembling at second petal by making a sl st just after 2 dc closed together, inserting hook at edge of a petal on the previous flower. Complete the flower.

Make a third flower, assembling it as established with a sl st to the flower just made, leaving 1 free petal on one side, and 2 on the other (see diagram).

Make 2 more flowers assembling them as shown (see diagram).

End triangular repeat with a flower joined to the others as shown (see diagram). Each triangular repeat consists of a total of 6 flowers.

To join the flower triangles to the top of the edging (or support strip), work with right side always facing across entire length.

With C, make a loop on the hook, ch 5, sc in top petal of the first flower, *ch 9, sc in top petal of next flower*. Repeat from * to *. End with 5 chs.

With C and right sides facing, ch 1 to turn, sc, sl st in st at edge of support strip, *sc in next 10 chs, skip 9 support strip sts, sl st in next st (to join)*. Repeat from * to *. End with sl st in last st of support strip. Fasten off.

Finish working around flower triangles, with right side always facing.

Row 7 (A): Insert hook in first st and pull up a loop, ch 6, sc in edge of first side petal, *ch 3, sc in edge of second side petal, ch 7, sc in edge of first petal on next flower, ch 7, sc in edge of first petal of bottom flower, ch 8, (ch 1, pic) 3x, ch 1, sl st in last of 8 chs, ch 8, sc in edge of third petal of bottom flower, ch 7, sc in edge of free petal on next flower, ch 7, sc in edge of first side petal of next flower, ch 3, sl st inserting hook in edge of 2 flowers to join to form the continuous edging (this is also the end of the repeat)*. Repeat from * to * on next flower triangle. End with ch 3, sc in next petal of last flower, ch 6, sl st in last st. Fasten off.

Row 8 (B): With right side facing, insert hook in first st and pull up a loop, [sl st in next 3, pic] 11x, *sl st in next 2, pass thread behind bottom group of pics and resume work on the other side of the same flower triangle, [sl st in next 3, pic] 8x, sl st in next 2, [sl st in next 3, pic) 8x on next flower triangle*. Repeat from * to *. End with sl st in next 3, sl st in last st. Fasten off.

BORDER 16

DIFFICULTY *

COLORS: (A) Deep Purple; (B) Wisteria; (C) Off-White

STITCHES USED: Slip stitch (sl st) • chain (ch) • single crochet (sc) • half double crochet (hdc) • double crochet (dc) • ch-3 picot (pic)

Worked with right side always facing. This edging is worked like a ribbon: The motif is repeated symmetrically on both sides of a central row.

With B, chain a multiple of 3 + 1 turning chain. Fasten off.

Row 1 (B): Insert hook in first ch and pull up a loop, ch 2 (to replace first hdc), hdc across. Fasten off.

Row 2 (C): Insert hook in first st and pull up a loop, ch 3, *dc, (yarn over, insert hook to work around dc just made, pull up a loop) 4x (9 loops on hook), yarn over and pull through first loop, yarn over and pull through remaining loops, ch 1 to close the st, skip 2 hdc*. Repeat from * to *. End with dc in last st. Fasten off.

Row 3 (B): Insert hook in first st and pull up a loop, sc across. Fasten off.

Row 4 (A): Insert hook in first st and pull up a loop, sl st in first 2, *pic, sl st in next 3*. Repeat from * to *. End with sl st in last 2. Fasten off.

Turn work to work on opposite side of Row 1. Repeat Rows 2–4 in corresponding colors. Fasten off.

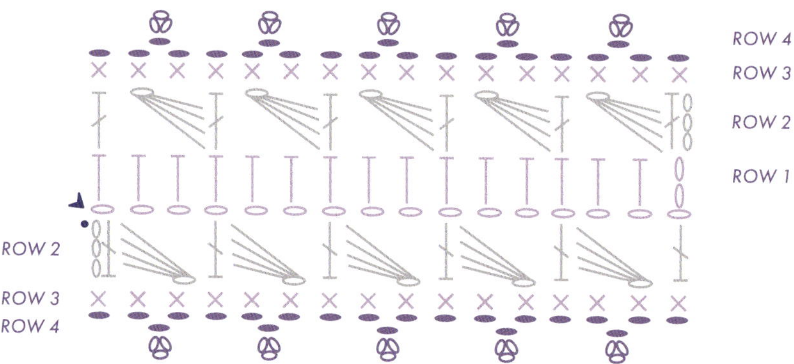

BORDER 17

DIFFICULTY **

COLORS: (A) Deep Purple; (B) Wisteria; (C) Off-White

STITCHES USED: Chain (ch) • single crochet (sc) • double crochet (dc) • treble crochet (tr)

This slightly rounded edging is worked with right side always facing. For a straight option, see instructions at the end of Row 4. With C, chain a multiple of 12 + 1.

Row 1: Ch 1 to turn, sc in first ch, *ch 4, skip 5 chs, (dc, ch 3, dc) in next st, ch 4, skip 5 chs, sc in next*. Repeat from * to *. Fasten off.

Row 2 (C): Sc in first st, *4 sc in ch-4 space, sc in next dc, 3 sc in ch-3 space, sc in next dc, 4 sc in next ch-4 space*. Repeat from * to *. End with sc in last st. Fasten off.

Row 3 (B): Insert hook in first st and pull up a loop, ch 3 (to replace first dc), *ch 1, skip 4 sc, [3 tr closed together in next, ch 3] 4x, 3 tr closed together in next, ch 1, skip 4 sc, dc in next sc*. Repeat from * to *. Fasten off.

Row 4 (A): Insert hook in third ch from Row 3 and pull up a loop, sc in same space, ch 3, sc in next ch, *skip a group of 3 tr, [(sc, ch 3, sc, ch 3, sc) in next ch-3 space] 4x, sc in ch before next dc, (sc, pic) in dc, sc in ch after dc*. Repeat from * to *. End with sc in ch before last dc, pic, sc in last dc.

For a straight option, work as follows between each rounded shape: sc around ch before and sc around ch after tr-groups from previous row.

Row 5: Now working on opposite site of starting chain with right side facing, insert hook in first ch and pull up a loop, sc in same space, *ch 3, 2 sc in next*. Repeat from * to * (working around the chs, covering them completely).

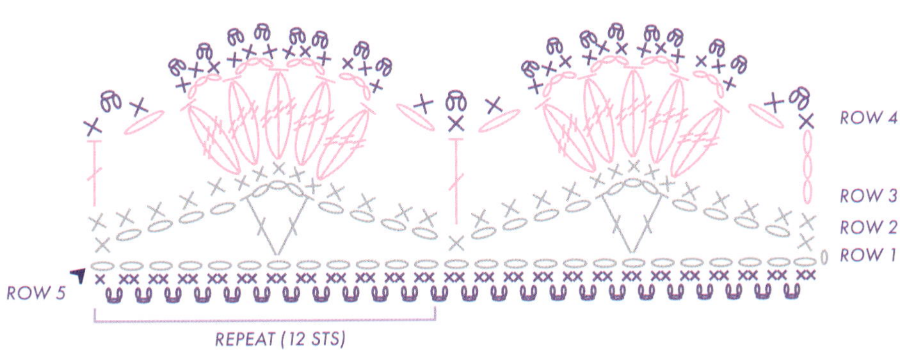

ABERDEEN

BORDER 18

DIFFICULTY ***

COLORS: (A) Deep Purple; (B) Wisteria; (C) Off-White

STITCHES USED: Slip stitch (sl st) • chain (ch) • single crochet (sc) • half double crochet (hdc) • double crochet (dc) • treble crochet (tr)

Worked with right side always facing. This edging consists of a string of flowers, which are then attached to the top edging.

To crochet the heart of the flower, with A, ch 8, sl st to form a ring.

Rnd 1: Ch 1, 16 sc in ring, sl st to close the rnd. Fasten off.

Rnd 2 (B or C): To make the petals, insert hook under sl st, *ch 4, tr in next 2 sts and closed together, ch 4, sl st in same st as last tr*. Repeat from * to * (8 petals). Fasten off. Crochet as many flowers as needed for desired length.

To begin the support strip with C, chain a multiple of 13 + 1 turning chain.

Row 1: Ch 2 (to replace first hdc), *ch 3, skip 3 chs, hdc in next*. Repeat from * to *. Fasten off.

For Rows 2 and 3, dc and tr are worked into the starting chs and made in front of the work.

Row 2 (B): Insert hook in first starting ch and pull up a loop, ch 3 (to replace first dc), sc in second starting ch from previous row, ch 1, *dc in starting ch after hdc from previous row, skip 1 ch, sc in next ch-3 space, ch 2*. Repeat from * to *. End with dc. Fasten off.

Row 3 (A): Insert hook at base of Row 2 starting chs and pull up a loop, ch 4 (to replace first tr), sc in next sc, ch 2, *tr in starting ch after next dc, sc in next ch-2 space, ch 2*. Repeat from * to *. End with tr. Fasten off.

Attach the flowers as you crochet Row 4.

Row 4 (A): Insert hook in top of starting ch from previous row and pull up a loop, ch 5, sl st in edge of a petal, ch 5, sc in next first sc, sc in next 7, *join the next petal of the flower as follows: [ch 1, sl st in edge of next petal, ch 1, sl st in last sc made], sc in next 8; join the third petal of the flower as follows: ch 4, sl st in edge of next petal, ch 4, sl st in first ch of previous ch-4 made; ch 4, sl st in edge of a petal on next flower, ch 4, sl st in last sc made, sc in next 8*. Repeat from * to *. End with ch 4, sl st in edge of next petal, ch 4, sl st in first of previous 4 chs, sc in last st. Fasten off.

BORDER 19

DIFFICULTY **

COLOR: Almond Green

STITCHES USED: Slip stitch (sl st) • chain (ch) • single crochet (sc) • half double crochet (hdc) • double crochet (dc)

Worked with right side always facing, fastening off at the end of each row, and beginning all rows on the right.

This edging consists of a central strip, on each side of which the same pattern is then worked asymmetrically.

With A, chain a multiple of 18.

Row 1: Ch 2 (to replace first hdc), hdc across.

Row 2: *Sc in next 6, form a ring as follows: ch 12, sl st in st at base of ring, sc in next 12*. Repeat from * to *. End with sc in last 6.

Row 3: Sl st in next 3, *skip 3 sc, 21 dc in 12-ch ring, skip 3 sc, sl st in next 12*. Repeat from * to *. End with sl st in last 3.

Now working opposite Row 1, with right side facing and working into the starting chains.

Row 4: Sc in next 15, *form a ring as follows: ch 12, sl st in st at base of ring, 18 sc*. Repeat from * to *. End with sc in last 15.

Row 5: Sl st in next 12, *skip 3 sc, 21 dc in ch-12 ring, skip 3 sc, sl st in next 12*. Repeat from * to *. End with sl st in last 12.

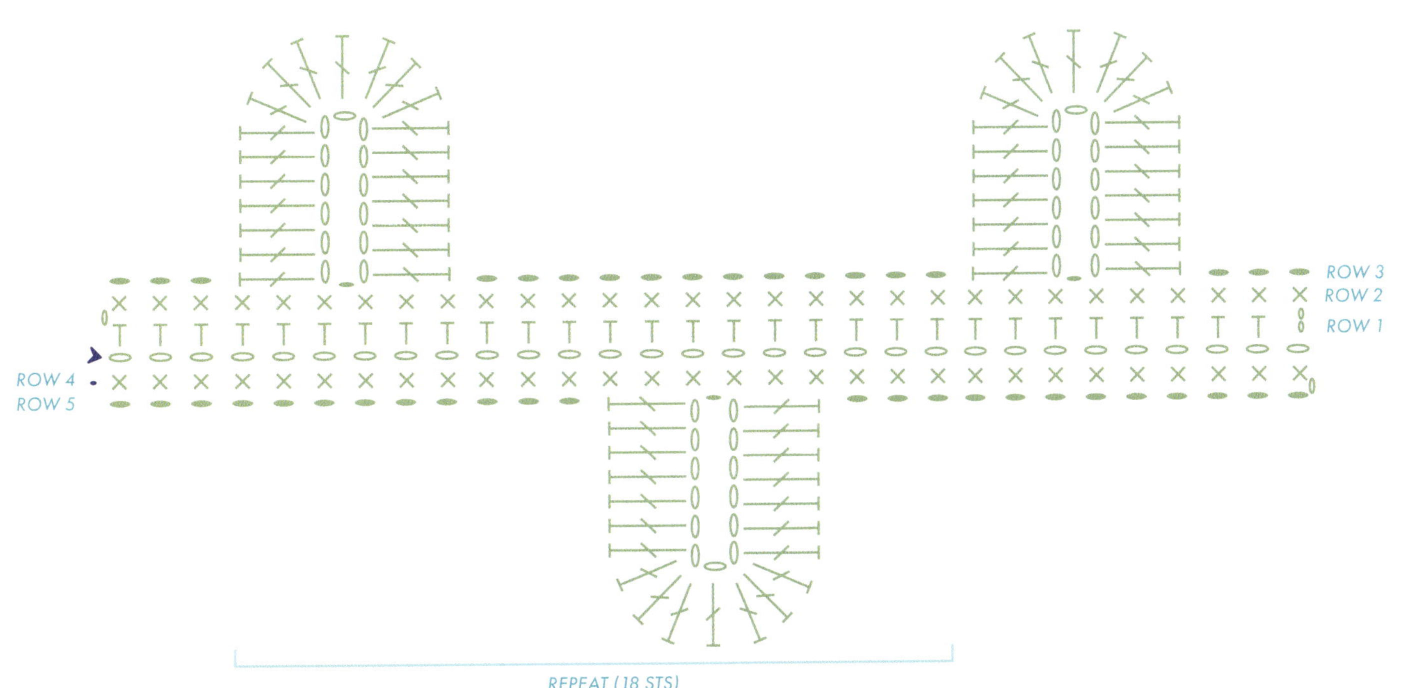

BORDER 20

DIFFICULTY ***

COLORS: (A) Ecru; (B) Almond Green

STITCHES USED: Slip stitch (sl st) • chain (ch) • single crochet (sc) • half double crochet (hdc) • double crochet (dc) • treble crochet (tr) • double treble crochet (dtr)

On the diagram, arrows indicate changes in direction.

Row 1 (A): *Ch 6, insert hook in fifth ch from hook and close 3 dtr together, ch 2, make the first big ring as follows: ch 25, sl st in first of these chs, ch 1*. Repeat from * to *, to desired length. End with 6 chs, insert hook in fifth ch from hook and close 3 dtr together, ch 1. Fasten off.

Row 2 (B): Insert hook in first ch and pull up a loop, sc in same space, *working around next dtr, (hdc, dc, tr, dc, hdc), sc in next ch, skip 1 ch, begin working in the big ring's chains (making sure their right side is facing before inserting the hook, see diagram), 7 sc, 3 hdc, 2 dc in next, (dc, tr) in next, 2 tr in next, (tr, dc) in next, 2 dc in next, 3 hdc, 7 sc. After having worked around the first ring, work is now on the left; this is normal. Reposition the edging in the direction of the work: from right to left. The ring just made is at the top. Push it to the bottom (its right side facing), the hook is on top. Flatten the ring, slightly pull the loop on the hook, skip 1 ch and sc in next ch from Row 1*. Repeat from * to *. End by working as follows around last dtr: hdc, dc, tr, dc, hdc, sc in last ch. Fasten off.

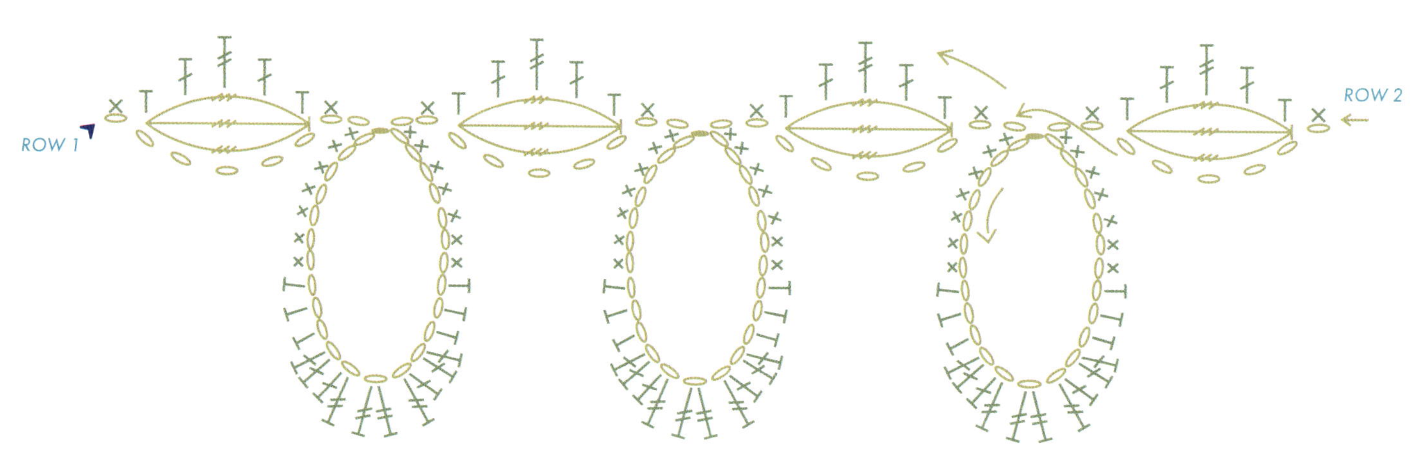

BORDER 21

DIFFICULTY **

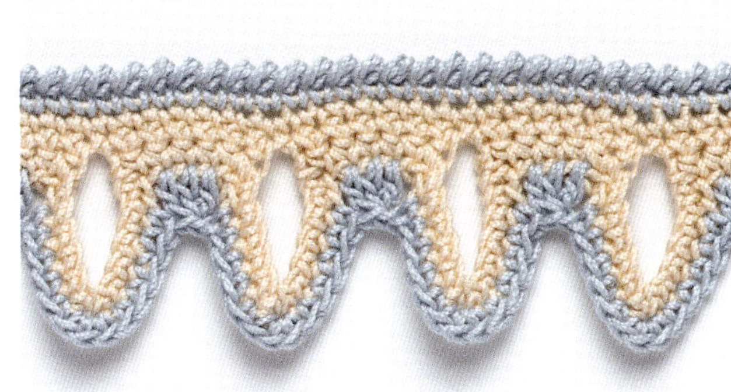

COLORS: (A) Ecru; (B) Grey Blue

STITCHES USED: Chain (ch) • single crochet (sc) • double crochet (dc) • crab stitch

With A, chain a multiple of 7 + 8 chains.

Row 1: Ch 1, sc across.

Row 2: Ch 1 to turn, sc in next 4, *ch 13, sc in next 7*. Repeat from * to *. End with sc in next 4.

Row 3: Ch 1 to turn, sc in next 3, *skip 1, 13 sc in ch-space, skip 1, sc in next 5*. Repeat from * to *. End with skip 1, sc in last 3. Fasten off.

Row 4 (B): Sc in first 2, skip 2, *sc in next 5, 3 sc in next, sc in next 5, skip 2, 3 dc closed together, skip 2*. Repeat from * to *. End with sc in last 2. Fasten off.

Row 5: Now working on opposite side of starting chain with right side facing, sc across. Work back across this row in crab stitch. Fasten off.

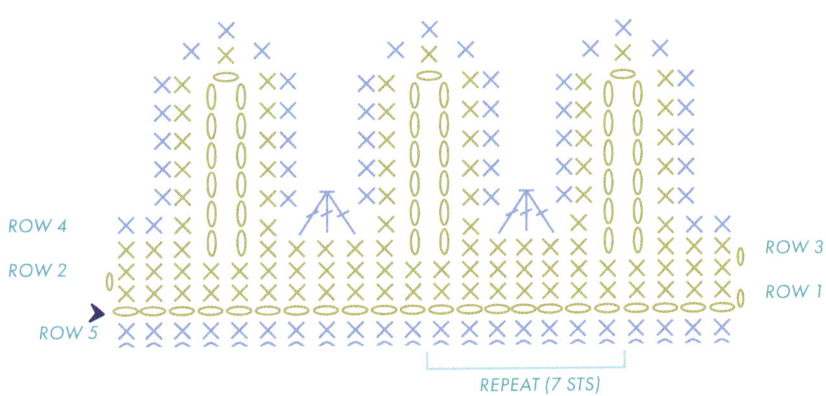

BORDER 22

DIFFICULTY ***

COLORS: (A) Salmon; (B) Almond Green; (C) Ecru

STITCHES USED: Slip stitch (sl st) • chain (ch) • single crochet (sc) • half double crochet (hdc) • double crochet (dc) • treble crochet (tr)

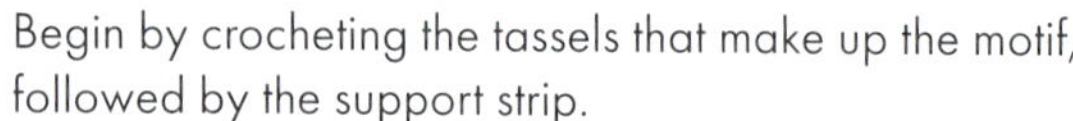

Begin by crocheting the tassels that make up the motif, followed by the support strip.

To make a group of 3 attached tassels, begin with Tassel C: With C, ch 11, sl st to close ring.

Rnd 1: Working in ring: 2 sc, 3 hdc, 4 dc, 5 tr, 4 dc, 3 hdc, 2 sc. End with sl st in first st. Fasten off.

Make Tassel B: With B, ch 9, sl st to close ring.

Rnd 1 (B): Working in ring: 2 sc, 3 hdc, 3 dc, 2 tr, sl st in Tassel C sl st, 2 tr, 3 dc, 3 hdc, 2 sc. End with sl st in first st. Fasten off.

Make Tassel A: With A, ch 6, sl st to close ring.

Rnd 1 (A): Ch 2, working in ring: 2 hdc, 2 dc, 2 tr, sl st in Tassel B sl st, 2 tr, 2 dc, 2 hdc, ch 2. End with sl st. Fasten off.

To make a pair of attached tassels, repeat Tassels C and B. Crochet several groups of two or three tassels to reach desired length.

To crochet the support strip, work as follows:

Row 1 (C): Ch 4, *sc in sl st of 3-tassel motif with its wrong side facing, ch 8, sc in sl st of 2-tassel motif with its wrong side facing, ch 8*. Repeat from * to *. End with ch 4.

Row 2: Ch 1 to turn, sc across. Fasten off.

Row 3 (A): Sc in next 8, *ch 3, skip 2, sc in next 7*. Repeat from * to *. End with sc in last 8. Fasten off.

Row 4 (B): Sc in next 4, *ch 3, skip 1, sc in next 2, ch 2, skip 2, sc in second ch of ch-3 space, ch 2, skip 2, sc in next 2*. Repeat from * to *. End with ch 3, skip 1, sc in last 4. Fasten off.

BORDER 23

DIFFICULTY **

COLORS: (A) Almond Green; (B) Grey Blue

STITCHES USED: Slip stitch (sl st) • chain (ch) • single crochet (sc) • half double crochet (hdc) • double crochet (dc) • treble crochet (tr)

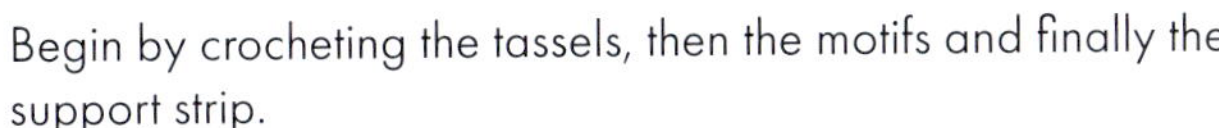

Begin by crocheting the tassels, then the motifs and finally the support strip.

To begin a tassel with A, ch 5, sl st to form a ring.

Rnd 1: Ch 3, 7 dc in ring, ch 3, sl st. Fasten off.

Rnd 2 (B): To crochet the motif and include the tassel, ch 13, sc in tassel ring, making sure its right side is facing, ch 13, sl st to close ring.

Rnd 3: With right side facing, insert hook in first ch-13 space of ring from previous rnd, sc in next 4, hdc in next, 2 hdc in next, hdc in next, dc in next 3, [2 tr in next] 3x, tr in next, 9 sc across tassel, in next ch-13 space: tr in next, [2 tr in next] 3x, dc in next 3, hdc in next, 2 hdc in next, hdc in next, sc in next 5, sl st to close. Fasten off.

Make the number of motifs required for desired length, alternating between colors as shown on the diagram.

To crochet the support strip, work as follows:

Row 1 (A): *Ch 7, sc in sc at top of motif, with its wrong side facing, ch 7*. Repeat from * to *.

For the next row, begin working with contrasting col to that of the motif. Change to next col at last yarn over of second tr, working over col not in use.

Row 2 (A and B): Insert hook in first ch, ch 4 (to replace first tr), tr in next, dc in next 2, hdc in next 2, sc in next 3, hdc in next 2, dc in next 2, tr in next 2 (change to next color at the last yarn over), *tr in next 2, dc in next 2, hdc in next 2, sc in next 3, hdc in next 2, dc in next 2, tr in next 2 (change to next color at the last yarn over)*. Repeat from * to *. Fasten off.

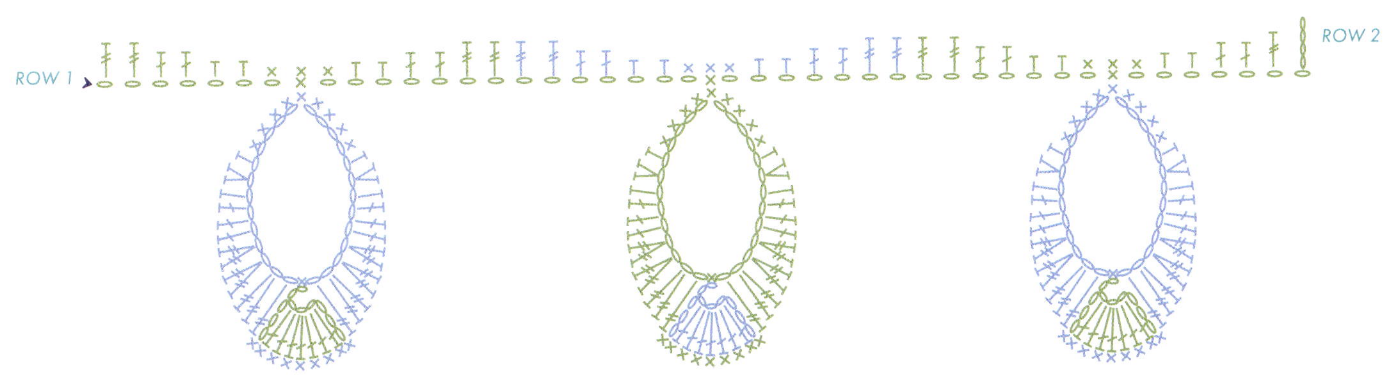

BORDER 24

DIFFICULTY **

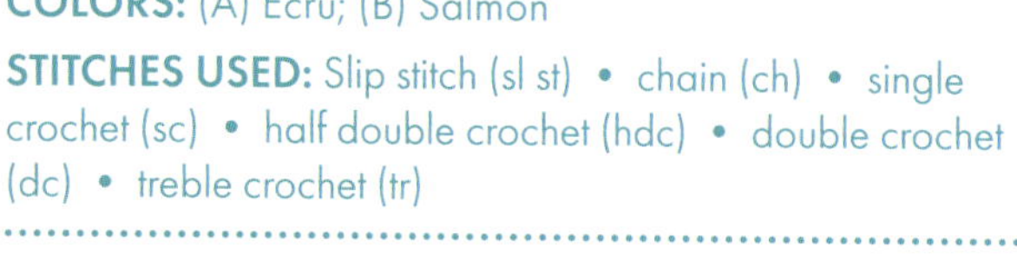

COLORS: (A) Ecru; (B) Salmon

STITCHES USED: Slip stitch (sl st) • chain (ch) • single crochet (sc) • half double crochet (hdc) • double crochet (dc) • treble crochet (tr)

Worked with right side always facing.

With A, chain a multiple of 27 + 4 chains.

Row 1: Ch 1 to turn, sl st in first, *sl st in next 2, sc in next 2, hdc in next 2, [2 dc in next, dc in next] twice, hdc in next 2, 2 hdc closed together skipping 3 chs between them, hdc in next 2, [dc in next, 2 dc in next] twice, hdc in next 2, sc in next 2*. Repeat from * to *. End with sl st in last 3. Fasten off.

Now working on the opposite side of the starting chain, with the right side facing.

Row 2 (B): Insert hook in the edge st and pull up a loop, sc in same space, *sl st in next, ch 4, 2 tr closed together in initial sl st, ch 4, sl st in initial sl st, sl st in next, sc in next 12, 3 sc in top ch, sc in next 12*. Repeat from * to *. End with sl st in next, ch 4, 2 tr closed together in initial sl st, ch 4, sl st in initial sl st, sl st in next, sc in last st. Fasten off.

Row 3 (B): Insert hook in edge st from Row 1 and pull up a loop, sc in next 3, *sc in next 2, ch 7, skip 5, 3 tr closed together in next dc, skip 11, 3 tr closed together in next dc, ch 7, skip 4, sc in next 2, ch 2, skip 2 sl sts*. Repeat from * to *, ending with sc in last 3 sl sts. Fasten off.

Row 4 (B): Insert hook in edge st from Row 3 and pull up a loop, sc in next 3, *sc in next 3, hdc in next 3, dc in next, 2 dc in next, tr in next, tr between 2 tr-groups from previous row, tr in next, 2 dc in next, dc in next, hdc in next 3, sc in next 3, sl st in next 2 chs*. Repeat from * to *, ending with sc in last 6. Fasten off.

Row 5 (A): Insert hook in edge st from Row 4 and pull up a loop, sl st across, inserting hook in back loops. Fasten off.

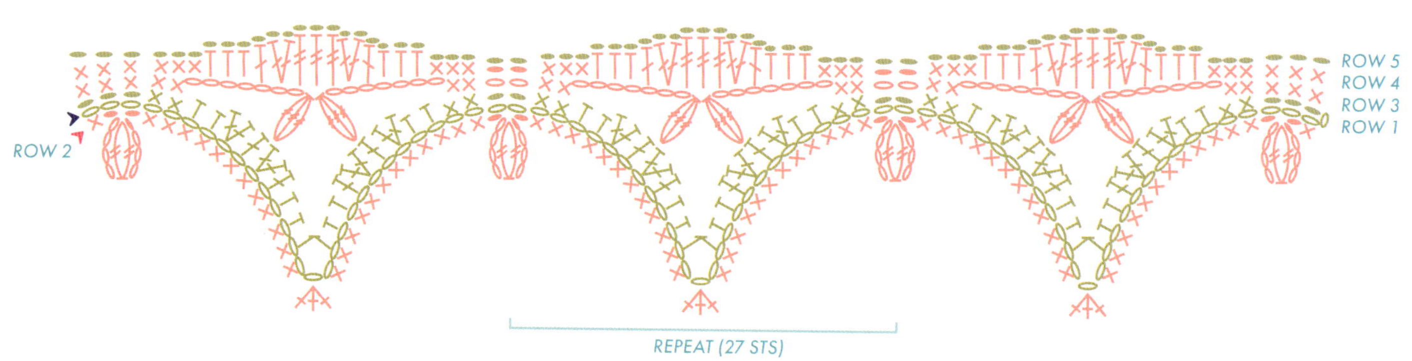

BORDER 25

DIFFICULTY **

COLORS: (A) Fuchsia; (B) Apple Green; (C) Yellow

STITCHES USED: Slip stitch (sl st) • chain (ch) • single crochet (sc) • half double crochet (hdc) • double crochet (dc)

This edging consists of several motifs, which are assembled and sewn onto a braided support strip.

With A, ch 6, sl st to close the ring.

Rnd 1: Ch 1, sc in next, 2 sc in next, sc in next, (2 sc, hdc) in next, (hdc, dc) in next, 3 dc in next, sl st to close. Fasten off.

Rnd 2 (C): Sc in next 2, [2 sc in next] twice, sc in next, 2 sc in next, sc in next, 2 sc in next, hdc in next, 3 hdc in next, 2 hdc in next, 3 hdc in next, sl st to close. Fasten off.

Rnd 3 (B): Sc in next 2, 2 sc in next, sc in next, 2 sc in next, sc in next, 2 hdc in next, hdc in next, 2 hdc in next, hdc in next 3, sc in next, 2 sc in next, sc in next 3, 2 sc in next, sc in next, 2 sc in next, sl st to close. Leave approximately 4 inches (10 cm) of yarn aside for finishing.

Create different motifs varying the colors.

To make the support braid, chain 80 in each of the three colors (A, B, and C). Fasten off. Tie the three lengths together at one end and braid them.

Sew the motifs to each other with the yarn kept aside, then sew them to the support braid with a length of yarn in the same color.

MURANO

BORDER 26

DIFFICULTY **

COLORS: (A) Apple Green; (B) Yellow; (C) Salmon; (D) Maroon

STITCHES USED: Slip stitch (sl st) • chain (ch) • single crochet (sc) • half double crochet (hdc) • double crochet (dc)

This edging consists of several motifs that are then assembled and sewn onto a support strip.

With C, ch 5, sl st to close the ring.

Rnd 1: Ch 1, 4 sc in first ch, [2 hdc in next] twice, (hdc, sc) in next, 2 sc in last. End with sl st in first st. Fasten off.

Rnd 2 (D): Insert hook in first st and pull up a loop, 2 sc in first, 2 dc in next, 3 dc in next, hdc in next 2, 3 hdc in next, [2 hdc in next] 4x, sc in last 2. End with sl st in first st. Fasten off.

Rnd 3 (A): Insert hook in first st and pull up a loop, sl st in first 2, hdc in next, 2 dc in next, 2 hdc in next, sc in next 9, sl st in next 8. End with sl st in first st. Fasten off.

Crochet motifs with the following colors:

Rnd 1: A; **Rnd 2:** B; **Rnd 3:** D

Rnd 1: A; **Rnd 2:** C; **Rnd 3:** B

Rnd 1: C; **Rnd 2:** B; **Rnd 3:** D

Rnd 1: D; **Rnd 2:** B; **Rnd 3:** A

Rnd 1: D; **Rnd 2:** C; **Rnd 3:** B

Join to a support strip consisting of chains, as follows: With C, ch 14, sc between 2 dc of last rnd of next motif, *ch 11, sc between 2 dc of last rnd of next motif*. Repeat from * to *, joining the different motifs. End with 14 chs. Fasten off.

With C, sc in next 3, ch 2, skip 2, sc in next, *[ch 2, skip 2, sc in next) twice between each motif, ch 2, skip (2 chs, sc (joining the motif to the previous row) and 2 chs), sc in next*. Repeat from * to *. End with sc in last 2.

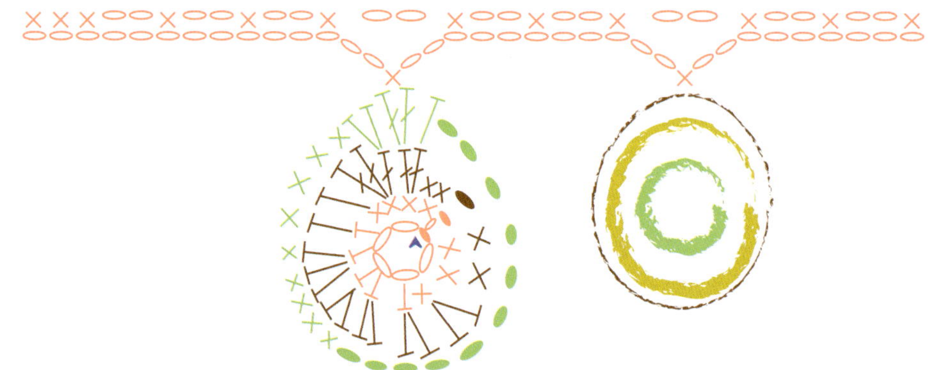

BORDER 27

DIFFICULTY ***

COLORS: (A) Apple Green; (B) Salmon; (C) Teal

STITCHES USED: Slip stitch (sl st) • chain (ch) • half double crochet (hdc) • double crochet (dc) • treble crochet (tr)

This edging consists of several motifs, which are then assembled and sewn onto a support strip.

With B, ch 7, sl st to close the ring.

Rnd 1: Ch 3 (to replace first dc), 8 dc in ring, ch 3. Do not fasten off. Change to next col.

Rnd 2 (A): 3 dc in dc row end, 4 dc and 1 hdc in ring, hdc in next 3 chs, sc in next 5 sts, sc in next—changing color at last yarn over.

Rnd 3 (C): Dc in the next dc, [2 dc in next] twice, skip 1 ch, 2 dc in second ch, skip 1 ch, sc in next 7 sts, 2 hdc in next. End with hdc in last 3. Fasten off (setting aside approximately 12 inches [30 cm] of yarn for finishing before cutting).

Make another motif as follows: Rnds 1 and 2: C; Rnd 3: A; Rnd 4: B.

Alternate motifs until you reach the desired length.

To make the support strip, chain a multiple of 14 + 1 in each of the three colors (A, B, and C). Assemble these lengths by making a sl st in every fifteenth ch on the previous length.

Attach the motifs to the strip as follows: In addition to the yarn set aside, cut a 6 inches (15 cm) length of yarn in each of the three colors. Tie two lengths together at 2½ inches (6 cm), pull them through the eye of a yarn needle and slide them on the wrong side of the motif so they exit near the third length.

On wrong side, weave 2 added lengths in. With yarn needle, pull length set aside through sl st in same col. Take the 3 lengths, pass them over and behind the 3 lengths of chains, bring them to the front on the right, and back to the front on the left; bring them behind, cross them again in the front, and with the help of the hook, bring them through the loop behind the work. Pull slightly to shape (see diagram). End by weaving ends in on wrong side of motif.

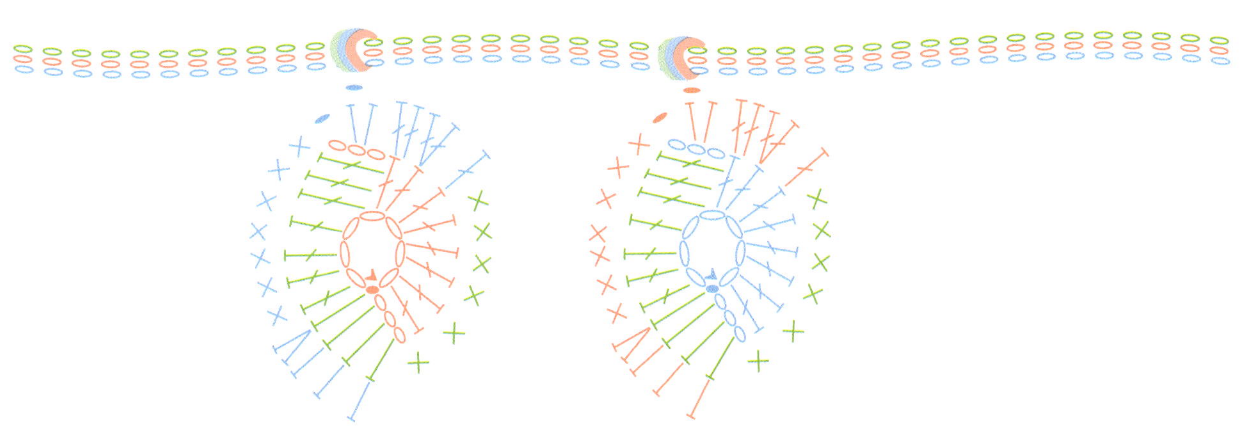

BORDER 28

DIFFICULTY ***

COLORS: (A) Fuchsia; (B) Yellow; (C) Teal

STITCHES USED: Slip stitch (sl st) • chain (ch) • single crochet (sc) • half double crochet (hdc) • double crochet (dc)

This edging consists of several motifs, which are then assembled and sewn onto a support strip.

Begin Motif 1 with A.

Rnd 1: Ch 4, 3 dc in first ch. Fasten off.

Rnd 2 (B): Insert the hook in last dc made and pull up a loop, ch 3, working around this dc as in a row end, make (3 dc, changing to next col at last yarn over, dc, and 3 hdc), 2 sc in next, (sc, sl st) in next. End with 2 sl sts. Fasten off.

Begin Motif 2 with A. Ch 6, sl st to close the ring.

Rnd 1: Sc in next, 2 sc in next, sc in next, (2 sc, hdc) in next, (hdc, dc) in next, 3 dc in next. End with sl st in first st. Fasten off.

Rnd 2 (C): Insert hook in first st and pull up a loop, ch 3, hdc in same space, 3 hdc in next, [2 hdc in next 2] twice, 2 sc in next, sc in next 2, 2 sc in next hdc, 2 sc in next dc, sl st in last 3, sl st to close.

Begin Motif 3 with A.

Rnd 1: Ch 5, 3 dc in first ch. Fasten off.

Rnd 2 (B): Insert hook in last dc made and pull up a loop, ch 3, working around this dc as in a row end (dc, 2 hdc, sc), 2 sc in next, sc in next 6. End with sl st in last dc from Rnd 1. Fasten off.

Rnd 3 (C): Insert hook in last sl st made and pull up a loop, ch 4, 3 dc in same st. End with sl st in 3rd starting ch from Rnd 2. Fasten off.

To make the support strip, crochet two chains of the required length, one with A and the other with C (make a swatch to calculate the number of stitches needed).

Tie the two chains together at regular intervals (approximately 10 sts between each knot). Link each motif to a knot with the corresponding col (see diagram). Thread an auxiliary length through a yarn needle, clamp it to the back of the motif and thread the needle through the knot in the support strip. Fasten off on the wrong side of the motif.

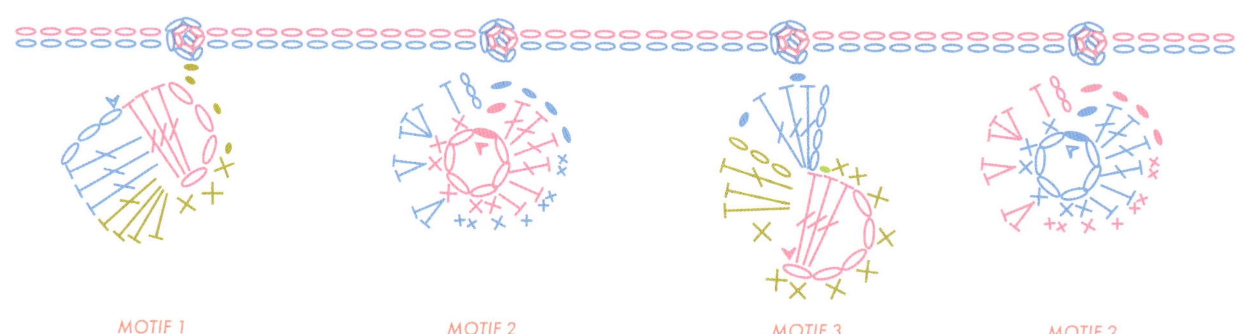

BORDER 29

DIFFICULTY ***

COLORS: (A) Fuchsia; (B) Yellow; (C) Teal; (D) Maroon

STITCHES USED: Slip stitch (sl st) • chain (ch) • single crochet (sc) • half double crochet (hdc) • double crochet (dc) • treble crochet (tr)

This edging consists of several motifs that are then assembled and sewn onto a support strip.

Rnd 1 (A): Ch 5, 3 dc in first ch, changing color at the last yarn over of the last dc.

Rnd 2 (B): Ch 4, 3 dc in last dc from Rnd 1, changing color at the last yarn over of the last dc.

Rnd 3 (C): In last dc from Rnd 1, make (3 tr, 2 dc, hdc). End with sl st in ch from Rnd 1. Fasten off.

Rnd 4 (D): Insert hook in fifth ch from Rnd 1 and pull up a loop, make (2 dc, 3 tr, dc) in st located between col A and C. End with sl st in fourth ch from Rnd 2. Fasten off.

To make the support strip, take 3 lengths of different col (A, C, and D), tie them together at regular intervals (approximately 2½ inches [6 cm]). Join each motif to a different colored area with a needle of auxiliary thread of the chosen col (the one that will be at the top, just below the knot). Conceal the thread on the wrong side of the motif, insert the needle into the knot and then back into the motif, repeating the operation; you can also combine the motifs by making a sl st into the knot of the support strip. Fasten off and weave ends through the thickness of the work.

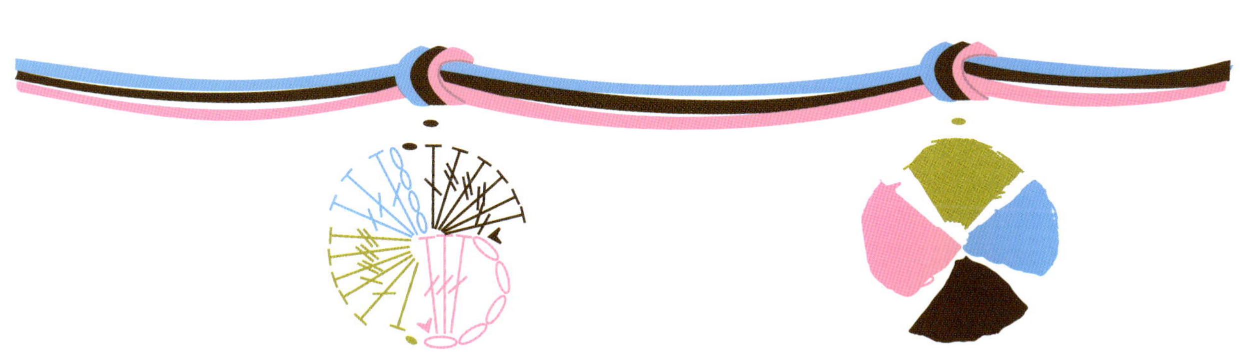

BORDER 30

DIFFICULTY **

COLORS: (A) Fuchsia; (B) Apple Green; (C) Yellow; (D) Salmon; (E) Maroon

STITCHES USED: Slip stitch (sl st) • chain (ch) • single crochet (sc) • half double crochet (hdc) • double crochet (dc)

This edging consists of several motifs that are then assembled.

Begin Motif 1 with B.

Rnd 1: Ch 4, hdc in first ch, change to next color at the last hdc.

Rnd 2 (E): 2 sc in hdc row end, [sc in next, 2 sc in next] twice, 2 sc in next, sc in next, 2 sc in next. End with sl st in first st. Fasten off.

Rnd 3 (D): Insert hook and pull up a loop, sc in next 4, 2 sc in next, sc in next, 2 sc in next, sc in next, sl st in next 5, sl st to close. Fasten off.

Crochet a second identical motif with the following col: Rnd 1: D; Rnd 2: C; Rnd 3: B. Join the motifs with a sl st in third sl st of last rnd of previous motif (you can assemble them randomly to increase the color play).

Begin Motif 2 with A. Ch 6, sl st to close ring. Fasten off.

Rnd 1 (C): 3 dc, 3 hdc, 3 sc in ring, sl st to close. Fasten off.

Rnd 2 (A): Insert hook in first st and pull up a loop, 2 sc in same st, sc in next (join to Motif 1 with a sl st in the corresponding st, as per diagram), 2 sc in next, sc in next (join to second Motif 1 with a sl st in the corresponding st, as per diagram), 2 sc in first st after join, sc in next, 2 sc in next, 2 sc in next, sc in next. End with sl st in first st. Fasten off.

Continue combining the different motifs as suggested in the book, with Motif 1 reversed every other instance. Feel free to play with the colors.

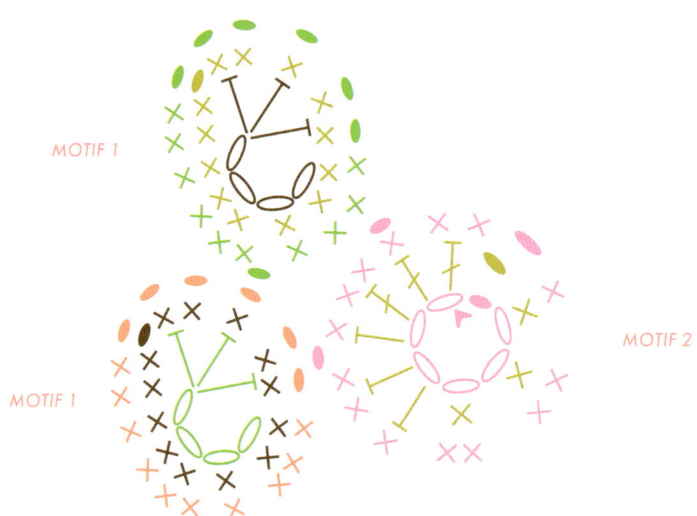

BORDER 31

DIFFICULTY ****

COLORS: Ecru

STITCHES USED: Slip stitch (sl st) • chain (ch) • single crochet (sc) • double crochet (dc) • ch-3 picot (pic)

This edging is worked in two parts. First, a support strip is worked over 9 chains, then a motif is crocheted on one side of the strip (the red arrows indicate the direction to follow to complete the work). Motif is worked over 8 rows.

To make the support strip, chain a multiple of 9 + 1 turning chain.

Rows 1–3: Sc in next 9, ch 1 to turn.

Row 4: Ch 3 (to replace first dc), dc in next 2, ch 4, skip 4, dc in next 2.

Row 5: Ch 3 (to replace first dc), dc in next, ch 4, skip 4, dc in next 3.

Rows 6–8: Repeat Row 1.

Repeat Rows 1–8 to desired length.

To make the motif, work on the side of the edging where there are 2 dc.

Row 1: Insert hook in first st of row, *sc in 3 sc row ends, 3 sc in dc row end, ch 25, now working in these chains, 24 sc starting in second ch from hook, now working on the support strip again: 3 sc in dc row end, sc in 3 sc row ends*. Repeat from * to *. End with 3 sc.

Row 2: On the right side of the edging, insert hook in st at the edge and pull up a loop, sc in same space, *working in 25 chs from previous row, 3 dc in first ch, [ch 1, skip 5, 5 dc in next] 3x, ch 1, skip 5, 15 dc in last ch, [ch 1, skip 5, 5 dc in next sc] 3x, ch 1, skip 5, 3 dc in last, skip 5, 2 sc*. Repeat from * to *. End with sc.

Row 3: On the right side of the edging, insert hook in st at the edge of the support strip and pull up a loop, make 11 sl sts on the straight side of the edging, sl st in next dc, ch 3, skip 2 dc, [dc in next ch, pic, ch 3, skip 2 dc, sc in next dc, ch 3, skip 2 dc] 3x, dc in next ch, pic, ch 5, skip 3 dc, dc in next, pic, *[ch 5, skip 2 dc, dc in next, pic] 3x, ch 3, skip 2 dc, [dc in next ch, ch 3, skip 2 dc, sc in next dc, ch 3, skip 2 dc] twice, ch 3, skip 2 dc, sc in next, ch 3, skip 2 dc, 2 dc closed together with the first dc in the ch on this motif, (skip 3 dc, 2 sc, 3 dc), and the second dc in the ch on the next motif, [ch 3, skip 2 dc, sc in next dc, ch 3, skip 2 dc, dc in ch, sl st in corresponding dc to join] 3x, ch 3, skip 3 dc, dc in next dc, sl st in corresponding pic to join*. Repeat from * to *. End at the opposite side of the edging by making a pic on top of each dc per the beginning, ch 3, skip 2 dc, sc in next dc, 10 sl sts. Fasten off.

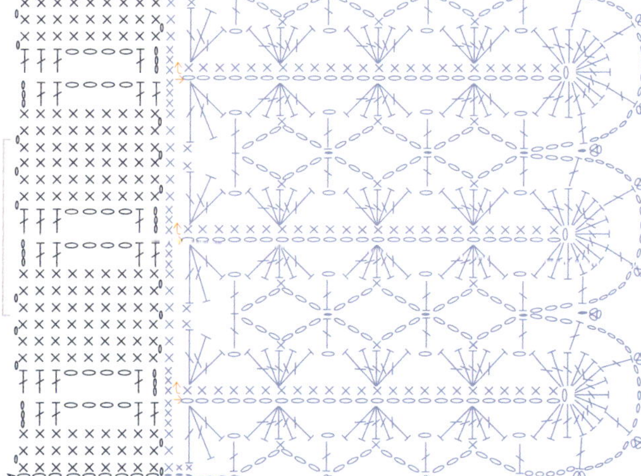

REPEAT (8 ROWS)

BORDER 32

DIFFICULTY ****

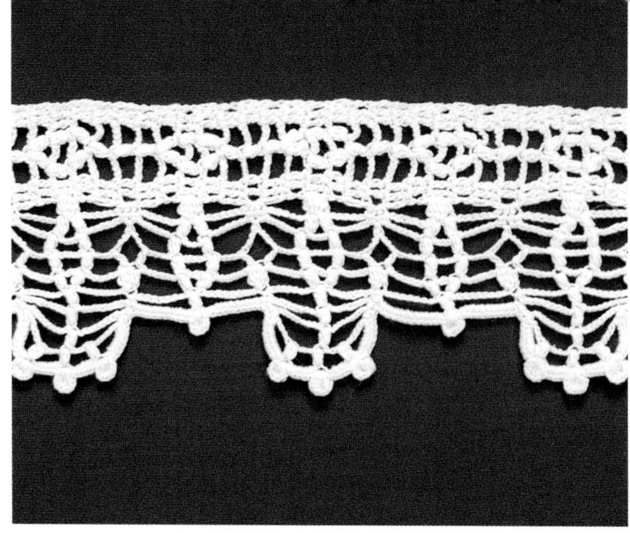

COLOR: Ecru

STITCHES USED: Slip stitch (sl st) • chain (ch) • single crochet (sc) • double crochet (dc) • puff [yarn over, insert hook in same stitch and pull up a long loop] 3x, yarn over and pull through first 6 loops, yarn over and pull through remaining 2 loops, close puff with a tight ch)

This edging is worked in two parts. First, a support strip is worked over 15 chains, then a motif is crocheted on one side of the strip. Motif is worked over 12 rows. Finish the edging with the same motif as before, adding 8 rows at the end.

Step 1: To make the support strip, chain a multiple of 15.

Row 1: Ch 3 to turn, 14 dc.

Row 2: Ch 3 (to turn and replace first dc), dc in next 2, ch 3, skip 3 dc, dc in next, ch 1, skip 1, dc in next, ch 3, skip 3 dc, dc in next 3.

Row 3: Ch 3 (to turn and replace first dc), dc in next 2, ch 4, skip 4, puff in next ch, ch 4, skip 4, dc in next 3.

Row 4: Ch 3 (to turn and replace first dc), dc in next 2, ch 1, skip 4, (puff, ch 4, puff) in puff from previous row, ch 1, skip 4, dc in next 3.

Row 5: Ch 3 (to turn and replace first dc), dc in next 2, ch 1, skip 1, puff in puff from previous row, ch 4, skip 4, puff in next puff, ch 1, skip 1, dc in next 3.

Row 6: Ch 3 (to turn and replace first dc), dc in next 2, ch 4, skip 1, puff in puff from previous row, skip 4 ch, puff in next puff, ch 4, skip 1, dc in next 3.

Row 7: Ch 3 (to turn and replace first dc), dc in next 2, ch 4, skip 4, puff between puffs from previous row, ch 4, skip 4, dc in next 3.

Rows 8–9: Ch 3 (to turn and replace first dc), dc in next 2 dc, ch 4, skip 4, puff in puff from previous row, ch 4, skip 4, dc in next 3.

Start again from Row 4.

Step 2: To create the motif, position the strip right side up and work on one long side.

Row 1: Insert hook at base of first dc from Row 2 and pull up a loop, 4 sc in dc row end, *ch 6, skip the length of 2 dc, 5 dc closed together in next dc row end, ch 6, skip the length of 2 dc, 3 sc in next dc row end*. Repeat from * to *. End with 4 sc in last dc row end.

Row 2: Ch 1 to turn, sc in next 4, *ch 6, skip 6 chs, (puff, ch 4, puff) in top of next dc-group, ch 6, skip 6 chs, sc in next 3 sc*. Repeat from * to *. End with 4 sc.

Row 3: Ch 1 to turn, sc in next 2, *ch 8, skip 6 chs, puff in puff from previous row, ch 5, skip 4 chs, puff in next puff, ch 8, skip 7, sc in next sc*. Repeat from * to *. End with 2 sc.

Row 4: Ch 1 to turn, sl st in second sc and first ch, ch 9, *puff in puff from previous row, ch 4, skip 5 chs, puff in next puff, ch 6, skip 3 chs, dc in next ch, skip 9, dc in next ch, ch 6, skip 3 chs*. Repeat from * to *. End with 9 chs, skip 7 chs, sl st in next ch. Turn.

Row 5: Sl st in first ch, ch 11, skip 8 chs, *puff in puff from previous row, skip 4 chs, puff in next puff, ch 8, skip 6 chs, 4 dc closed together, making 2 dc in each of next 2 dc, ch 8*. Repeat from * to *. End with 11 chs, skip 8 chs, sl st in next ch. Turn.

Row 6: Sl st in first ch, ch 11, skip 10 chs, *puff in puff from previous row, ch 9, skip 8 chs, sc in next dc-group, ch 9*. Repeat from * to *. End with 11 chs, skip 8 chs, sl st in next. Fasten off.

Row 7: To create the tips of the large motif, insert hook in first sc of previous row and pull up a loop, sc in same st, ch 10, skip 9 chs, puff in next puff, ch 10, skip 9 chs, sc in next sc, turn.

Row 8: Ch 1 in first st, ch 10, skip 9 chs, puff in puff from previous row, ch 10, skip 9 chs, sl st in next ch, turn.

Row 9: Ch 1 in first st, ch 6, skip 5 chs, puff in next ch, ch 4, skip 3 chs, puff in next puff, ch 4, skip 3 chs, puff in next ch, ch 6, skip 5 chs, sl st in next ch. Fasten off.

Row 10: Insert hook in sc from Row 3 of motif and pull up a loop, sc in same st, sc in next 4, * 11 sc over next 11 chs, (sl st, ch 3, 4 dc closed together, ch 3, sl st) in next puff, 10 sc over next 9 chs, sc over the first ch of Rows 7 and 8, 7 sc over next 6 chs, (sl st, ch 3, 4 dc closed together, ch 3, sl st) in next puff, 5 sc over next 4 chs, (sl st, ch 3, 4 dc closed together, ch 3, sl st) in next puff, 5 sc over next 4 chs, 7 sc over next 6 chs, sc under last ch of Rows 7 and 8*. Repeat from * to *, beginning with 10 sc over next 9 chs. End with 11 sc over 11 chs, 5 sc. Fasten off.

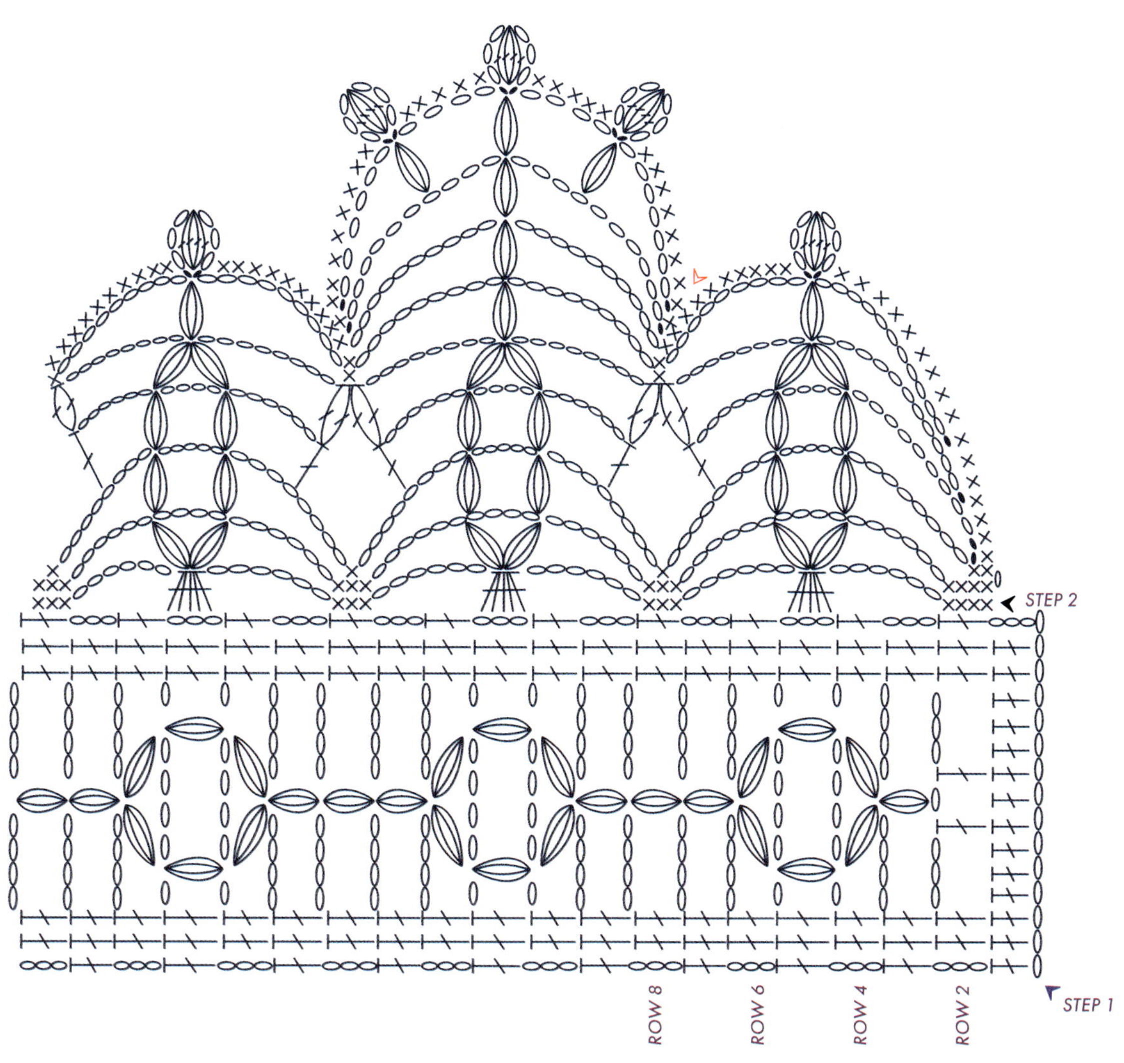

BORDER 33

DIFFICULTY ****

COLOR: Ecru

STITCHES USED: Slip stitch (sl st) • chain (ch) • single crochet (sc) • half double crochet (hdc) • double crochet (dc) • treble crochet (tr) • ch-3 picot (pic)

This edging is worked back and forth in rows. The motif is worked over a multiple of 16 + 1. At the beginning and end of each row, add 6 sts to finish the motifs at the end, for a total of 12 more sts in all.

Chain a multiple of 16 + 13 chains.

Row 1: Ch 2 (to replace first hdc), hdc across, turn.

Row 2: Ch 1, sc in first st, *ch 13, skip 7, sc in next*. Repeat from * to *. End with ch 6, tr in last. Fasten off.

Row 3: In this row, alternate with the chains from the previous row passing once in front before making the sc, and once behind before making the next sc; insert hook at base of last tr and pull up a loop, ch 13, skip 7 sts from Row 1, *sc in next, ch 13, skip 7 sts*. Repeat from * to * alternating the position of the chs. End with sc in next, ch 6, tr in last st from Row 2, turn.

Row 4: Ch 1, sc in first st, *ch 3, sc in seventh ch of each ch-13 space from previous row*. Repeat from * to *. End with ch 3, sc in tr.

Row 5: Ch 1 to turn, sc across.

Row 6: Ch 3 (to turn and replace first dc), *ch 1, skip 1, dc in next*. Repeat from * to *.

Row 7: Ch 1 to turn, sc in same st, *ch 3, 3 pics, sl st at base of first pic, ch 3, skip 3, sc in next*. Repeat from * to *. Fasten off.

Row 8: Begin in the second pic of the first group of pics, sc in same space, *6 dc in second pic of next group, sc in second pic of next group, ch 9, skip a group of 3 pics, sc in second pic of next group*. Repeat from * to *. End with 6 dc in second pic of group before last, sc in second pic of last group.

Row 9: Ch 3 (to turn and replace first dc), 5 dc, *make 3 petals as follows: ch 3, 2 dc closed together at base of ch-3, 3 dc closed together in fourth ch of ch-9 space, ch 3, 2 dc closed together in previous dc-group, skip 5, dc in next 6 dc*. Repeat from * to *.

Row 10: Ch 3 (to turn and replace first dc), 2 dc in next, dc in next 2, 2 dc in next, dc in next, *ch 3, skip 1 petal, make the fourth petal as follows: Close 3 dc together in center of the petals, ch 3, skip 1 petal, dc in next, 2 dc in next, dc in next 2, 2 dc in next, dc in next*. Repeat from * to *.

Row 11: Ch 3 (to turn and replace first dc), 2 dc closed together, ch 2, skip 2, 3 dc closed together, *skip 3 chs, (tr, ch 3, tr, ch 3, tr) in next petal, skip 3 chs, 3 dc closed together, ch 2, skip 2, 3 dc closed together*. Repeat from * to *. Turn.

Row 12: *Ch 3, 2 dc closed together, ch 3, sc in next dc-group, ch 3, skip ch, dc in next, ch 1, skip ch, (dc, ch 1, dc) in next st, ch 1, skip ch, dc in next, ch 3, skip ch, sc in dc-group*. Repeat from * to *. End with ch 3, 2 dc closed together, ch 3, sc in last. Turn.

Row 13: Sl st in first 3 chs from previous row, sc in next st, *ch 4, 2 dc in next dc, ch 1, skip ch, dc in next, ch 1, skip ch, dc in next, ch 1, skip ch, 2 dc in next, ch 4, sc in next dc-group*. Repeat from * to *. Turn.

Row 14: Ch 2 (to replace first hdc), *ch 3, skip 4 chs, dc in next 9, ch 3, skip 4 chs, hdc in next sc.* Repeat from * to *.

Row 15: Ch 1 to turn, sc in first st, pic, *ch 4, skip 3 chs, (tr, pic, tr) in next st, pic, [tr, pic] 7x, (tr, pic, tr) in next st, ch 4, skip 3 chs, (sc, pic) in next*. Repeat from * to *.

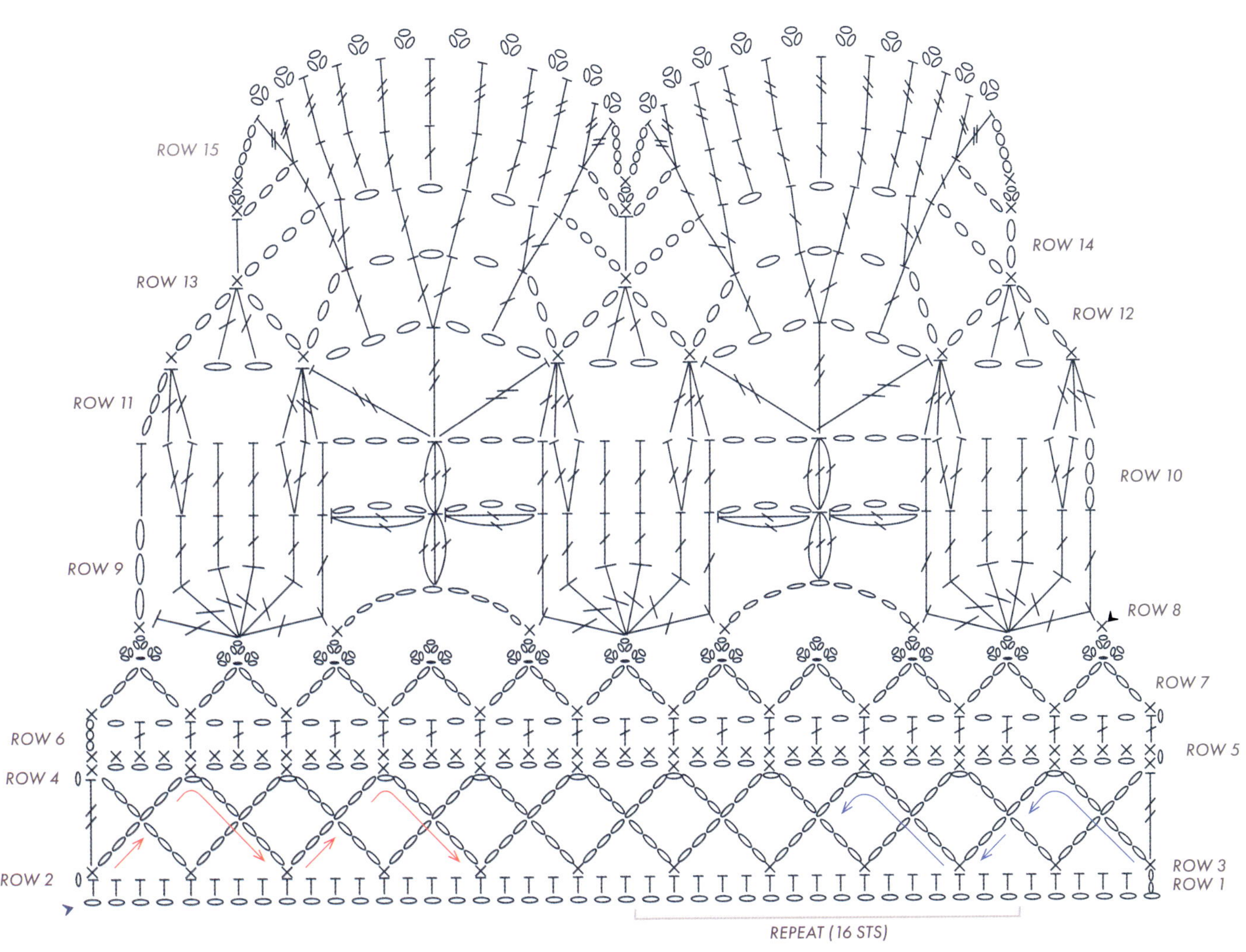
ROW 15
ROW 14
ROW 13
ROW 12
ROW 11
ROW 10
ROW 9
ROW 8
ROW 7
ROW 6
ROW 5
ROW 4
ROW 3
ROW 2
ROW 1
REPEAT (16 STS)

BORDER 34

DIFFICULTY ****

COLOR: Ecru

STITCHES USED: Slip stitch (sl st) • chain (ch) • single crochet (sc) • double crochet (dc) • ch-3 picot (pic) • crab stitch

This edging is worked back and forth in rows. Tips are completed independently. The motif is worked over a multiple of 54 + 1. At the beginning and end of each row, add 6 sts to finish the motifs at the end, for a total of 12 more sts in all.

Chain a multiple of 54 + 13 chains.

Row 1: Ch 3 (to replace first dc), [ch 2, skip 2, dc in next] 10x, ch 2, skip 2, 3 dc closed together in next, [ch 2, skip 2, dc in next] 11x. Turn.

Row 2: Ch 7, skip 2, sc in next dc, *[ch 2, skip 2, 3 dc closed together in next dc, ch 2, skip 2, sc in next dc, ch 7, skip 5, sc in next dc] twice, ch 2, skip 2 ch and dc, dc in next 2 chs, 3 dc in next dc-group, dc in next 2 chs, ch 2, skip 3, sc in next dc, ch 7, skip 5, sc in next dc, ch 2, skip 2, 3 dc closed together in next dc, ch 2, skip 2, sc in next dc, ch 7, skip 5, sc in next dc*. Repeat from * to *, ending with ch 3, dc in last st.

Row 3: Ch 1 to turn, sc in first st, ch 7, skip 6, *sc in next dc-group, ch 7, sc in fourth ch of next ch-space, ch 7, sc in next dc-group, ch 7, sc in fourth ch of next ch-space, skip 6, ch 2, [(dc, ch 1, dc, ch 1) in next dc, skip next dc] 4x, ch 1, sc in fourth ch of next ch-space, ch 7*. Repeat from * to *. End with ch 7, sc in first ch-7 space. Turn.

Row 4: Ch 7, sc in fourth ch of ch-space, ch 2, *skip 3 chs, dc in next sc, ch 2, skip 3 chs, [sc in fourth ch of next ch-space, ch 7] twice, sc in fourth ch of next ch-space, ch 2, skip 6, [dc in next dc, 3 dc closed together in next ch] 7x, dc in next dc, ch 2, [sc in fourth ch of next ch-space, ch 7] twice, sc in fourth ch of next ch-space, ch 2*. Repeat from * to *. End with ch 3, skip 3 chs, dc in last sc.

Row 5: Ch 1 to turn, sc in first st, *ch 3, skip 6, 5 dc in next dc, ch 3, sc in fourth ch of next ch-space, ch 7, sc in fourth ch of next ch-space, ch 3, skip 6, [3 dc closed together in next dc, ch 2, skip next 3-dc-group] 8x, ch 1, skip 6, sc in fourth ch of next ch-space, ch 7, sc in fourth ch of next ch-space*. Repeat from * to *. End with ch 3, sc in last st. Turn.

Row 6: Ch 3 (to replace first dc), 2 dc closed together in same st, *ch 3, skip 5, 5 dc in third dc of next dc-group, ch 3, skip 5, 3 dc closed together in next sc, skip 3, dc in next ch, ch 6, skip 7, [dc in next dc-group, ch 1, 3 dc closed together between next 2 chs, ch 1] 3x, (dc, ch 2, 3 dc closed together) in next dc-group, skip 2 chs, (3 dc closed together, ch 2, dc) in next dc-group, [ch 1, 3 dc closed together between next 2 chs, ch 1, dc in next dc-group] 3x, ch 6, skip 7, dc in next ch, skip 3, 3 dc closed together in next sc*. Repeat from * to *. End with ch 3, skip 5, 5 dc in third dc of last dc-group, ch 3, skip 5, 3 dc closed together in last st. Turn.

Row 7: Ch 3 (to replace first dc), *ch 3, skip 3 chs, [3 dc closed together in next dc, ch 2, skip 1] twice, 3 dc closed together in next dc, ch 3, skip 3, dc in next dc-group, ch 5, skip 7, [3 dc closed together in next dc, ch 2, skip 3] 3x, 3 dc closed together in next dc-group, ch 3, 3 dc closed together between next dc-groups, ch 3, skip 3, [3 dc closed together in next dc, ch 2, skip 3] 3x, 3 dc closed together in next dc, ch 5, skip 7 chs, dc in next dc-group*. Repeat from * to *. End with ch 3, skip 3 chs, [3 dc closed together in next dc, ch 2, skip 1] twice, 3 dc closed together in next dc, ch 3, skip 3 chs, dc in last dc-group. Turn.

Row 8: Ch 3, *ch 2, skip 3 chs, [dc in next dc-group, ch 1, dc between next 2 chs, ch 1] twice, dc in next dc-group, ch 2, skip 3 chs, dc in next dc-group, ch 4, skip (5 chs, 1 dc-group, 1 ch), 3 dc closed together in next ch, ch 2, [skip 1 dc-group and 1 ch, 3 dc closed together in next ch, ch 2] 2x, [3 dc closed together in next ch-3 space, ch 3, 3 dc closed together in same ch-3 space] twice, [ch 2, skip 1 dc-group and 1 ch, 3 dc closed together in next ch] 3x, ch 2, skip 2 chs*. Repeat from * to *. End with 5 chs, skip 3 chs, sl st in next ch.

Row 9: 3 sl sts, *ch 3, skip 2 chs, 3 dc closed together, [pic, ch 2, close 3 dc together with first dc in same st as previous dc] 3x, pic, ch 3, skip 2 chs**, sc in next dc, ch 3, skip 4 chs, dc in next 12, skip 1 ch, dc between next 2 dc-groups, skip 1 ch, dc in next 12, ch 3, skip 4 chs, sc in next dc*. Repeat from * to *. End at **, sc in third starting ch. Fasten off.

Resume work on the second motif as shown in the diagram.

Row 10: Insert hook in first dc and pull up a loop, ch 3 (to replace first dc), dc in next 10, ch 2, skip 1, 3 dc closed together in next st, ch 2, skip 1, dc in next 9, 2 dc closed together. Turn.

Row 11: Ch 3 (to replace first dc), 3 dc closed together, ch 3, skip 1, 4 dc closed together in next st, ch 3, skip 1, 3 dc closed together, ch 3, skip 2 chs, 5 dc closed together in next dc-group, ch 3, skip 2 chs, 3 dc closed together, ch 3, skip 1, 4 dc closed together in next st, ch 3, skip 1, 4 dc closed together. Turn.

Row 12: Ch 3 (to replace first dc), 3 dc closed together, ch 3, skip 2, 4 dc closed together in next st, ch 3, skip 3, 4 dc closed together in next st, ch 1, skip 3, 4 dc closed together in next st, ch 3, skip 3, 4 dc closed together in next st, ch 3, skip 2. End with 4 dc closed together. Turn.

Row 13: Ch 3 (to replace first dc), 3 dc closed together, ch 2, skip 2, 4 dc closed together in next st, ch 2, skip 2, 4 dc closed together in next st, ch 2, skip 2, 4 dc closed together in next st, ch 2, skip 2, 4 dc closed together. Turn.

Row 14: Ch 3 (to replace first dc), 2 dc closed together, ch 1, skip 1, 3 dc closed together in next st, ch 1, skip 3, 3 dc closed together in next st, ch 1, skip 1. End with 3 dc closed together. Turn.

Row 15: Ch 3 (to replace first dc), skip 1, begin 3 dc without closing them, skip 1, begin 1 dc and close it with the previous 3. End with pic. Fasten off. Repeat Rows 10–15 to finish remaining tips.

Row 16: With right side facing and working on the opposite side of the foundation chain, insert the hook in the fifth chain from the turning chain in Row 1. *Crab stitch in the next 2 chs, skip 1 ch.* Repeat from * to * across.

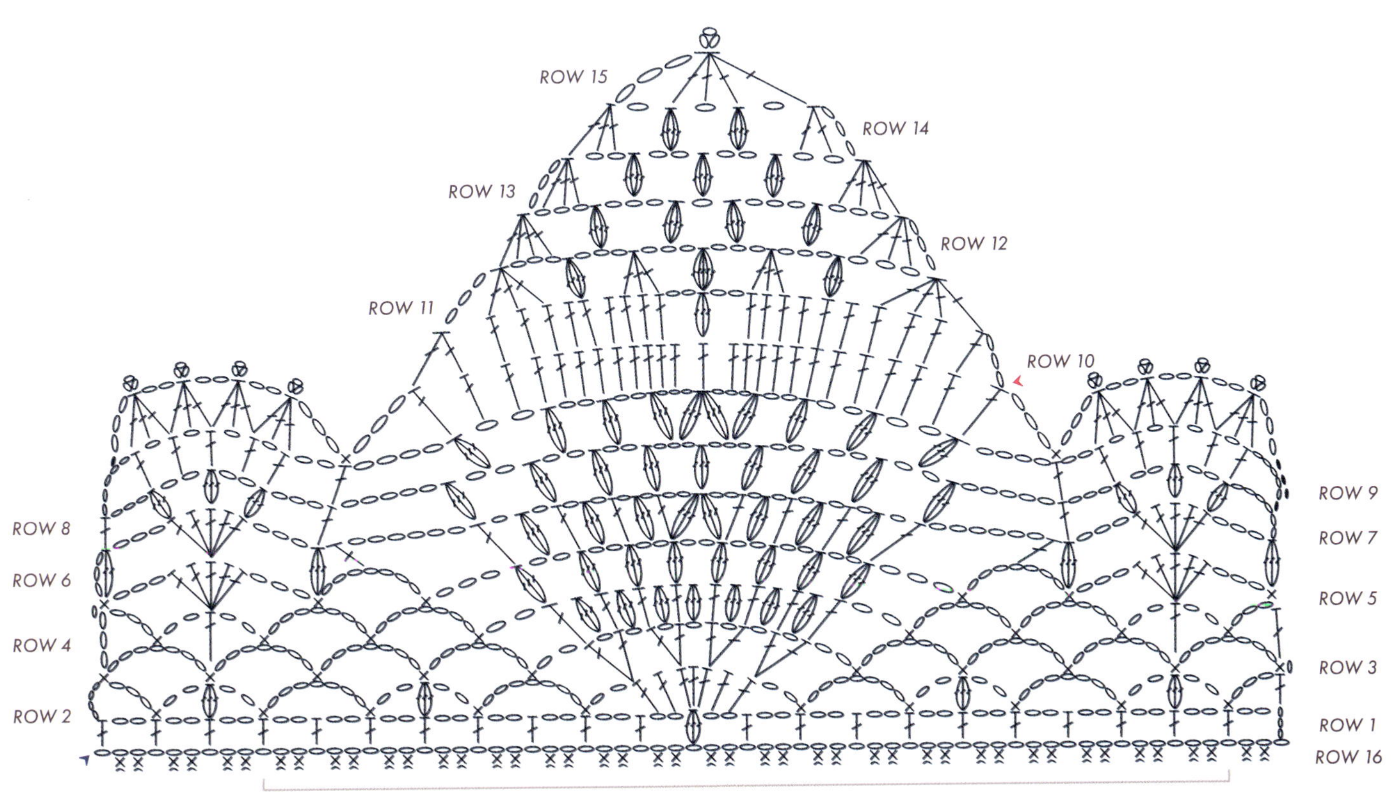

CHICAGO

BORDER 35

DIFFICULTY ****

COLOR: Ecru

STITCHES USED: Chain (ch) • single crochet (sc) • treble crochet (tr) • ch-3 picot (pic)

This edging is made in two parts. First, a support strip is crocheted over 28 chains, then the motif is crocheted on one side of the strip. The motif is worked over 8 rows.

To make the support strip, chain a multiple of 28 + 1 turning chain.

Row 1: Ch 4, insert hook in tenth ch from hook, *sc in next 4, ch 4, skip 4 chs*. Repeat from * to *. End by skipping 3 chs, sc in last.

Row 2: Ch 4 (to replace first tr), tr in next 3, *ch 4, skip 4, tr in next 4*. Repeat from * to *.

Row 3: Ch 1 (to turn), sc in same st, ch 3, skip 3, *4 sc in next ch-4 space, ch 4, skip 4*. Repeat from * to *. End with ch 3, sc in last.

Row 4: Ch 1 (to turn), *4 sc in ch-space, ch 4, skip 4*. Repeat from * to *. End with 4 sc.

Row 5: Repeat Row 3.

Repeat Rows 2–5 to desired length. End with a Row 3.

To crochet the motif, position the strip on the wrong side and work in row ends on one side.

Row 1: Insert hook in st at edge, sc in same st, *4 sc in tr row end, ch 4, skip 2 row ends, sc in next row end, ch 6, skip tr row end, sc in next row end, ch 4*. Repeat from * to *. End with 4 sc in tr row end and sc at the edge.

Row 2: Ch 1 to turn, sc in first st, sc in next 4, *skip (4 chs and sc), (8 tr, ch 3, 8 tr) in next ch-6 space, skip (sc and 4 chs), sc in next 4 sts*. Repeat from * to *. End with 5 sc.

Row 3: Ch 4, skip (4 sc and 2 tr), *tr in next 6, (2 tr, ch 1, 2 tr) in ch-3 space, tr in next 6, skip (2 tr, 4 sc, 2 tr)*. Repeat from * to *. End with ch 3, skip (2 tr and 4 sc), sc in last.

Row 4: Ch 1 to turn, sc in first st, skip (3 chs and 3 tr), ch 5, [tr in next, pic, ch 1] 5x, (tr, pic, ch 1) in ch-space, [tr in next, pic, ch 1] 4x, 2 tr closed together (with the first tr in the next st, and the second one in the fourth tr of the next motif), ch 1, *[tr in next, pic, ch 1] 4x, (tr, pic, ch 1) in ch-space, [tr in next, pic, ch 1] 4x, 2 tr closed together (with the first tr in the next st, and the second one in the fourth tr of the next motif)*. Repeat from * to *. End with [tr in next, pic, ch 1] 5x, ch 5, sc in last st.

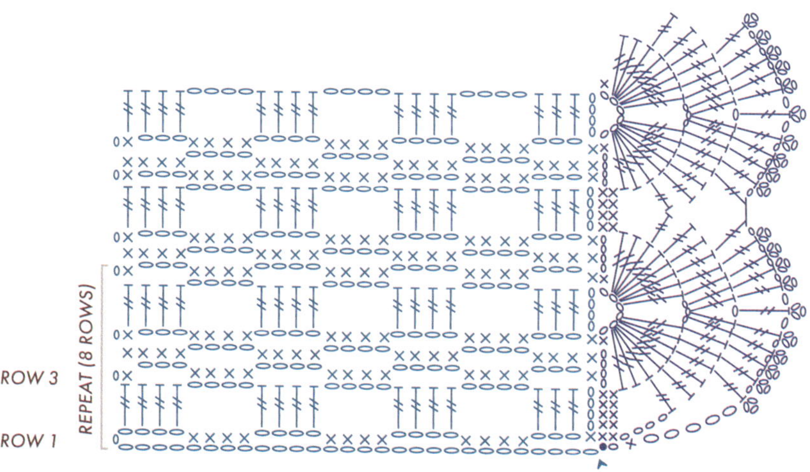

BORDER 36

DIFFICULTY **

COLORS: (A) Black; (B) Red; (C) White

STITCHES USED: Slip stitch (sl st) • chain (ch) • single crochet (sc) • half double crochet (hdc) • double crochet (dc)

The elements of this edging are crocheted independently and then joined to a strip.

With C, ch 3.

Rows 1–3: Ch 1 to turn, sc in next 3, leave thread on standby behind work.

Rows 4–6 (B): Ch 1 to turn, sc in next 3, leave thread on standby behind work.

Rows 7–9 (A): Ch 1 to turn, sc in next 3, leave thread on standby behind work.

Repeat to desired length, carrying yarn behind work. For the motif (an ocean liner), 10 squares are required.

Motifs will be joined to edging in Row 5 of its top portion. Look at the photo for help with assembly.

Crochet the boat hull (First Start on diagram) with A.

Row 1: Ch 1, ch 1 to turn, 2 sc in first ch.

Row 2: Ch 1 to turn, sc in next, 2 sc in next.

Row 3: Ch 1 to turn, 2 sc in first st, sc in next 2.

Row 4: Ch 1 to turn, sc in next 3, 2 sc in next.

Row 5: Ch 1 to turn, 2 sc in first st, sc in next 4.

Row 6: Ch 1 to turn, sc in next 5, 2 sc in next.

Rows 7–24: Ch 1 to turn, sc in next 7.

Row 25: Ch 1 to turn, skip 1, sc in next 6.

Row 26: Ch 1 to turn, sc in next 4, 2 sc closed together.

Row 27: Ch 1 to turn, skip 1, sc in next 4.

Row 28: Ch 1 to turn, sc in next 2, 2 sc closed together.

Row 29: Ch 1 to turn, skip 1, sc in next 2.

Row 30: Ch 1 to turn, 2 sc closed together.

Create the base of the boat's hull (Second Start on diagram) with B. Insert hook in first st and pull up a loop, make 19 sc.

Make the top of the boat (Third Start on diagram) with C.

Row 1: Insert hook in first st on hull and pull up a loop, make 30 sc.

Row 2: Ch 1 to turn, sl st in next 8, ch 2 (to replace first hdc), hdc in next 18.

Row 3: Ch 1 to turn, sc in next 5, ch 1, hdc in next 13.

Row 4: Sl st in first st, ch 3, skip 1, hdc in next 6, change to next col at last yarn over of last hdc (do not cut C), hdc in next 4 with B.

Row 5 (B): Ch 3 (to replace first dc), dc in next, [dc in next, sl st in support strip] twice.

Pick up C, sl st in next 3, ch 3, dc in next, sl st in support strip, ch 3. End with sl st in next st. Fasten off.

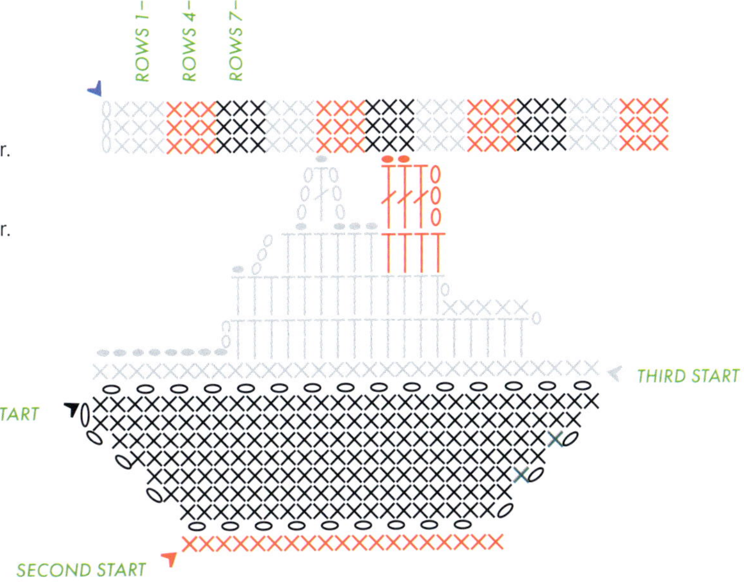

BRIGHTON

BORDER 37

DIFFICULTY **

COLORS: (A) Red; (B) White

STITCHES USED: Slip stitch (sl st) • chain (ch) • single crochet (sc) • half double crochet (hdc)

The elements of this edging are crocheted independently and joined to a strip.

To make a buoy: With A, ch 20, sl st to close ring.

Rnd 1: Ch 2 (to replace first hdc), hdc in each ch (19 total), sl st to close.

Rnd 2: Ch 1, *sc in next 4, 2 sc in next*. Repeat from * to *. End with sc in next 4, sl st in first st to close. Fasten off.

Rnd 3 (B): Insert hook in an initial starting ch and pull up a loop, make 3 long sc in same st from Rnd 1, [ch 5, skip 4 sts from Rnd 1, 3 long sc in next] 3x, ch 5, sl st in first st, ch 7, sl st in first ch. Fasten off.

Crochet the number of motifs required to reach desired length, alternating cols.

To make the support strip, using A, ch 7, *sl st in top ch-7 ring, making sure the motif's right side is facing, ch 13*. Repeat from * to *. End with 8 chs, ch 1 to turn, sc across. Fasten off.

With B, begin again with right side facing and sc across. Fasten off.

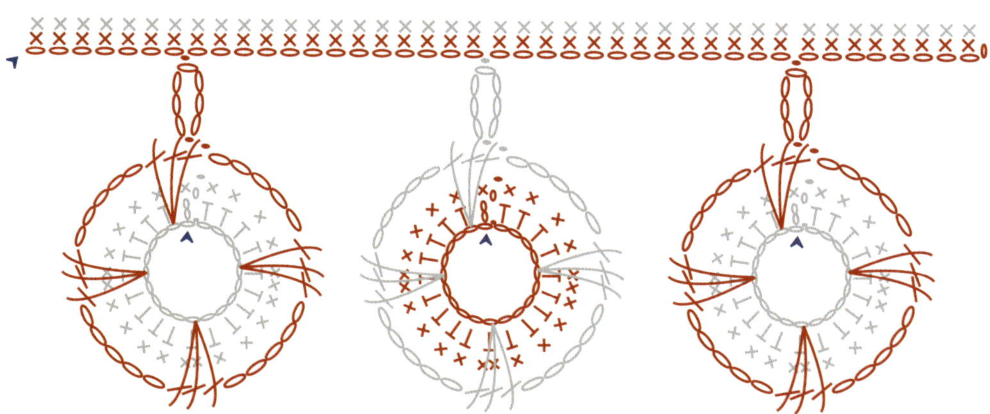

BORDER 38

DIFFICULTY **

COLORS: (A) Grey; (B) Red

STITCHES USED: Slip stitch (sl st) • chain (ch) • single crochet (sc) • half double crochet (hdc) • double crochet (dc) • ch-3 picot (pic)

The elements of this edging are crocheted independently and then joined to a strip.

Rnd 1 (A): Ch 4 (to replace first dc), (ch 3, dc in first starting ch) 5x, ch 3, sl st in fourth starting ch.

Rnd 2: *3 sc in next ch-3 space, sc in next dc*. Repeat from * to *. End with 3 sc and sl st to close. Fasten off.

Rnd 3 (B): Working in back loops around, ch 2 (to replace first hdc), hdc in next, *2 hdc in next st, hdc in next 3*. Repeat from * to *. End with 2 hdc in next st, hdc in next, sl st to close. Fasten off.

Rnd 4 (A): Insert hook in first hdc and pull up a loop, sc in same st, pic, *sc in next 4, pic*. Repeat from * to *. End with sc in next 4, sl st to close. Fasten off.

Crochet the required number of motifs to reach desired length, alternating cols.

To make the support strip, using A, ch 12, *sl st in pic making sure the motif's right side is facing, ch 16*. Repeat from * to *. End with 12 chs. With B, insert hook in first st and work across as follows: *sc in next, ch 3, skip 3*. Repeat from * to *. End with sc in last.

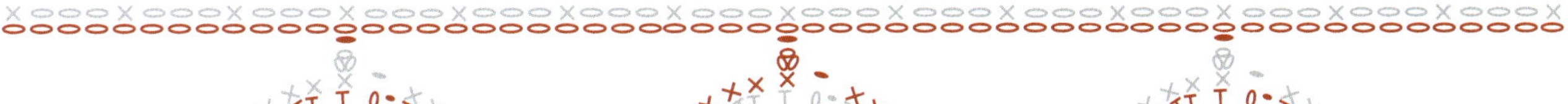

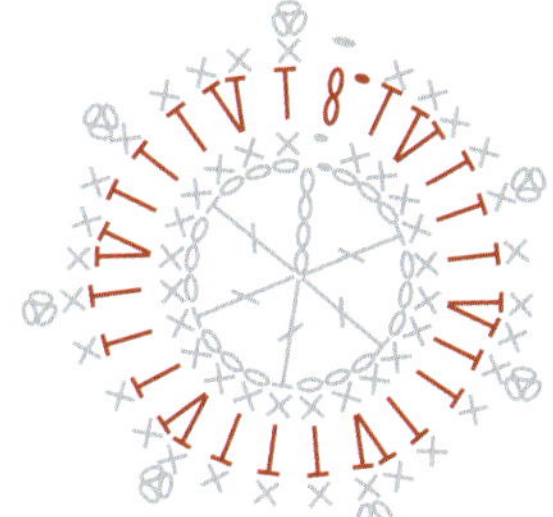

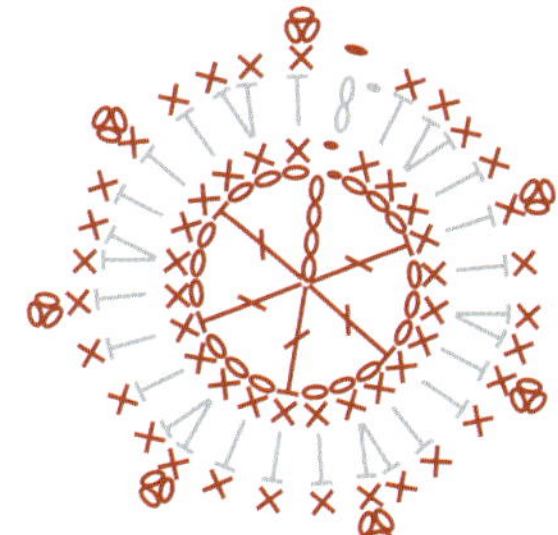

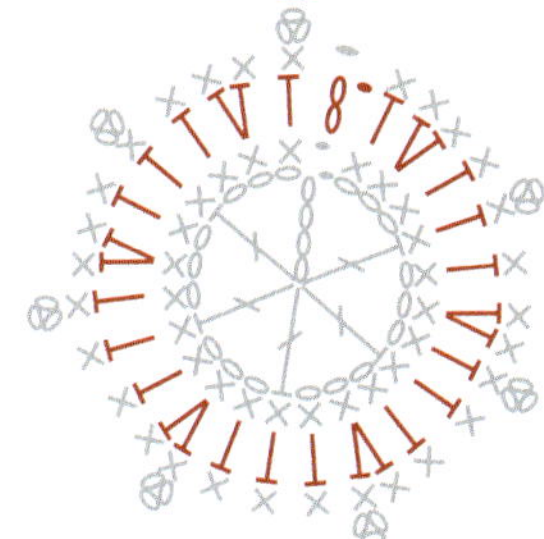

BORDER 39

DIFFICULTY ***

COLORS: (A) Blue; (B) White; (C) Red

STITCHES USED: Slip stitch (sl st) • chain (ch) • single crochet (sc) • half double crochet (hdc) • double crochet (dc) • treble crochet (tr) • ch-3 picot (pic)

The elements of this edging are crocheted independently and then joined to a support strip.

With A, ch 21.

Row 1: Pic, tr in fourth ch from hook, dc in next, hdc in next, sc in next 9, hdc in next, dc in next, tr in next, sl st in last. End with pic. Fasten off.

Row 2 (B): On right side (Second Start), insert hook at base of tr and pull up a loop, sl st in next 6, ch 3, 3 dc closed together, pic, ch 3, sl st in next 6. Fasten off.

Row 3 (A): On right side (Third Start), insert hook in fourth sc from Row 1, ch 3 (to replace first dc), 2 dc closed together, ch 11, make a 6-ch ring closed with a sl st in sixth ch from hook.

Row 4: With thread behind work, 13 sc in ring. End with sl st in next 11 chs, ch 3, sl st in next sc from Row 1. Fasten off.

Make another anchor, alternating A and B, join them with a sl st.

With C, make the support strip as follows: ch 11, *sl st in seventh sc in ring, ch 15*. Repeat from * to *. End with 11 chs. Last row: ch 1 to turn, sc across. Fasten off.

BORDER 40

DIFFICULTY *

COLORS: (A) Blue; (B) White; (C) Red; (D) Black

STITCHES USED: Slip stitch (sl st) • chain (ch) • single crochet (sc) • half double crochet (hdc) • double crochet (dc)

The elements of this edging are crocheted independently and then joined to a support strip.

With A, ch 11.

Rows 1–3 (A): Ch 1 to turn, sc in next 11. Fasten off.

Row 4 (B): Insert hook in first st and pull up a loop, ch 3 (to replace first dc), dc in next 8, 2 dc closed together. Turn.

Rows 5–9: Ch 2 (to replace first hdc), hdc in next 8, turn. Change to next color at last yarn over of last hdc of last row.

Rows 10–11 (C): Ch 2 (to replace first hdc), hdc in next 8, turn. Fasten off after last row.

Row 12 (B): Insert hook in first st and pull up a loop, sc in next 9, turn.

Row 13: Ch 1, sc in next 9. Fasten off.

Row 14 (D): Insert hook and pull up a loop, sc in next 9, turn.

Row 15: Sl st in first st, ch 3 (to replace first dc), 2 dc closed together, dc in next 3, ch 3, skip next sc, sl st in last. Fasten off.

Crochet the other motifs, changing col as shown in the diagram. Make the number of motifs required to reach desired length.

With A, crochet the support strip as follows: ch 11, *3 sc in the top of the lighthouse (with right side facing), ch 15*. Repeat from * to *. End with 11 chs. Last row: ch 1 to turn, sc in next 2, *ch 3, skip 3, sc in next st*. Repeat from * to *. End with sc in last 2. Fasten off.

BORDER 39

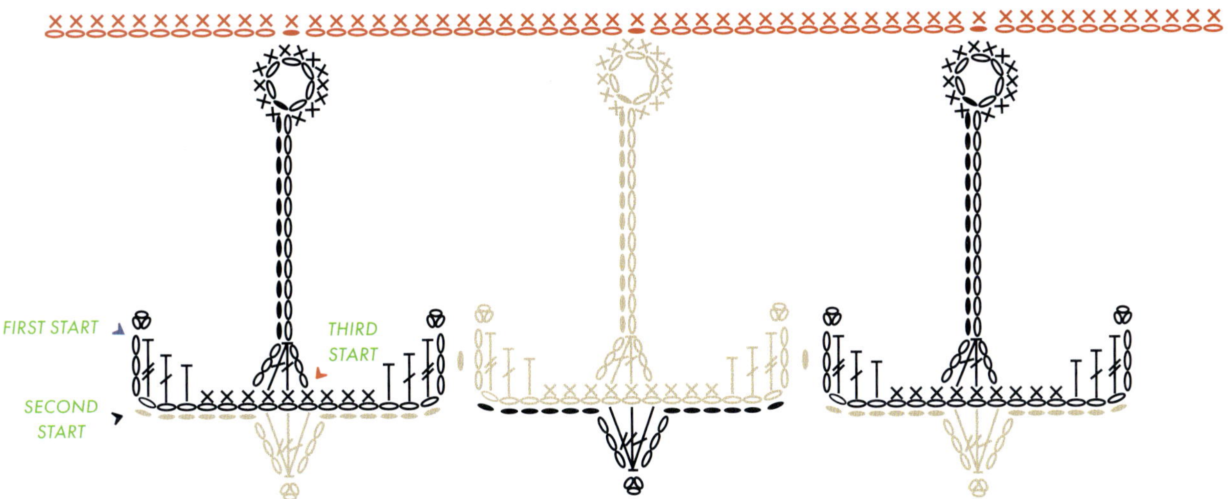

BORDER 40

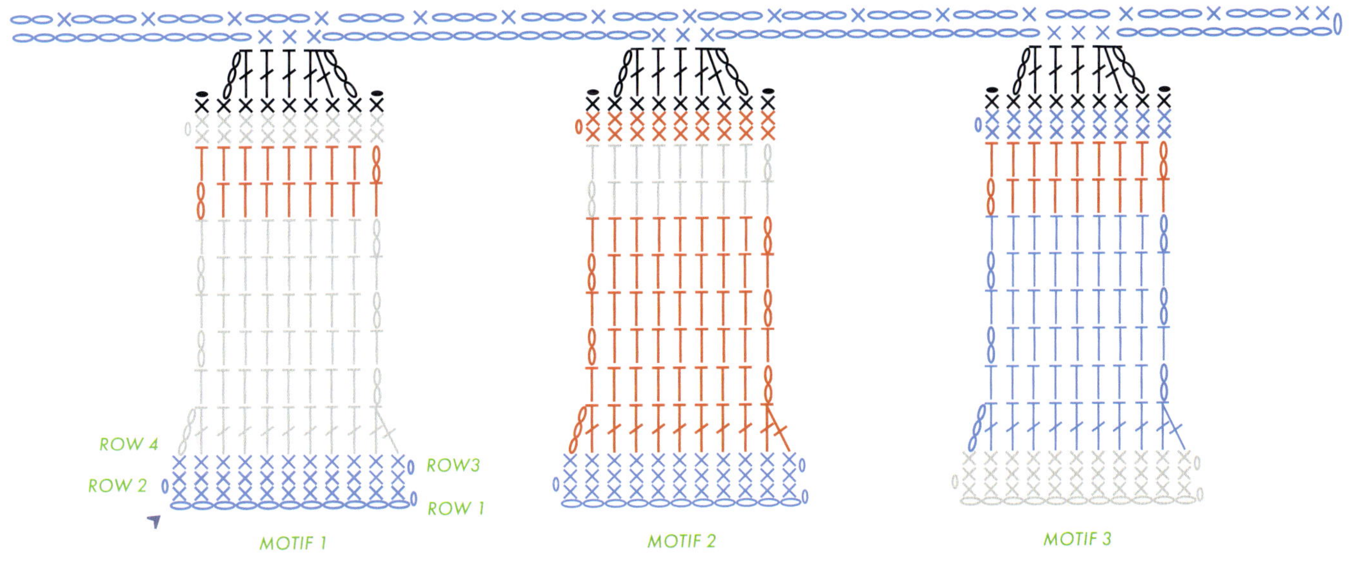

BORDER 41

DIFFICULTY *

COLORS: (A) Blue; (B) White; (C) Red • Red embroidery thread for the pom-poms

STITCHES USED: Slip stitch (sl st) • chain (ch) • single crochet (sc)

The elements of this edging are crocheted independently and then joined to a strip.

With A, ch 6, sl st to close ring.

Rnd 1: Ch 1, 9 sc in ring, sl st in first st.

Rnd 2: Ch 1, *sc in next, 2 sc in next*. Repeat from * to *. End with sc in next, sl st in first st.

Rnd 3: Ch 1, *sc in next 3, 2 sc in next*. Repeat from * to *. End with sc in next, sl st in first st.

Rnd 4: Ch 1, *sc in next 2, 2 sc in next*. Repeat from * to *. End with sc in next, sl st in first st.

Rnd 5: Ch 1, *sc in next 3, 2 sc in next*. Repeat from * to *. End with sc in next, sl st in first st.

Rnd 6: Ch 1, *sc in next 2, 2 sc in next*. Repeat from * to *. End with sc in next, sl st in first st.

Rnd 7: Ch 1, sc around. End with sl st in first st.

Make ⅔-inch (1.5 cm) pom-poms with the red thread. Place them in the center of each beret and attach them, hiding the ends in the work.

Crochet the support strip starting each row on the same side. With A, ch 15, *sc in 3 sts on a beret, ch 20*. Repeat from * to * to desired length. End with 15 chs. Fasten off. With B, *sc in next 3, ch 3, skip 3*. Repeat from * to *, ending with sc in last 3. Fasten off. With C, sc in first, ch 3, skip 2, *sc in next 3, ch 3, skip 3*. Repeat from * to *. Fasten off.

DISK DETAIL

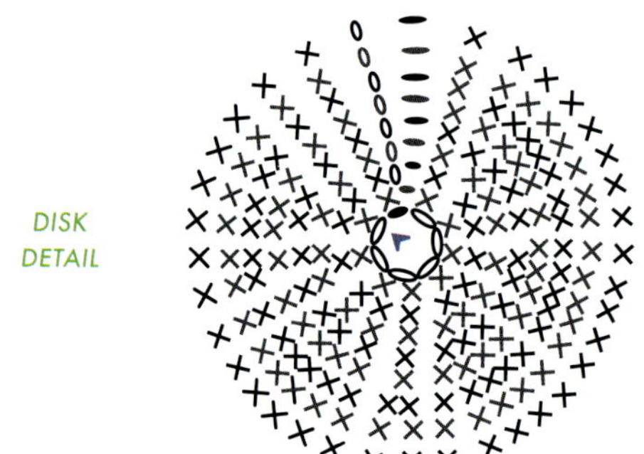

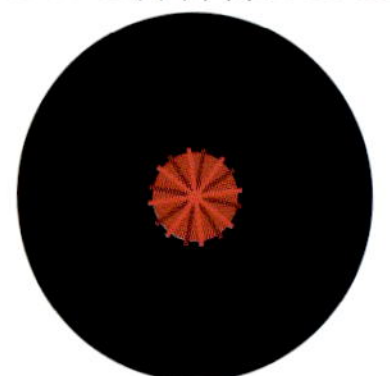

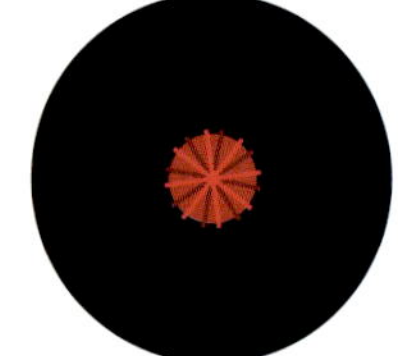

BORDER 42

DIFFICULTY *

COLOR: Black

STITCHES USED: Slip stitch (sl st) • chain (ch) • single crochet (sc) • double crochet (dc) • treble crochet (tr) • ch-3 picot (pic)

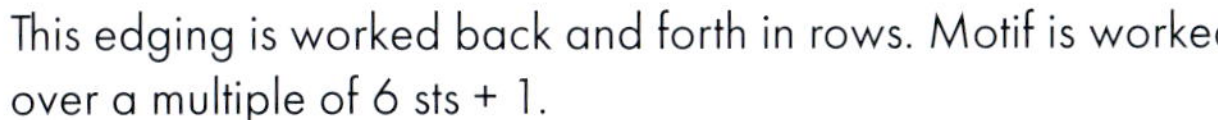

This edging is worked back and forth in rows. Motif is worked over a multiple of 6 sts + 1.

Chain a multiple of 6 + 1.

Row 1: Ch 3 (to replace first dc), *ch 1, skip 1, dc in next*. Repeat from * to *. Turn.

Row 2: Ch 3 (to replace first dc), *ch 1, skip 1, dc in next*. Repeat from * to *. Turn.

Row 3: Ch 7, skip 3, *sc in next dc, ch 7, skip 5*. Repeat from * to *. End with ch 7, skip 3, sc in last. Turn.

Row 4: Sl st in first 3 chs, sc in next, *ch 4, tr in next sc, ch 4, sc in fourth ch of ch-7 space*. Repeat from * to *. End with ch 4, sc in fourth ch of last space. Turn.

Row 5: Ch 9, skip 4 chs, *(sc, ch 7, sc) in tr, ch 7, skip (ch 4, sc, ch 4)*. Repeat from * to *. End with ch 3, skip 4 chs, tr in last sc. Turn.

Row 6: Ch 4 (to replace first tr), 2 tr closed together at base of starting ch, *ch 3, sc in fourth ch of ch-7 space, ch 3, 3 tr closed together in next ch-space*. Repeat from * to *. Turn.

Row 7: Ch 4 (to replace first tr), pic, *ch 4, sc in sc from previous row, ch 4, skip 3 chs, (tr, pic) in next tr-group*. Repeat from * to *. Turn.

Row 8: Sc in first pic, *ch 4, pic, ch 4, sc in next pic*. Repeat from * to *. Fasten off.

BORDER 43

DIFFICULTY **

COLOR: Black

STITCHES USED: Slip stitch (sl st) • chain (ch) • single crochet (sc) • double crochet (dc) • treble crochet (tr) • ch-3 picot (pic) • crab stitch

This edging is worked back and forth in rows. Motif is worked over a multiple of 20 sts + 1.

Chain a multiple of 20 + 1.

Row 1: Ch 1 to turn, sc across. Turn.

Row 2: Ch 3 (to replace first dc), *ch 1, skip 1, dc in next*. Repeat from * to *. Turn.

Row 3: Ch 3 (to replace first dc), *ch 1, skip 1, dc in next*. Repeat from * to *.

Row 4: Ch 1 to turn, sc in first st, *ch 8, skip 9, (tr, ch 3, tr) in next, ch 8, skip 9, sc in next*. Repeat from * to *.

Row 5: Ch 1 to turn, sc in first st, *ch 4, skip 8 chs, 3 tr closed together in next tr, ch 5, 3 tr closed together in next ch, ch 5, skip 1 ch, 3 tr closed together in next ch, ch 5, 3 tr closed together in next tr, ch 4, skip 8 chs, sc in next sc*. Repeat from * to *. Turn.

Row 6: *Ch 4, skip 4 chs, [3 tr closed together in next st, ch 4, skip 2 chs, 3 tr closed together in next ch, ch 4, skip 2 chs] 3x, 3 tr closed together in next tr-group, ch 4, skip 4 chs, sc in next st*. Repeat from * to *. Turn.

Row 7: *Ch 4, [skip 5, (sc, pic) 3x in next ch-4 space, sc in same space] 6x, ch 4, skip 4 chs, sl st in next*. Repeat from * to *. Fasten off.

Row 8: Now working across the starting chain, crab stitch across. Fasten off.

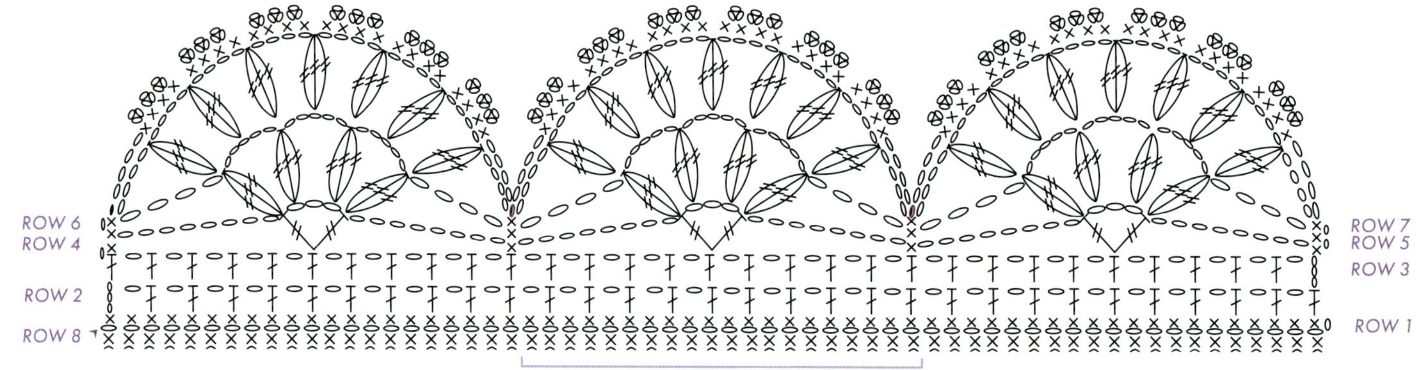

BORDER 44

DIFFICULTY ***

COLOR: Black

STITCHES USED: Slip stitch (sl st) • chain (ch) • single crochet (sc) • treble crochet (tr) • double treble crochet (dtr) • ch-3 picot (pic) • crab stitch

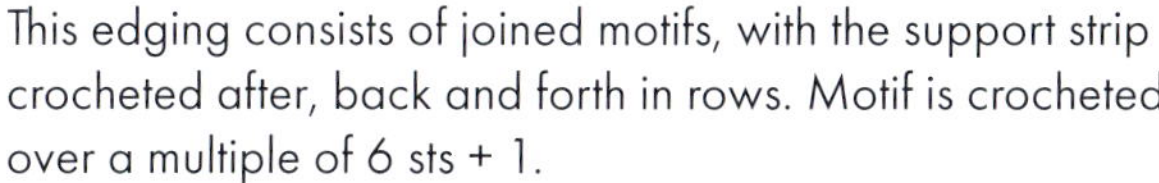

This edging consists of joined motifs, with the support strip crocheted after, back and forth in rows. Motif is crocheted over a multiple of 6 sts + 1.

To begin the motif: ch 7, sl st to close.

Rnd 1: 16 sc in ring, sl st to close.

Rnd 2: Ch 4 (to replace first tr), 3 tr closed together in first sc, pic, *ch 5, skip sc, tr in next sc, ch 5, skip sc, 4 tr closed together in next st, pic*. Repeat from * to *. End with ch 5, skip sc, tr in next, ch 5, sl st to close.

Continue, making the required number of motifs to reach desired length.

Progressively assemble the motifs by, at the joining pic, making a sl st instead of the second ch (making joining pic as follows: ch 1, sl st in corresponding pic of previous motif, ch 1, sl st in same st).

To crochet the support strip, insert hook in side pic of last motif joined and pull up a loop.

Row 1: Ch 6 (for motif height), tr in next tr on first motif, ch 6, sc in next pic on first motif, ch 6, 2 tr closed together in tr on first motif and tr on next motif, *ch 6, sc in pic of same motif, ch 6, 2 tr closed together in tr on same motif and tr on next motif*. Repeat from * to *. End with 6 chs, close tr in tr on last motif and dtr in last side pic together. Turn.

Row 2: Ch 4 (to replace first tr), *ch 2, skip 1, 4 tr closed together, ch 2, skip 1, tr in next st*. Repeat from * to *.

Row 3: Ch 1 to turn, sc across.

Row 4: End with a finishing row in crab stitch. Fasten off.

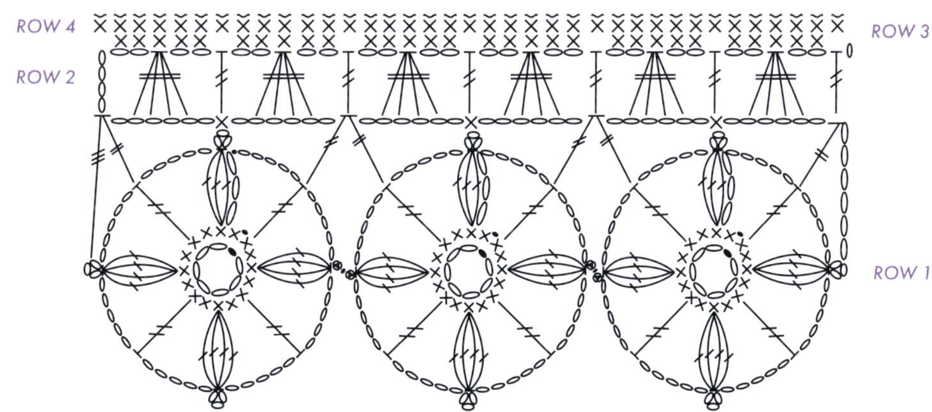

BORDER 45

DIFFICULTY **

COLOR: Black

STITCHES USED: Slip stitch (sl st) • chain (ch) • single crochet (sc) • half double crochet (hdc) • double crochet (dc) • treble crochet (tr) • ch-3 picot (pic)

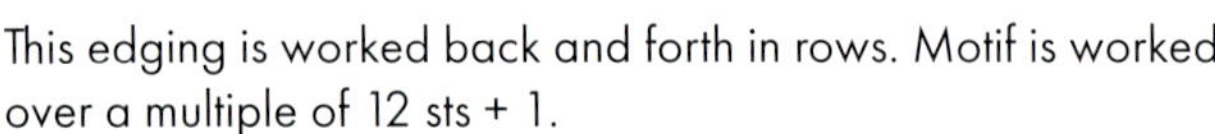

This edging is worked back and forth in rows. Motif is worked over a multiple of 12 sts + 1.

Chain a multiple of 12 + 1.

Row 1: Ch 3 (to replace first dc), ch 1, skip 1, *3 dc closed together in next, ch 2, skip 2*. Repeat from * to *. End with ch 1, skip 1, dc in last.

Row 2: Ch 1 to turn, sc across. Turn.

Row 3: Ch 3 (to replace first dc), *skip 2, dc in sc after next dc-group, ch 1, dc in sc before same dc-group*. Repeat from * to *. End with dc in last. Turn.

Row 4: Ch 1, sc in next 6, *(follow the arrows on the diagram) ch 6, ch 1 to turn, turn work and crochet 6 sc in these chs, sl st in base row, turn work and place thread behind work, crochet again in these 6 sc, ch 5, crochet again in the 6 chs: sc in 6 chs, now working in sts from previous row, sc in next 12*. Repeat from * to *. End with sc in next 6.

Row 5: Ch 1 to turn, sc in first st, *ch 3, skip 4 sts, tr in next sc on base row, ch 2, [dc, ch 1] 8x in ch-5 space, dc in same space, ch 2, skip 6 sc, tr in next sc, ch 3, skip 4 sc, sc in next*. Repeat from * to *. Fasten off.

Row 6: Insert the hook in the sc at the beginning of Row 5, ch 4 (to replace first tr), *ch 1, skip (3 chs, tr, ch 1), sc in next ch, [ch 1, pic, ch 1, skip dc, hdc in next ch] 8x, ch 1, pic, ch 1, skip dc, sc in next ch, ch 1, skip (1 ch, tr, ch 3), tr in next sc*. Repeat from * to *, joining the first and second pics of next motif with sl st in last and second-to-last pic of previous motif (see diagram). Fasten off.

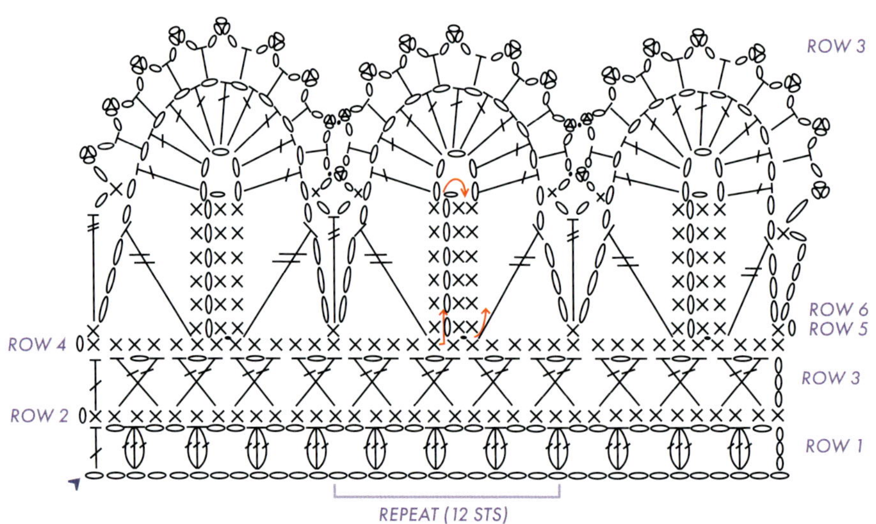

BORDER 46

DIFFICULTY ***

COLOR: Black

STITCHES USED: Slip stitch (sl st) • chain (ch) • single crochet (sc) • double crochet (dc) • treble crochet (tr) • ch-3 picot (pic)

This edging is worked back and forth in rows. Motif is crocheted on a multiple of 12 sts + 1.

Chain a multiple of 12 + 1.

Row 1: Ch 3 (to replace first dc), 2 dc closed together in first st, *ch 5, skip 5, 3 dc closed together in next st*. Repeat from * to *.

Row 2: Ch 1 to turn, *sc in dc-group from previous row, ch 5, skip 5, 5 dc in next dc-group, ch 5, skip 5*. Repeat from * to *. End with ch 5, skip 5, sc in last. Turn.

Row 3: Ch 5, skip 2 chs, tr in next, ch 4, skip 2 chs, *3 dc closed together in first dc of group from previous row, ch 2, skip dc, dc in next dc of same group, ch 2, skip dc, 3 dc closed together in last dc of same group, ch 4, skip 2 chs, 2 tr closed together with the first one in the next chain, and the second one in the third ch of the next 5-ch-space, ch 4, skip 2 chs*. Repeat from * to *. End with ch 4, skip 2 chs, 2 tr closed together with the first one in the next ch, and the second one in the last sc. Turn.

Row 4: Ch 3 (to replace first dc), pic, 2 dc in same space, *ch 3, skip 4 chs, (sl st, ch 3, dc) in next dc-group, ch 3, skip 2 chs, sc in next dc, ch 3, skip 2 chs, (dc, ch 3, sl st) in next dc-group, ch 3, skip 4 chs, (3 dc, pic, 2 dc) in next st*. Repeat from * to *. End with ch 3, skip 4 chs, (3 dc, pic) in last st. Fasten off.

Now finish each tip independently.

Row 5: Insert hook in third ch of last motif (see diagram) and pull up a loop, ch 3, (dc, ch 3, 2 dc closed together) in same st, skip (3 chs, sc and 3 chs), 2 dc closed together in next dc, ch 3, 2 dc closed together in same st. Turn.

Row 6: Ch 3 (to replace first dc), dc in same st, ch 2, skip 3 chs, 3 dc closed together between dc-groups from previous row, ch 2, skip 3 chs, 2 dc closed together in last. Turn.

Row 7: Ch 3 (to replace first dc), dc in same space, skip 2 chs, 2 dc closed together in next st, skip 2 chs, 2 dc closed together in last. Turn.

Row 8: Ch 3, 2 dc closed together, pic. Fasten off.

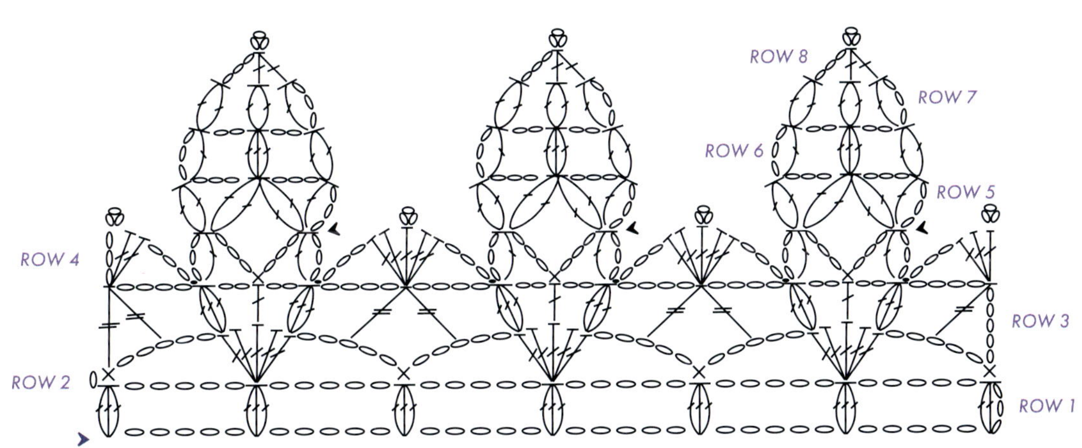

BORDER 47

DIFFICULTY **

COLOR: Black

STITCHES USED: Slip stitch (sl st) • chain (ch) • single crochet (sc) • double crochet (dc) • treble crochet (tr) • ch-3 picot (pic)

This edging is worked back and forth in rows. The motif is worked over a multiple of 32 sts + 1.

Chain a multiple of 32 + 1.

Row 1: Ch 1 to turn, sc across.

Row 2: Ch 3, dc in first st, ch 3, skip 2, *4 dc closed together with the first 2 in the next st, skipping 1, and the next 2 in the next st, ch 2, skip 2, 2 dc closed together in next st, ch 1, 2 dc closed together in same st, ch 2, skip 2*. Repeat from * to *. End with 4 dc closed together with the first 2 in the next st, skipping 1, and the next 2 in the next st, ch 3, skip 2, 2 dc closed together in last st. Turn.

Row 3: Ch 4 (to replace first tr), ch 5, skip 3, *sc in next st, skip 3, insert hook between dc-groups from previous row and make (3 dc, ch 1, 3 dc), skip 3, sc in next st, ch 9, skip 7*. Repeat from * to *. End with sc in next st, skip 3, (3 dc, ch 1, 3 dc) between dc-groups, skip 3, sc in next st, ch 5, tr in last st.

Row 4: Ch 1 to turn, sc in first st, *ch 1, skip (chs and sc), tr in next st, 2 tr in next st, tr in next st, 3 tr in next ch, tr in next st, 2 tr in next st, tr in next st, ch 1, sc in central ch of next ch-space, ch 1, skip (4 chs and sc), tr in next st, 2 tr in next st, ch 3, 2 tr closed together in next 2 tr, ch 3, 2 tr in next st, tr in next st, ch 1, sc in central ch of next ch-space*. Repeat from * to *. End with ch 1, skip (chs and sc), tr in next st, 2 tr in next st, tr in next st, 3 tr in next ch, tr in next st, 2 tr in next st, tr in next st, ch 1, sc in last. Turn.

Row 5: Ch 5, skip 3, *tr in next st, 2 tr in next st, tr in next st, (tr, ch 2, tr) in next st, tr in next st, 2 tr in next st, tr in next st, ch 2, skip (2 tr, ch 1, sc, ch 1), 3 tr closed together, ch 4, skip 3 chs, 3 tr in next st, ch 4, skip 3 chs, 3 tr closed together, ch 2, skip (ch 1, sc, ch 1, 2 tr)*. Repeat from * to *. End with tr in next st, 2 tr in next st, tr in next st, (tr, ch 2, tr) in next st, tr in next st, 2 tr in next st, tr in next st, skip 3, tr in last st. Turn.

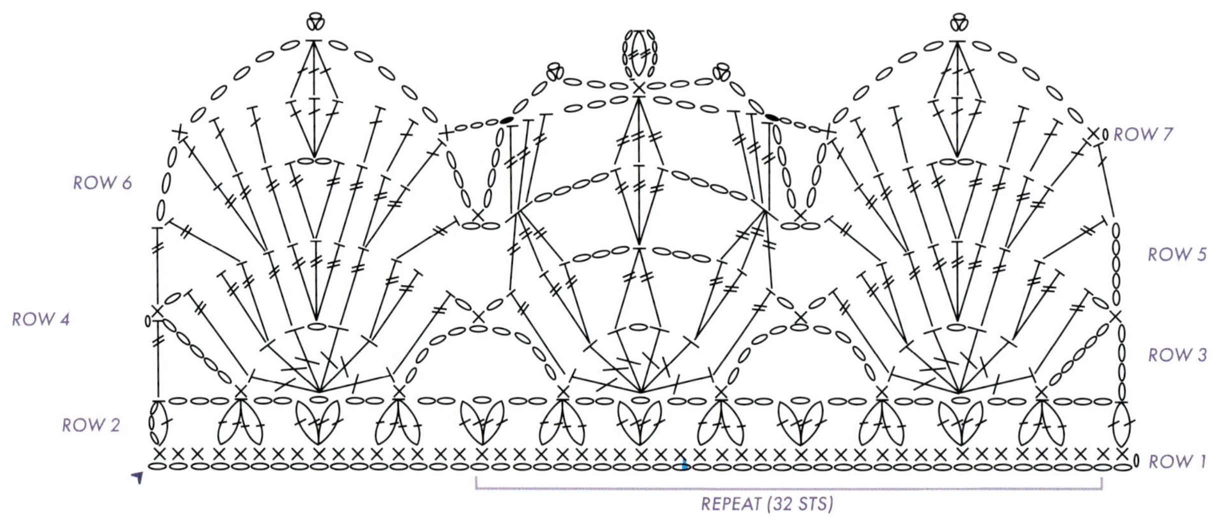

Row 6: *Ch 3, skip 1, dc in next 3, skip 1, 3 dc in next ch-2 space, skip 1, dc in next 3, ch 3, skip 1, sc in next ch-2 space, ch 4, 3 tr in next tr-group, ch 3, skip 4 chs, 3 tr closed together, ch 3, skip 4 chs, 3 tr in next tr-group, ch 4, sc in next ch-space*. Repeat from * to *. End with ch 3, skip 1, dc in next 3, skip 1, 3 dc in next ch-2 space, skip 1, dc in next 3, dc in last. Turn.

Row 7: Ch 1, *sc in second dc, ch 5, skip 2, 3 dc closed together, pic, ch 5, skip 2, sc in next dc from previous row, ch 3, sl st in next tr, ch 2, pic, ch 3, skip 5, sc in next st, ch 4, 2 tr closed together in sc, ch 4, sl st at base, ch 3, pic, ch 2, skip 5, sl st in next tr, ch 3*. Repeat from * to *. End with sc in first tr of last section, ch 5, skip 2, 3 dc closed together, pic, ch 5, skip 2, sc in last dc. Fasten off.

BORDER 48

DIFFICULTY ***

COLOR: Ecru

STITCHES USED: Slip stitch (sl st) • chain (ch) • double crochet (dc) • ch-3 picot (pic)

The motifs of this border are worked height-wise back and forth in rows.

Ch 9, dc in first ch.

Row 1: Ch 3 (to turn and replace first dc), 10 dc in ch-space, dc in fifth ch of ch-space.

Row 2: Turn, (ch 1, pic) 3x, ch 1, (dc, ch 4, dc) in sixth dc.

Repeat these two rows to desired height.

Last Row: Turn, sl st in each dc, *sl st in next ch, ch 2, skip 2 chs, sl st in presenting dc, (ch 1, pic) 3x, ch 1*. Repeat from * to *. Fasten off.

BORDER 49

DIFFICULTY ****

COLOR: Ecru

STITCHES USED: Chain (ch) • single crochet (sc) • half double crochet (hdc) • double crochet (dc) • treble crochet (tr) • ch-3 picot (pic) • puff ([yarn over, insert hook in same stitch and pull up a long loop] 3x, yarn over and pull through first 6 loops, yarn over and pull through remaining 2 loops, close puff with a tight ch)

The motifs of this border are crocheted on a support strip, which is crocheted first, in rows, height-wise.

Row 1: Ch 3, pic, ch 1, dc in first ch. Turn.

Row 2: Ch 5, dc in dc of previous row, dc in next ch. Turn.

Row 3: Ch 3, pic, ch 1, dc in next dc. Turn.

Repeat Rows 2–3 to desired length. End with Row 3.

Begin working on the resulting length.

Row 4: Ch 4, *skip the length of the dc, sc in third ch of next ch-5 space, ch 1, skip the length of the dc, puff in first ch of ch-space, ch 3, skip next ch, puff in next ch, ch 3, skip next ch, puff in next ch, ch 1*. Repeat from * to *. End by skipping the length of a dc, sc in last st of row. Turn.

Row 5: Ch 2, *sc in first puff, *[(hdc, dc, tr, pic, dc and hdc) in next ch-3 space, sc in next puff] 2x, skip next ch, (sc, pic) in next sc*. Repeat from * to *. Fasten off.

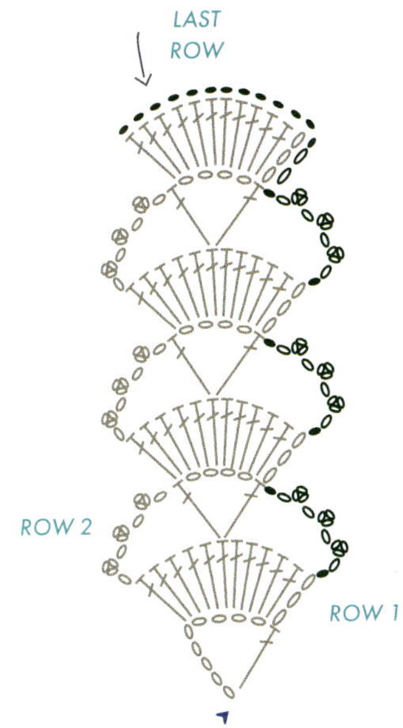

BORDER 50

DIFFICULTY ****

COLOR: Ecru

STITCHES USED: Slip stich (sl st) • chain (ch) • single crochet (sc) • double crochet (dc) • ch-3 picot (pic)

This is a rounded border.

Chain a multiple of 4 + 1.

Row 1: Ch 1, sc in first st, *ch 3, skip 3 chs, sc in next*. Repeat from * to *. Turn.

Row 2: Ch 1, sc in first st, ch 1, skip next, *sc in next, ch 3, skip 3*. Repeat from * to *. End with sc in next, ch 1, skip next, sc in last. Turn.

Row 3: Ch 3 (to replace first dc), (dc, pic, dc) in first sc, ch 3, skip 3, *(2 dc, pic, dc) in next ch, ch 3, skip 3*. Repeat from * to *. End with (2 dc, pic, dc) in last. Turn.

Row 4: Ch 1, *sl st in pic, ch 2, (2 dc, pic, dc) in second ch from previous row, ch 2*. Repeat from * to *. End with sl st in last pic. Fasten off.

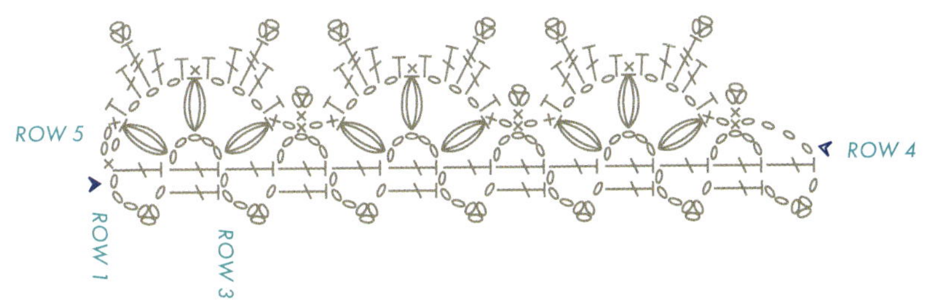

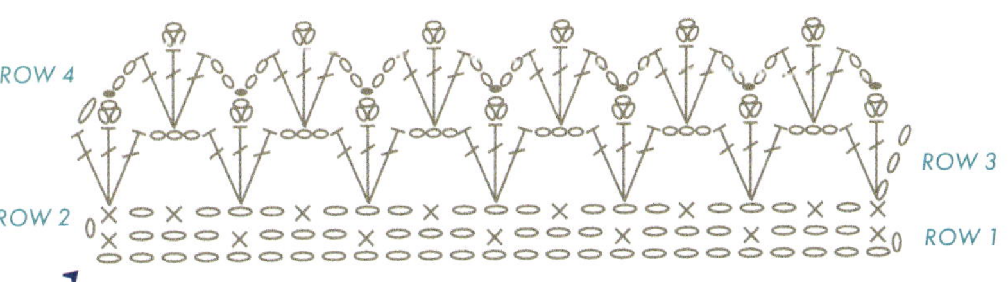

BORDER 51

DIFFICULTY ****

COLOR: Ecru

STITCHES USED: Slip stitch (sl st) • chain (ch) • single crochet (sc) • half double crochet (hdc) • double crochet (dc) • treble crochet (tr) • ch-3 picot (pic)

This is a rounded border.

Chain a multiple of 4 + 1.

Row 1: Ch 1, sc across. Turn.

Row 2: Ch 3 (to replace first dc), *ch 1, skip next st, (dc, ch 1, dc) in next st, ch 1, skip next st, dc in next st*. Repeat from * to *.

Row 3: Ch 1 to turn, sc in first st, *ch 2, skip 2 sts, (2 dc, tr, pic, 2 dc) in next ch, ch 2, skip 2 sts, sc in next dc*. Repeat from * to *. Turn.

Row 4: Ch 3 (to replace first dc), ch 3, skip 4 sts, *sl st in next pic, ch 5, skip 9 sts*. Repeat from * to *. End with sl st in next pic, ch 2, skip 4 sts, dc in last st. Turn.

Row 5: Ch 3 (to replace first dc), pic, 2 hdc in next ch, 2 sc in next, *skip sl st, 2 sc in next, 2 hdc in next, (dc, pic) in next, 2 hdc in next, 2 sc in next*. Repeat from * to *. End with 2 sc in next, 2 hdc in next, (dc, pic) in last. Fasten off.

BORDER 52

DIFFICULTY ****

COLOR: Ecru

STITCHES USED: Slip stitch (sl st) • chain (ch) • half double crochet (hdc) • treble crochet (tr) • ch-3 picot (pic) • puff ([yarn over, insert hook in same stitch and pull up a long loop] 3x, yarn over and pull through first 6 loops, yarn over and pull through remaining 2 loops, close puff with a tight ch)

Chain a multiple of 6 + 1, while following instructions for Row 1.

Row 1: *Ch 1, pic*. Repeat from * to *.

Row 2: Ch 3 to turn, 2 long hdc in first pic, pic, *skip (ch 1, pic, ch 1), 3 tr in next pic, 3 pic, sl st in first pic, 3 tr in skipped pic, skip 1 ch, (puff, pic) in next pic*. Repeat from * to *. Fasten off.

BORDER 53

DIFFICULTY ****

COLOR: Ecru

STITCHES USED: Slip stitch (sl st) • chain (ch) • single crochet (sc) • double crochet (dc) • treble crochet (tr) • double treble crochet (dtr)

The motifs of this border are crocheted height-wise, back and forth in rows.

Ch 10, sl st to form a ring.

Row 1: Ch 4 (to replace first tr), tr in ring, (ch 5, dc in top of tr just made, 2 tr in ring) 3x, ch 2, 8 tr in ring.

Row 2: Ch 1 to turn, sc in first st, [ch 1, sc] 7x, ch 10, sc in ch after next tr, ch 4, sc in third ch of ch-5 ring, turn.

Row 3: Working in ch-10 ring from Row 2, tr in ring, [ch 5, dc in previous tr, 2 tr in ring] 3x, ch 2, 8 tr in ring. End with dtr in fifth sc of previous row.

Start again at Row 2 and repeat these last two rows to desired length. Fasten off.

BORDER 51

ROW 5
ROW 4
ROW 3
ROW 2
ROW 1

BORDER 52

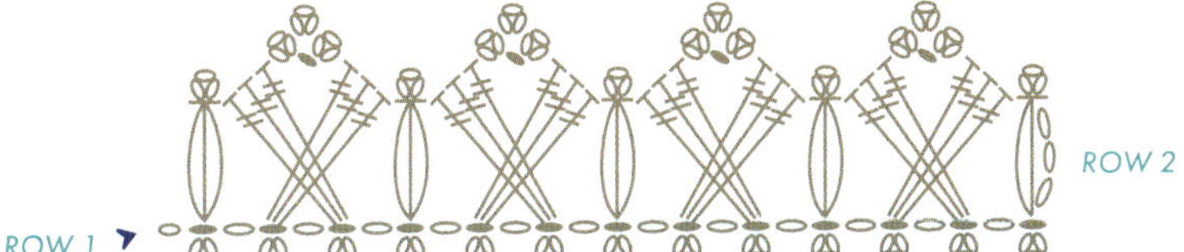

BORDER 53

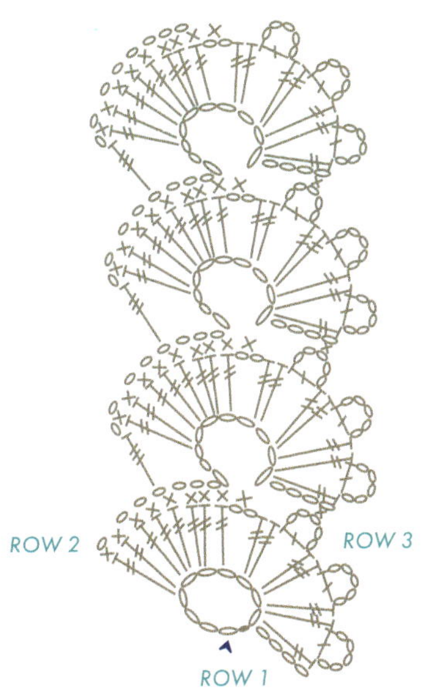

BORDER 54

DIFFICULTY ***

COLOR: Ecru

STITCHES USED: Chain (ch) • single crochet (sc) • double crochet (dc) • treble crochet (tr)

The motifs of this border are crocheted height-wise, back and forth in rows.

Ch 9.

Row 1: Ch 3 (to replace first dc), dc in fourth ch from hook, ch 3, skip 3, sc in next, ch 5, sc in next, ch 3, skip 3, 2 dc in last st. Turn.

Row 2: Ch 4 (to replace first tr), tr in first, 2 tr in next, ch 3, skip 3, 2 sc in ch-5 ring, ch 3, skip 3, 2 tr in next, 2 tr in next st. Turn.

Repeat these 2 rows to desired height. Fasten off.

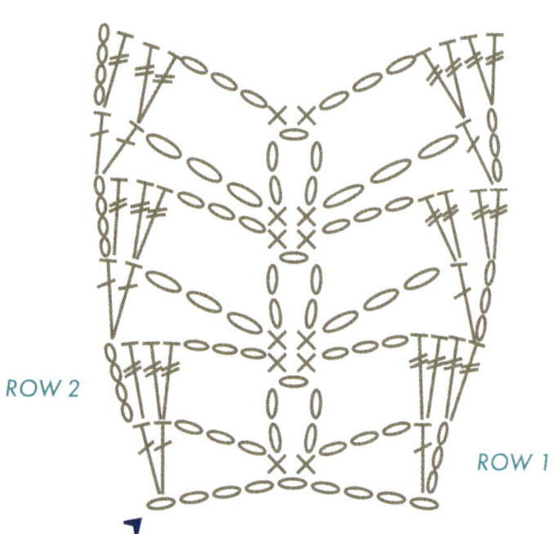

BORDER 55

DIFFICULTY ****

COLOR: Ecru

STITCHES USED: Chain (ch) • single crochet (sc) • half double crochet (hdc) • double crochet (dc) • treble crochet (tr) • ch-3 picot (pic)

This edging is working over a multiple of 11 sts + 14.

Row 1: Ch 7, pic, *ch 11, pic*. Repeat from * to *. End with 7 chs.

Row 2: Ch 1 to turn, *sc in next, ch 1, skip 1, sc in next, ch 6, skip (ch 4, pic, ch 4)*. Repeat from * to *. End with sc, ch 1, skip 1, sc in last.

Row 3: Ch 1 to turn, (sc, pic sc) in first ch-space, *(hdc, 2 dc, pic, 4 tr, pic, 2 dc, hdc) in next ch-6 space, skip sc, (sc, pic, sc) in next ch-space*. Repeat from * to *. Fasten off.

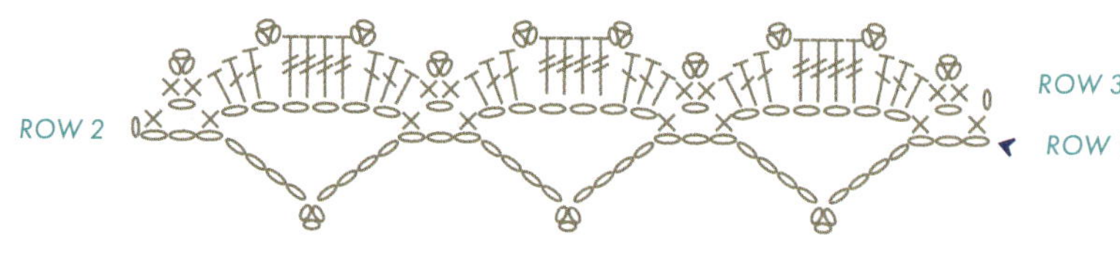

BORDER 56

DIFFICULTY **

COLORS: (A) Greige; (B) Pink

STITCHES USED: Slip stitch (sl st) • chain (ch) • single crochet (sc) • long single crochet • half double crochet (hdc) • double crochet (dc) • treble crochet (tr)

This edging is made in three steps: circles are crocheted independently, then joined at regular intervals on an edging crocheted at the top and bottom.

Begin the circles with A, ch 6, sl st to close the ring.

Rnd 1: Ch 3 (to replace first dc), 15 dc in ring, sl st to close. Fasten off.

Join the motifs with A.

Row 1: Insert hook in a st on one of the circles and pull up a loop, sc in same st, *ch 7, join a new circle by making an sc in a st*. Repeat from * to *. Fasten off.

Row 2 (B): Insert hook in first st and pull up a loop, sc in same st, *sc in next, hdc in next, dc in next, tr in next, dc in next, hdc in next, sc in next, insert hook in the center of the circle and make a long sc*. Repeat from * to *, alternating between a long single crochet in the center of the circle and a sc in the sc. Fasten off.

Next, with right side facing, join the motifs on the other side of the edging. Repeat Rows 1 and 2, alternating between sc and long sc in Row 2 as indicated in the diagram. Fasten off.

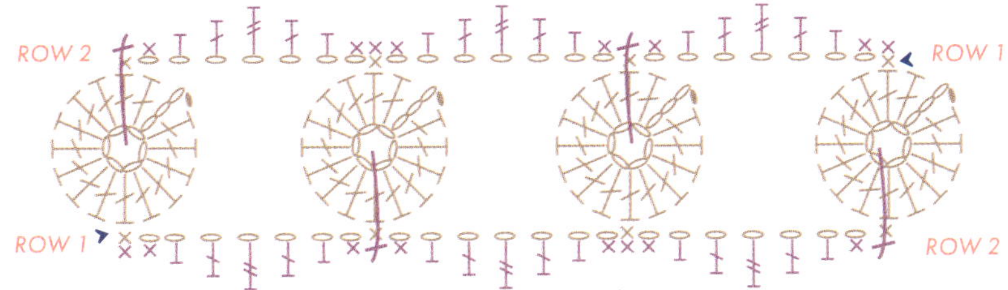

BORDER 57

DIFFICULTY ***

COLORS: (A) Pink; (B) Maroon

STITCHES USED: Slip stitch (sl st) • chain (ch) • single crochet (sc) • half double crochet (hdc) • double crochet (dc)

This edging consists of several motifs crocheted with alternating colors and progressively joined with sl sts as you go.

With A, ch 13. 8 dc in first ch, hdc in next 4, 2 hdc in next, 2 hdc in next changing to next col at last yarn over. With B, [2 sc in next, sc in next] twice, 2 sc in next, hdc in next, (hdc, 3 dc) in next, skip 2 initial dc, sc in next dc. Fasten off.

Make a second motif starting with B. Join the motifs with a sl st after fourth and fifth initial dc, made into first and second sc of previous motif.

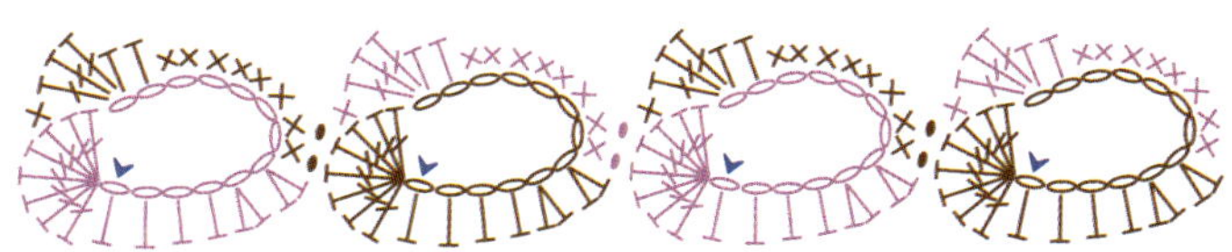

BORDER 58

DIFFICULTY **

COLORS: (A) Greige; (B) Maroon

STITCHES USED: Chain (ch) • single crochet (sc) • half double crochet (hdc) • double crochet (dc) • treble crochet (tr)

This edging consists of a central strip onto which we will work on both sides.

With A, chain a multiple of 15 + 1 turning chain.

Row 1: *Sc in next 2, hdc in next, dc in next, tr in next, dc in next, hdc in next*. Repeat from * to *. End with sc in last 2. Fasten off.

Row 2 (B): Insert hook in first st and pull up a loop, *sc in next 5, skip 2, 7 dc between next 2 sc, skip 2, sc in next 3*. Repeat from * to *. End with sc in last 5. Fasten off.

Turn edging to work on opposite side of starting chain, with right side facing.

Row 3: Insert hook in first st and pull up a loop, ch 3 (to replace first dc), 3 dc in next st, skip 2, sc in next 3, *sc in next 5, skip 2, 7 dc between next 2 sc, skip 2, sc in next 3*. Repeat from * to *. End with sc in next 5, skip 2, 3 dc in st before last, dc in last. Fasten off.

ROW 2

ROW 1

ROW 3

REPEAT (15 STS)

BORDER 59

DIFFICULTY **

COLORS: (A) Greige; (B) Maroon; (C) Dark Maroon

STITCHES USED: Slip stitch (sl st) • chain (ch) • single crochet (sc) • half double crochet (hdc) • double crochet (dc)

This edging is composed of several motifs with alternating colors, progressively joined with sl sts as you go.

With C, ch 14, sl st to close ring. Fasten off.

Rnd 1 (A): Insert hook in first st of rnd and pull up a loop, *sc in next 2, 2 sc in next*. Repeat from * to *. End with sc in last 2, sl st in first st to close. Fasten off.

Rnd 2 (B): Insert hook in first st of rnd and pull up a loop, [sc in next, (hdc, dc) in next st, (dc, hdc) in next st, sc in next] 3x, sl st in next 3, ch 2, skip 2, sl st in next 2, sl st in first st to close. Fasten off.

Make a second motif starting with C, then B, then A. Join the motifs with a sl st at the top of the (hdc, 2 dc, hdc) petal, making the sl st after the first dc of the motif to join, and under the ch-2 space of the previous motif (see diagram).

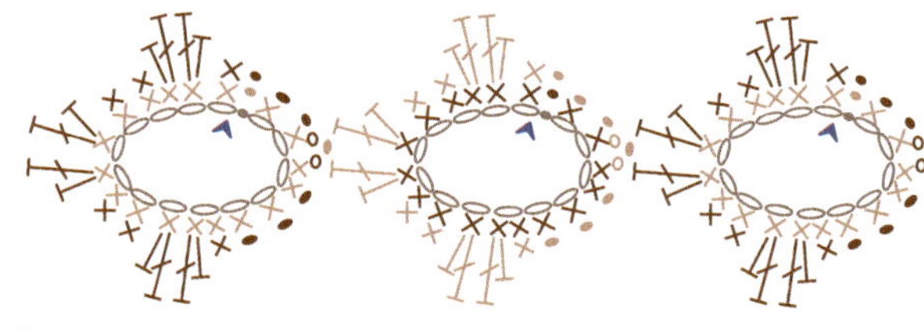

BORDER 60

DIFFICULTY **

COLORS: (A) Greige; (B) Dark Maroon

STITCHES USED: Chain (ch) • single crochet (sc) • double crochet (dc) • ch-3 picot (pic)

This edging consists of a central strip crocheted height-wise, onto which we will work on both long sides.

Make the central strip as long as needed (1 motif = 4 groups of dc).

With B, *ch 6, 4 dc closed together in second ch*. Repeat from * to *. End with 1 ch. Fasten off.

Row 1 (A): Insert hook in first ch and pull up a loop, (sc, pic) in same st, *ch 3, sc in middle of dc row end on central strip, 6 dc in next ch, sc in middle of next dc row end on central strip, ch 3, 3 dc closed together in next ch*. Repeat from * to *. End with ch 3, (sc, pic) in last ch on central strip.

Turn to work on second long side with right side facing.

Row 2: Insert hook in first ch and pull up a loop, ch 3 (to replace first dc), 2 dc closed together in same st, *ch 3, sc in third ch of central strip ch-5 space, skip 2 chs, 6 dc in next ch, sc in third ch of next central strip ch-5 space, ch 3, skip 2 chs from central strip, (sc, pic) in next ch, ch 3, sc in third ch of central strip ch-5 space, skip 2 chs, 6 dc in next ch, sc in third ch of next central strip ch-5 space, ch 3, skip 2 chs from central strip, 3 dc closed together in next ch*. Repeat from * to *. Fasten off.

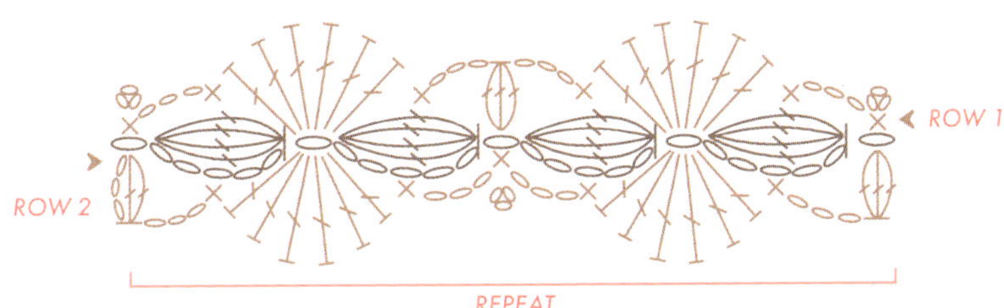

BORDER 61

DIFFICULTY **

COLORS: (A) Grey Blue; (B) White Sand

STITCHES USED: Slip stitch (sl st) • chain (ch) • single crochet (sc) • double crochet (dc) • treble crochet (tr) • ch-3 picot (pic)

This edging is composed of several motifs joined with sl sts.

With B, ch 7, sl st to close the ring.

Rnd 1: 16 sc in ring, sl st to close.

Rnd 2: Ch 3 (to replace first dc), [ch 1, dc in next, pic, (ch 1, dc in next) 3x] 3x, ch 1, dc in next, pic, [ch 1, dc in next] 2x, ch 1, sl st in third starting ch. Fasten off.

Rnd 3 (A): Insert hook under a ch from previous rnd and pull up a loop, sc in same st, *ch 5, skip 2, dc in next pic, pic, ch 5, skip 2, sc around next ch, ch 4, 3 tr closed together in next dc, ch 4, sc around next ch*. Repeat from * to *. End with sl st in first sc. Fasten off.

Continue as established until you've made the number of motifs required for desired length. Join the motifs with a sl st to replace the second ch in the joining pic (make the pic as follows: ch 1, sl st in corresponding pic on previous motif, ch 1, sl st in same st).

BORDER 62

DIFFICULTY **

COLORS: (A) Grey Blue; (B) White Sand

STITCHES USED: Slip stitch (sl st) • chain (ch) • single crochet (sc) • half double crochet (hdc) • treble crochet (tr) • ch-3 picot (pic)

This edging consists of multiple motifs joined with sl sts.

With A, ch 10, sl st to close the ring.

Rnd 1: (Ch 5, 4 tr closed together in ring, ch 5, sc in ring) 5x. Fasten off.

Rnd 2 (B): Insert hook in last st made and pull up a loop, ch 4 (to replace first tr), ch 2, tr in same st, [ch 5, skip 1 tr-petal from previous rnd, (tr, ch 2, tr) in next sc] 4x, ch 5, sl st in fourth starting ch.

Rnd 3: Ch 2 (to replace first hdc), hdc around (43 hdc total, 1 in each ch), sl st in second starting ch. Fasten off.

Rnd 4 (A): In this rnd, make the sc between the hdc from the previous rnd; insert hook after last hdc made and pull up a loop, *2 sc, pic*. Repeat from * to * (for a total of 22 pics). End with sl st in first st. Fasten off.

Continue as established, making the necessary number of motifs to reach desired length. Join the motifs with a sl st to replace the second ch in the joining pic (make the pic as follows: ch 1, sl st in corresponding pic on previous motif, ch 1, sl st in same st).

Motifs are joined over 2 pics.

BORDER 61

BORDER 63

DIFFICULTY **

BORDER 62

COLORS: (A) Grey Blue; (B) White Sand

STITCHES USED: Slip stitch (sl st) • chain (ch) • single crochet (sc) • double crochet (dc) • ch-3 picot (pic)

This edging consists of multiple motifs joined with sl sts.

With B, ch 7, sl st to close the ring.

Rnd 1: 10 sc in ring, sl st in first st to close.

Rnd 2: Ch 3 (to replace first dc), *ch 2, dc in next*. Repeat from * to *. End with ch 2, sl st in third starting ch. Fasten off.

Rnd 3 (A): Insert hook in first dc from previous rnd and pull up a loop, ch 3, 3 dc closed together in next ch-2 space, ch 3, sc in next dc*. Repeat from * to *. End with sc in first dc from previous rnd, sl st. Fasten off.

Rnd 4 (B): Insert hook in last st from previous rnd and pull up a loop, ch 3, dc in top of dc-group from previous rnd, pic, ch 3, sc in sc from previous rnd*. Repeat from * to *. End with sc, sl st. Fasten off.

Continue as established, making the necessary number of motifs to reach desired length. Join the motifs with a sl st to replace the second ch in the joining pic (make the pic as follows: ch 1, sl st in corresponding pic on previous motif, ch 1, sl st in same st).

Motifs are joined over 2 pics.

BORDER 63

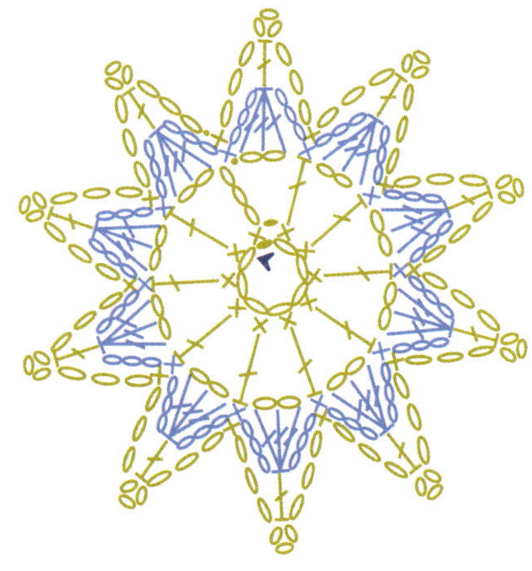

BORDER 64

DIFFICULTY **

COLORS: (A) Grey Blue; (B) White Sand

STITCHES USED: Slip stitch (sl st) • chain (ch) • single crochet (sc) • double crochet (dc) • ch-3 picot (pic)

This edging consists of multiple motifs joined with sl sts.

With A, ch 6, sl st to close the ring.

Rnd 1: (Sc in ring, ch 3) 8x, sl st in first st. Fasten off.

Rnd 2 (B): Insert hook in second ch of a ch-3 space and pull up a loop, ch 3 (to replace first dc), 2 dc in same st, *ch 1, pic, ch 1, skip sc, 3 dc in second ch of next ch-3 space*. Repeat from * to *. End with ch 1, pic, ch 1, sl st in first st. Fasten off.

Rnd 3 (A): Insert hook behind pic from previous rnd and pull up a loop, *sc in next ch, sc in first dc from previous rnd, ch 3, 2 dc closed together, ch 3, sc in next ch, carry thread behind next pic*. Repeat from * to *. End with sl st behind pic. Fasten off.

Continue as established, making the necessary number of motifs to reach desired length. Assemble the motifs on a peak as you crochet the last round, making a sl st in the top of a dc-group from last rnd of previous motif.

BORDER 65

DIFFICULTY **

COLORS: (A) Grey Blue; (B) White Sand

STITCHES USED: Slip stitch (sl st) • chain (ch) • single crochet (sc) • treble crochet (tr) • ch-3 picot (pic)

This edging consists of multiple motifs joined with sl sts.

With A, ch 8, sl st to close ring.

Rnd 1: Ch 4 (to replace first tr), 34 tr in ring, sl st to close. Fasten off.

Rnd 2 (B): Insert hook in first tr from previous rnd and pull up a loop, *ch 4, skip 4, sc in next st*. Repeat from * to *. End with sc in first st.

Rnd 3: Sl st in first sc from previous rnd, *ch 4, 4 tr closed together in ch-4 sp, ch 4, sl st in next sc*. Repeat from * to *. Fasten off.

Rnd 4 (A): Insert hook in a sl st from previous rnd and pull up a loop, *ch 6, sc in tr-group from previous rnd, pic, ch 6, long sc in sc from Rnd 2*. Repeat from * to *. Fasten off.

Continue as established, making the necessary number of motifs to reach desired length. Join the motifs with a sl st to replace the second ch in the joining pic (make the pic as follows: ch 1, sl st in corresponding pic on previous motif, ch 1, sl st in same st).

Each motif is assembled on a peak so there are two points at the top and three at the bottom.

BORDER 64

BORDER 66

DIFFICULTY **

COLORS: (A) Grey Blue; (B) White Sand

STITCHES USED: Slip stitch (sl st) • chain (ch) • single crochet (sc) • double crochet (dc) • treble crochet (tr) • ch-3 picot (pic)

This edging consists of multiple motifs joined with sl sts.

With A, ch 9, sl st to close the ring.

Rnd 1: 16 sc in ring, sl st to close.

Rnd 2 (A): Ch 4 (to replace first tr), 2 tr closed together in first st, pic, *ch 4, skip 1, (3 tr closed together, pic) in next st*. Repeat from * to *. End with ch 4, sl st in top of first tr-group.

Rnd 3 (B): Insert hook behind last pic made in previous rnd and pull up a loop; in this rnd, crochet around the chs of each ch-space, *sl st, ch 3, close [dc, long dc in dc from first rnd, dc] together, pic, ch 3, sl st in same ch-space, carry thread behind next pic*. Repeat from * to * in each ch-space. Fasten off.

Continue as established, making the necessary number of motifs to reach desired length. Join the motifs with a sl st to replace the second ch in the joining pic (make the pic as follows: ch 1, sl st in corresponding pic on previous motif, ch 1, sl st in same st). Motifs are joined over 2 pics.

BORDER 65

BORDER 66

BORDER 67

DIFFICULTY **

COLORS: (A) White; (B) Red

HOOKS: 2 sizes, such as D (3.125 mm) and E-4 (3.5 mm)

STITCHES USED: Slip stitch (sl st) • chain (ch) • single crochet (sc) • half double crochet (hdc) • double crochet (dc) • crab stitch

This edging consists of several circles crocheted into each other.

With B, ch 33, sl st to close the ring.

Rnd 1 (B, smaller hook): Ch 3 (to replace first dc), dc in next, *2 dc in next st, dc in next 2*. Repeat from * to *. End with 2 dc in next st, sl st in third starting ch.

Rnd 2 (B, larger hook): Ch 3 (to replace first dc), 2 dc closed together in same st, *ch 2, skip 1, 3 dc closed together in next st*. Repeat from * to *. End with 3 dc closed together in next st, ch 2, sl st in third starting ch. Fasten off.

Rnd 3 (A, larger hook): Insert hook in first dc-group and pull up a loop, in same group make (sc, ch 3, sc), *insert hook in next dc from Rnd 1 and make a long hdc, (sc, ch 3, sc) in next dc-group*. Repeat from * to *. End with long hdc in next dc from Rnd 1, sl st in first st. Fasten off.

Rnd 4 (A, smaller hook): Insert hook in a ch from initial starting ch, crab st around.

Make a second motif by crocheting a new starting chain and, before closing it with a sl st, wrap it around the previous circle. Make sure not to twist the chs when joining. Repeat Rnds 1–3. Work as established to desired length.

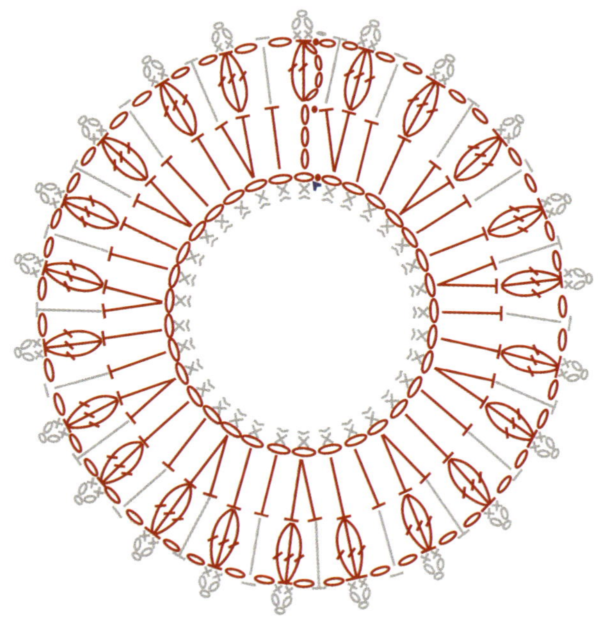

LINKED MOTIFS

BORDER 68

DIFFICULTY **

COLORS: (A) White; (B) Red; (C) Light Brown; (D) Green

STITCHES USED: Chain (ch) • single crochet (sc) • double crochet (dc) • treble crochet (tr)

This edging is crocheted in two parts: a central strip is crocheted height-wise, then we crochet on one long side.

Motif 1: With D, ch 5, 4 tr closed together in first ch, changing to next col at last yarn over.

Motif 2: With C, ch 5, 4 tr closed together in top of tr-group from previous rnd, changing to previous col at last yarn over (carry the yarn behind the work, loosely enough so as not to distort the tr). Work as established in Motif 2 alternating between C and D to desired height. On last motif, close the tr without changing col. Fasten off.

Resume work on the length of the strip just made, positioning the motifs on their right side.

Row 1 (B): Insert hook in st at the edge and pull up a loop, ch 3 (to replace first dc), dc in same st, *ch 2, sc in middle of tr row end, ch 2, 2 dc closed together between motifs*. Repeat from * to *. End with 2 dc closed together in st at edge. Fasten off.

Row 2 (A): On right side, sc in dc-group, *ch 2, skip 2 chs, sc in next sc, ch 3, sc in same st, ch 2, skip 2 chs, sc in next dc-group*. Repeat from * to *. Fasten off.

BORDER 69

DIFFICULTY **

COLORS: (A) Light Brown; (B) Green

STITCHES USED: Slip stitch (sl st) • chain (ch) • half double crochet (hdc) • double crochet (dc) • treble crochet (tr) • ch-3 picot (pic)

This edging is crocheted height-wise, with motifs made progressively while alternating colors.

With A, ch 6, sl st to close the ring.

Motif 1: Ch 2, hdc, 2 dc, 2 tr, pic, ch 3, sl st in ring.

Motif 2: Ch 6, sl st in first, turn work, ch 2, hdc, 2 dc, 2 tr, pic, ch 3, sl st in ring.

Continue repeating these 2 motifs. To change to B, yarn over and pull up a loop, ch 6, sl st in first st. Turn work and, with B, make 2 motifs, carrying A along the ring to hide it within the sts and pick it back up as needed. Work as established, making 2 motifs with each color, to desired length.

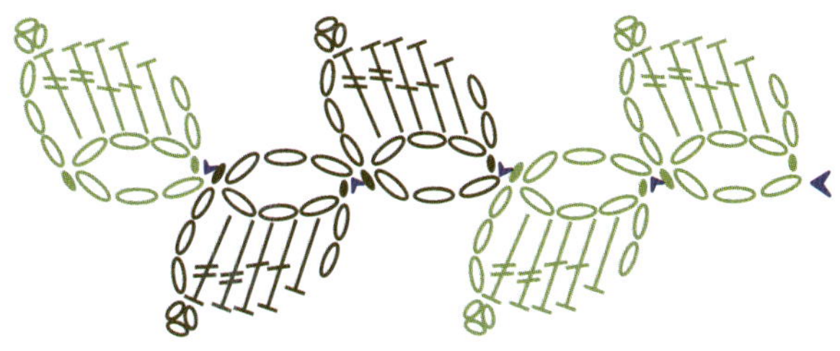

BORDER 70

DIFFICULTY **

COLORS: (A) White; (B) Dark Gray

HOOKS: 3 sizes, such as 2 mm, 2.5 mm, and 3 mm

STITCHES USED: Slip stitch (sl st) • chain (ch) • single crochet (sc) • half double crochet (hdc) • double crochet (dc) • ch-3 picot (pic)

This edging is composed of several circles joined by a crocheted ring.

With B, ch 48, sl st to close the ring.

Rnd 1 (B, medium hook): Sc around, sl st to close.

Rnd 2: Ch 2 (to replace first hdc), *ch 2, skip 1, hdc in next st*. Repeat from * to *. End with ch 2, sl st in first hdc. Fasten off.

Rnd 3 (A, large hook): Insert hook between 2 chs from previous rnd and pull up a loop, sc in same space, *ch 3, skip 3, 3 hdc closed together between next 2 chs from previous rnd, ch 3, skip 3, sc between next 2 chs from previous rnd*. Repeat from * to *. End with sl st in first st. Fasten off.

Rnd 4 (B, large hook): Insert hook in first sc from previous rnd and pull up a loop, ch 3 (to replace first dc), *ch 3, sc in top of hdc-group from previous rnd, ch 3, dc in next sc*. Repeat from * to *. End with sl st to close. Fasten off.

Rnd 5 (A, large hook): Insert hook in first ch from previous rnd and pull up a loop, sc in 3 chs, *hdc in next sc, sc in next 3 chs, pic, skip next dc, sc in next 3 chs*. Repeat from * to *. End with pic and sl st in first st. Fasten off.

Rnd 6 (B, small hook): Work a rnd of sl sts inside the motif to tighten the interior circle: skipping a ch every so often to make a total of 38 sl sts. Fasten off.

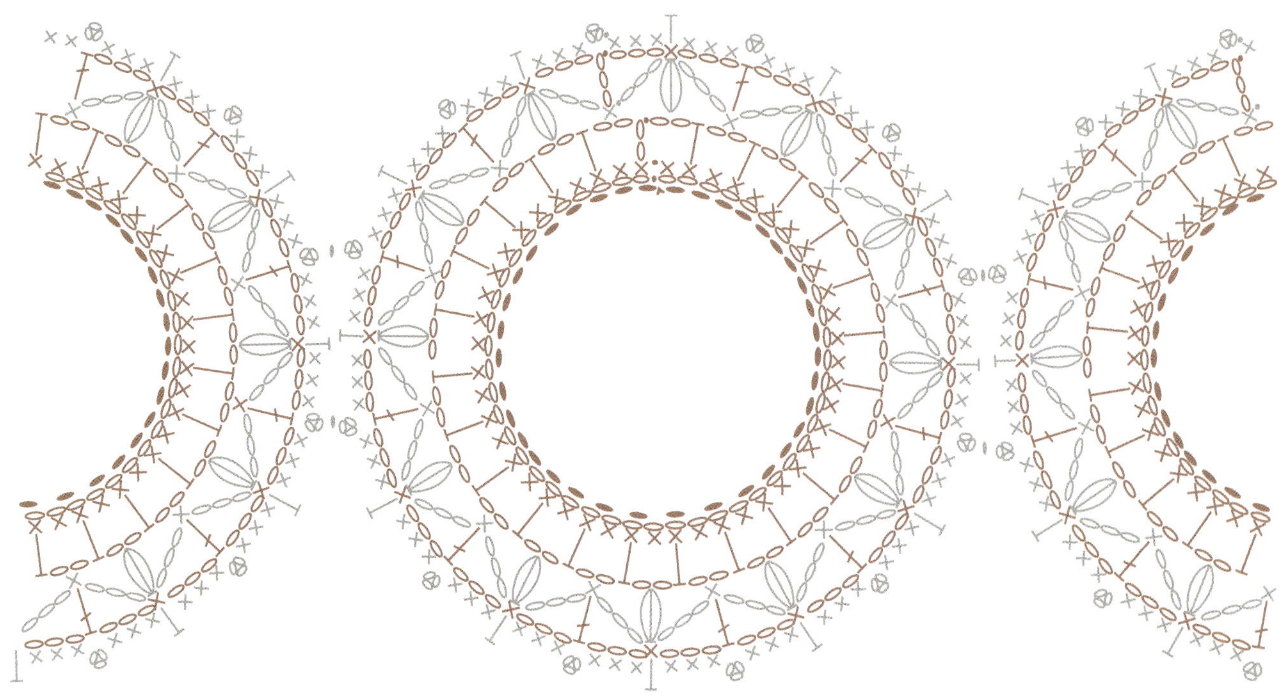

BORDER 71

DIFFICULTY **

COLORS: (A) White; (B) Brown; (C) Olive Green

STITCHES USED: Chain (ch) • single crochet (sc) • double crochet (dc)

This edging is crocheted in three parts: a central strip onto which we will crochet on both sides.

With B, chain a multiple of 8 + 1.

Row 1: Ch 1 to turn, sc in first st, *ch 3, skip 3, sc in next st*. Repeat from * to *. End with sc in last. Fasten off.

Row 2 (C): On one side of the central strip (color changes require thread to be carried loosely behind work between motifs), insert hook in first st and pull up a loop, *ch 4, 3 dc in same st, skip 3 chs from Row 1, sc in next sc working as follows: insert hook in sc, yarn over and pull up a loop, yarn over with A, pull through both loops on hook to complete the color change*. Repeat from * to * alternating between A and C. Fasten off.

Row 3 (A): On the other side of the central strip, with right side of motifs facing, crochet as established in previous row, starting with A to alternate col on opposite sides. Fasten off.

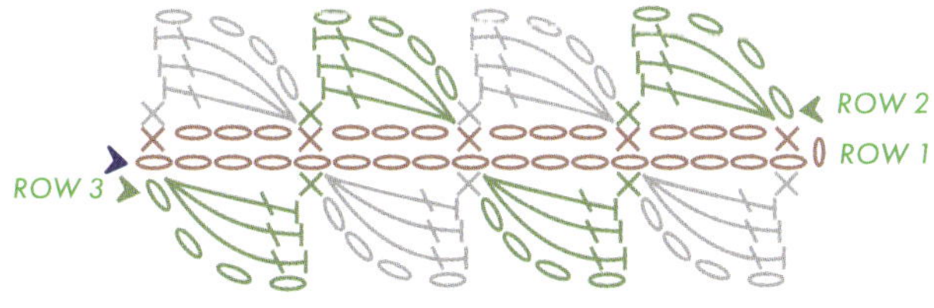

BORDER 72

DIFFICULTY **

COLORS: (A) Red; (B) Light Green

STITCHES USED: Slip stitch (sl st) • chain (ch) • double crochet (dc)

This edging is crochet height-wise, progressively crocheting the motifs while alternating colors

With A, ch 6, sl st to close the ring.

Motif 1: Ch 3, 4 dc in ring, ch 3, sl st in ring.

Motif 2 (B): Yarn over with next col and pull up a loop, ch 6, sl st in first ch, turn work, ch 3, 4 dc in ring, ch 3, sl st in ring, carrying A on ring to hide it inside the sts made.

Repeat Motifs 1 and 2 alternating colors to desired length.

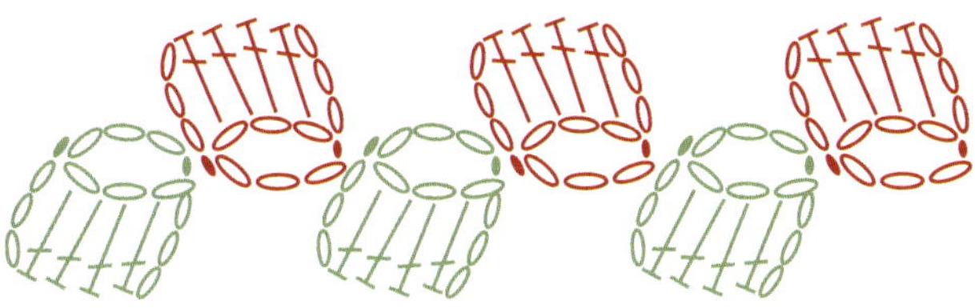

LONDON

BORDER 73

DIFFICULTY **

COLORS: (A) Gray; (B) Teal; (C) Dark Blue

STITCHES USED: Chain (ch) • half double crochet (hdc) • double crochet (dc) • crab stitch

Worked with right side always facing.

With A, chain a multiple of 19.

Row 1: Ch 4 (to replace first dc), 4 dc in fifth ch from hook, *(dc in next st, skip next st) 8x, dc in next st, 5 dc in next st, 5 dc in next st*. Repeat from * to *. End with 5 dc in last st. Fasten off.

Row 2 (C): Insert hook in first st and pull up a loop, ch 2 (to replace first hdc), hdc in each st across. Fasten off.

Row 3 (B): Insert hook in first st and pull up a loop, repeat Row 1. Fasten off.

Row 4 (A): With right side of last row facing, insert hook in last st made and pull up a loop, crab stitch across. Fasten off.

Row 5 (B): Turn border to work on opposite side of starting chains with right side of Row 1 facing, insert hook and pull up a loop, crab stitch across. Fasten off.

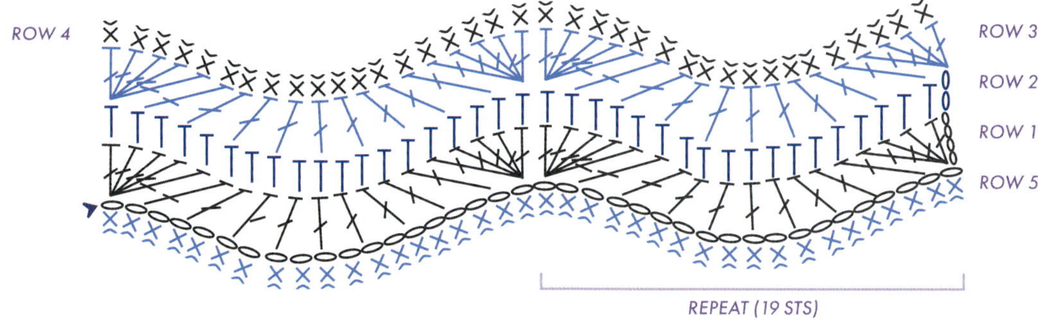

BORDER 74

DIFFICULTY **

COLORS: (A) Purple; (B) Gray; (C) Ivory

STITCHES USED: Chain (ch) • single crochet (sc) • half double crochet (hdc) • double crochet (dc)

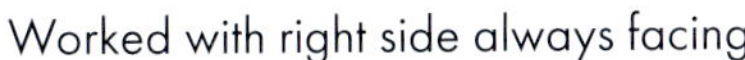

Worked with right side always facing.

With A, chain a multiple of 21 + 1.

Row 1: Ch 1 to turn, 3 sc in first ch, *sc in next 9, skip 2 chs, sc in next 9, 5 sc in next ch*. Repeat from * to *. End with 3 sc in last. Fasten off.

Row 2 (B): Ch 2 (to replace first hdc), hdc in first st, *hdc in next 10, skip 2, hdc in next 10, 3 hdc in next*. Repeat from * to *, ending with 2 hdc in last st. Fasten off.

Row 3 (C): 2 sc in first st, *sc in next 10, skip 2, sc in next 10, 3 sc in next st*. Repeat from * to *. End with 2 sc in last st. Fasten off.

Row 4 (A): Ch 3 (to replace first dc), dc in first st, *[ch 1, skip next st, 3 dc closed together in next st] 5x, skip 2 sts, 3 dc closed together in next st, [ch 1, skip next st, 3 dc closed together in next st] 5x*. Repeat from * to *. Fasten off.

Row 5 (C): 2 sc in first st, *sc in next 9, sc in space between next two dc-groups, skip dc-group, sc in next 9, 5 sc in next dc-group*. Repeat from * to *. End with 2 sc in last dc-group. Fasten off.

Row 6 (B): Ch 2 (to replace first hdc), hdc in first st, hdc in next 9, skip 3, hdc in next 10, 3 hdc in next, *hdc in next 10, skip 3, hdc in next 10, 3 hdc in next st*. Repeat from * to *. End with 2 hdc in last st. Fasten off.

Row 7 (C): 2 sc in first st, sc in next 9, skip 2, sc in next 10, 3 sc in next st, *sc in next 10, skip 2, sc in next 10, 3 sc in next st*. Repeat from * to *. End with 2 sc in last st. Fasten off.

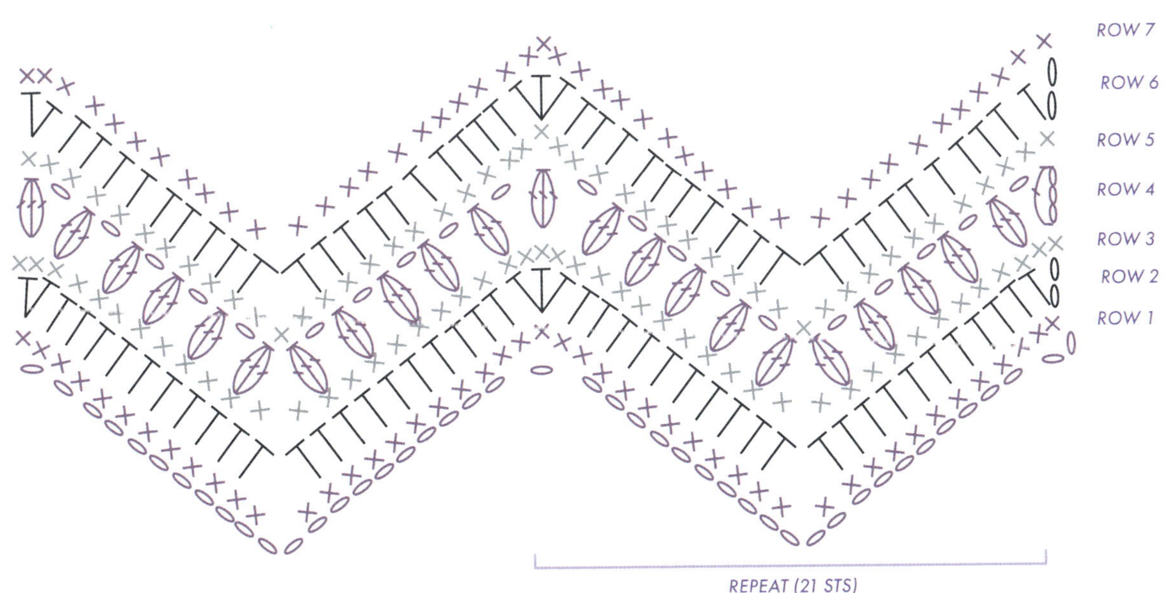

BORDER 75

DIFFICULTY ***

COLORS: (A) Gray; (B) Ivory; (C) Olive

STITCHES USED: Chain (ch) • single crochet (sc) • double crochet (dc) • puff ([yarn over, insert hook in same stitch and pull up a long loop] 3x, yarn over and pull through first 6 loops, yarn over and pull through remaining 2 loops, close puff with a tight ch)

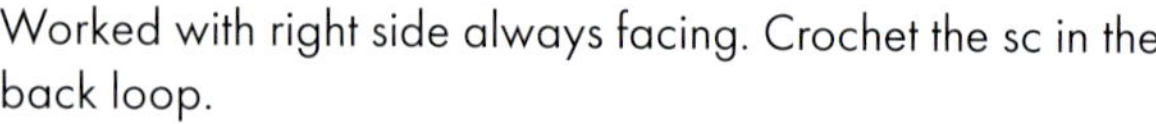

Worked with right side always facing. Crochet the sc in the back loop.

With A, chain a multiple of 21.

Row 1: Ch 3 (to replace first dc), dc in first st, *dc in next 3, ch 1, skip 1, puff in next st, ch 1, skip 1, dc in next 3, skip 2, dc in next 3, ch 1, skip 1, puff in next st, ch 1, skip 1, dc in next 3, ch 2*. Repeat from * to *. End with 2 dc in last st. Fasten off.

Row 2 (B): Ch 3 (to replace first dc), dc in first st, *dc in next 3, ch 1, skip 1, puff in next st, ch 1, skip puff, dc in next 2, skip 4, dc in next 2, ch 1, skip puff, puff in next st, ch 1, skip 1, dc in next 3, ch 3*. Repeat from * to *. End with 2 dc in last st. Fasten off.

Row 3 (C): Ch 3 (to replace first dc), ch 1, dc in first st, *dc in next 3, ch 1, skip 1, puff in next st, ch 1, skip puff, dc in next 2, skip 2, dc in next 2, ch 1, skip puff, puff in next st, ch 1, skip 1, dc in next 3, ch 3, skip 1*. Repeat from * to *. End with (dc, ch 1, dc) in last st. Fasten off.

Row 4 (A): Ch 3 (to replace first dc), ch 1, dc in first st, *dc in next 3, ch 1, skip 1, puff in next st, ch 1, skip puff, dc in next 2, skip 2, dc in next 2, ch 1, skip puff, puff in next st, ch 1, skip 1, dc in next 3, ch 3, skip 1*. Repeat from * to *. End with (dc, ch 1, dc) in last st. Fasten off.

Row 5 (C): On right side, sc across. Fasten off.

Row 6 (B): Turn edging and with right side of first row facing, insert hook in last starting ch and pull up a loop, sc across. Fasten off.

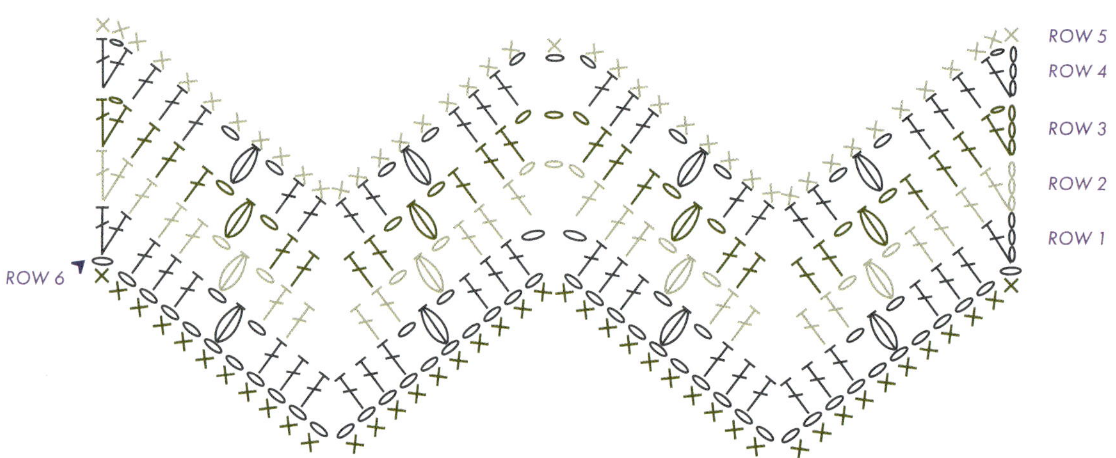

BORDER 76

DIFFICULTY ***

COLORS: (A) Olive; (B) Gray; (C) Ivory

STITCHES USED: Chain (ch) • single crochet (sc) • half double crochet (hdc) • puff ([yarn over, insert hook in same stitch and pull up a long loop] 3x, yarn over and pull through first 6 loops, yarn over and pull through remaining 2 loops, close puff with a tight ch)

Worked with right side always facing. Crochet the sc in the back loop.

With A, chain a multiple of 18 + 9.

Row 1: Ch 1, sc in next 9, *hdc in next, [ch 1, skip 1, puff in next] 3x, ch 1, skip 1, hdc in next, sc in next 9*. Repeat from * to *. End with hdc in next, sc in next 9. Fasten off.

Row 2 (B): Sc across (in the back loop of the sc, behind the puffs from the previous row, and over the chs). Fasten off.

Row 3 (C): Insert hook in first st and pull up a loop, ch 3, [ch 1, skip 1, puff in next] 3x, *ch 1, skip 1, hdc in next, sc in next 9, hdc in next, [ch 1, skip 1, puff in next] 3x*. Repeat from * to *. End with ch 1, hdc in last. Fasten off.

Rows 4–5 (A): Repeat Row 2.

Resume work on the opposite side of the starting chain.

Row 6 (A): Turn edging and with right side of the first row facing, insert hook and pull up a loop. Work as per Row 1.

Row 7 (B): Crocheting in the back loops of the chs, insert hook and pull up a loop, sc in first st, *ch 2, sc in next 2*. Repeat from * to *. Fasten off.

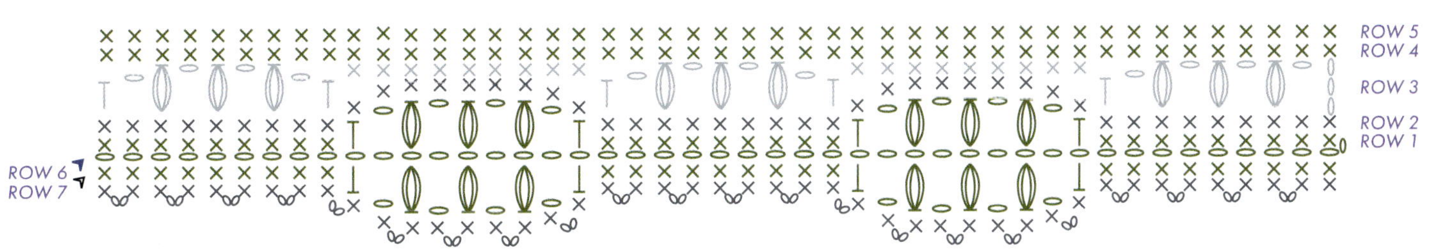

BORDER 77

DIFFICULTY ***

COLORS: (A) Purple; (B) Gray; (C) Ivory

STITCHES USED: Slip stitch (sl st) • chain (ch) • single crochet (sc) • half double crochet (hdc) • double crochet (dc) • treble crochet (tr)

Worked with right side always facing. Crochet all sc in the back loop of the stitch of the previous row.

With A, chain a multiple of 14 + 3 chs.

Row 1: Ch 1 to turn, *sc in next 3, hdc in next 2, dc in next 2, tr in next 3, dc in next 2, hdc in next 2*. Repeat from * to *. End with 3 sc. Fasten off.

Turn work to continue working on the other side of the starting chain.

Row 2 (B): Insert hook in first st and pull up a loop, sc across working in the back loop of the sts. Fasten off.

Row 3 (C): Insert hook in first st and pull up a loop, ch 3 (to replace first dc), *3 dc closed together in next st, ch 2, skip 2 sts*. Repeat from * to *. End with ch 1, skip next st, dc in last st. Fasten off.

Row 4 (B): Repeat Row 2.

Row 5 (A): Repeat Row 2.

Row 6 (B): Insert hook in first st and pull up a loop, sl st across working in the back loop of the sts. Fasten off.

Row 7: Insert hook in first st of Row 1 and pull up a loop, sc in first, *ch 2, sc in next 2*. Repeat from * to *. Fasten off.

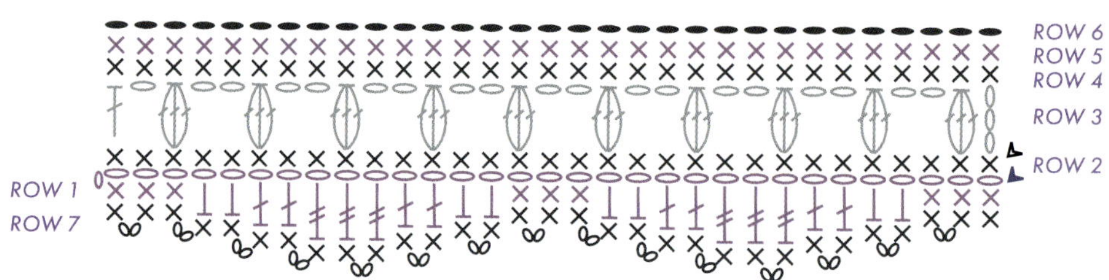

BORDER 78

DIFFICULTY ***

COLORS: (A) Teal; (B) Dark Blue; (C) Gray

STITCHES USED: Chain (ch) • single crochet (sc) • double crochet (dc)

Worked with right side always facing. Crochet all sc in the back loop of the stitch of the previous row.

With A, chain a multiple of 10 + 3 chs.

Row 1: Ch 1 to turn, *sc in next 3, skip 3 chs, 7 dc in next st, skip 3 chs*. Repeat from * to *. End with sc in last 3. Fasten off.

Row 2 (B): Sc across working in the back loop of the sts. Fasten off.

Row 3 (C): Insert hook in first st and pull up a loop, ch 3 (to replace first dc), 4 dc closed together, *ch 3, sc in next 3, ch 3, 7 dc closed together*. Repeat from * to *, ending with 5 dc closed together. Fasten off.

Row 4: Ch 3 (to replace first dc), 5 dc in first st, *skip 3 chs, sc in next 3, skip 3 chs, 7 dc in next st*. Repeat from * to *. End with skip 3 chs, sc in next 3, skip 3 chs, 5 dc in last st. Fasten off.

Turn border to work on opposite side of starting chain with the right side facing.

Row 5 (B): Insert hook in first st and pull up a loop, *sc in next 2, ch 2*. Repeat from * to *. End with sc in last 3. Fasten off.

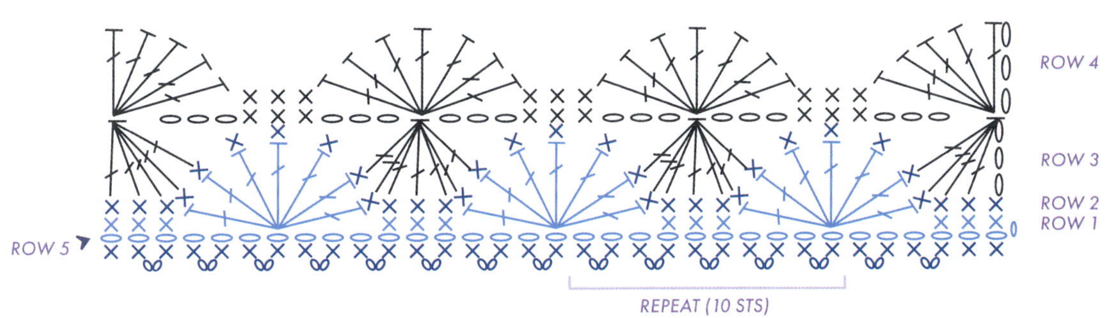

BORDER 79

DIFFICULTY *

COLOR: Black

STITCHES USED: Slip stitch (sl st) • chain (ch) • single crochet (sc) • half double crochet (hdc) • ch-3 picot (pic)

This edging is worked back and forth in rows. Repeat is crocheted over a multiple of 8 sts + 1.

Chain a multiple of 8 + 1.

Row 1: Ch 2 (to replace first hdc), *ch 3, skip 3, hdc in next*. Repeat from * to *.

Row 2: Ch 1 to turn, sc across.

Row 3: Ch 1 to turn, sc in first st, *ch 6, skip 3, sc in next st*. Repeat from * to *.

Row 4: Ch 1 to turn, *3 sc in first half of ch-space, ch 7, 3 sc in second half of next ch-space, pic*. Repeat from * to *. End with 3 sc in second half of next ch-space. Turn.

Row 5: Sl st in last st from previous row, *ch 4, (sc, pic) in fourth ch of next ch-space, ch 4, sl st in next pic*. Repeat from * to *. End with ch 4, sl st in last st. Fasten off.

BORDER 80

DIFFICULTY *

COLOR: Black

STITCHES USED: Slip stitch (sl st) • chain (ch) • treble crochet (tr) • ch-5 picot (pic)

This edging is crocheted height-wise.

Make a ch-5 pic, sl st in first ch, ch 5, ch-5 pic, sl st in first ch, ch 5, tr in first pic, ch-5 pic, sl st in tr (turn the completed part of the strip to the left), *ch 5, tr in pic, ch-5 pic, sl st in tr (turn strip before making the sl st).* Repeat from * to *, to desired height. Fasten off.

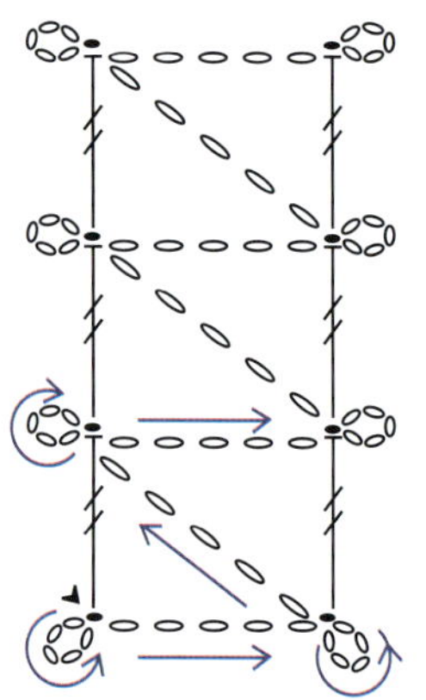

BORDER 81

DIFFICULTY *

COLOR: Black

STITCHES USED: Chain (ch) • single crochet (sc) • double crochet (dc) • treble crochet (tr)

This edging is crocheted height-wise.

Ch 7.

Row 1: Ch 1 to turn, sc in next 7 chs. Turn.

Row 2: Ch 4 (to replace first tr), ch 1, skip 2, 4 tr in next st, ch 1, skip 2, tr in last st. Turn.

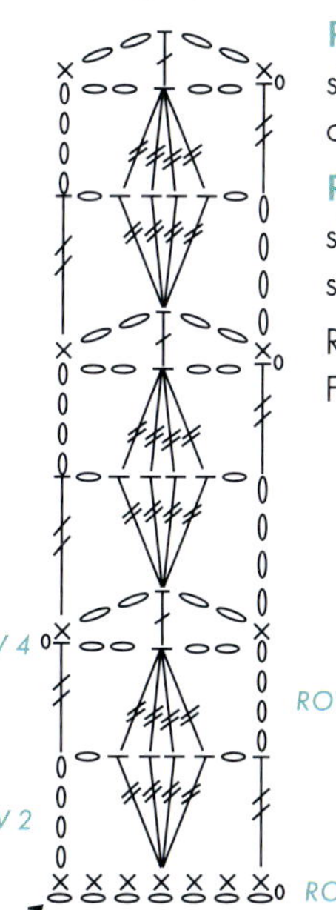

Row 3: Ch 4 (to replace first tr), ch 2, skip ch, 4 tr closed together, ch 2, skip ch, tr in last st.

Row 4: Ch 1 to turn, sc in first tr, ch 2, skip 2 chs, dc in next st, ch 2, skip 2 chs, sc in last st.

Repeat from Row 2 to desired height. Fasten off.

BORDER 82

DIFFICULTY **

COLOR: Black

STITCHES USED: Slip stitch (sl st) • chain (ch) • single crochet (sc) • half double crochet (hdc) • double crochet (dc) • treble crochet (tr) • ch-3 picot (pic)

This edging is crocheted back and forth in rows.

Chain a multiple of 12 + 1.

Row 1: Ch 1 to turn, sc across. Turn.

Row 2: Ch 3 (to replace first dc), *ch 2, close next 4 sts together: dc in first st, skip 2, [2 hdc in next st, skip 2, dc in next st], ch 2, dc in same st as previous dc*. Repeat from * to * making the first dc in the same st as last dc made (see diagram). End with dc in last st. Turn.

Row 3: Ch 1 to turn, sc in first st, *ch 2, pic, ch 2, skip 5, sc in next dc*. Repeat from * to *.

Row 4: Ch 3 (to replace first dc), *ch 3, (tr, ch 1, tr, ch 1, tr) in next sc, ch 3, dc in next st*. Repeat from * to *. Turn.

Row 5: Sl st in first st, *ch 3, skip 3 chs, (sc, pic) in next tr, sc in next tr, ch 4, pic, ch 4, sc in same tr, pic, sc in next tr, ch 3, skip 3 chs, sl st in next dc*. Repeat from * to *. Fasten off.

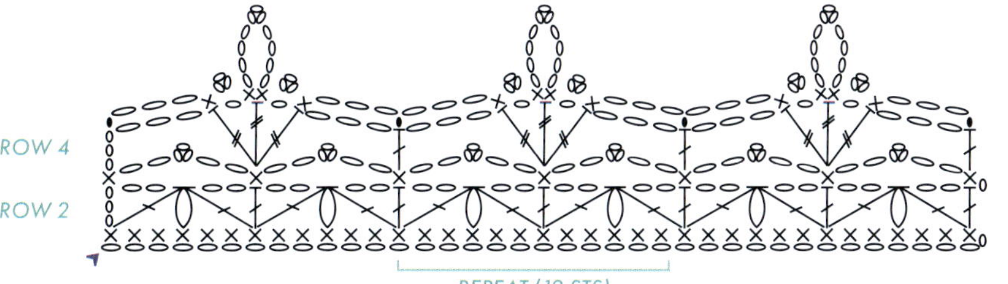

BORDER 83

DIFFICULTY **

COLOR: Black

STITCHES USED: Slip stitch (sl st) • chain (ch) • single crochet (sc) • double crochet (dc) • double treble crochet (dtr) • ch-3 picot (pic)

This edging is crocheted back and forth in rows.

Chain a multiple of 12 + 1.

Row 1: Ch 1, sc across. Turn.

Row 2: Ch 3 (to replace first dc), *skip 5, dtr in next st, ch 5, dc in same st, ch 5, dtr in same, skip 5 sc, dc in next sc*. Repeat from * to *. Turn.

Row 3: Ch 3 (to replace first dc), 2 dc closed together in first st, pic, *ch 5, skip 5 chs, (sl st, pic) in next dc, ch 5, skip 5 chs, 3 dc closed together and pic in next dc*. Repeat from * to *. Fasten off.

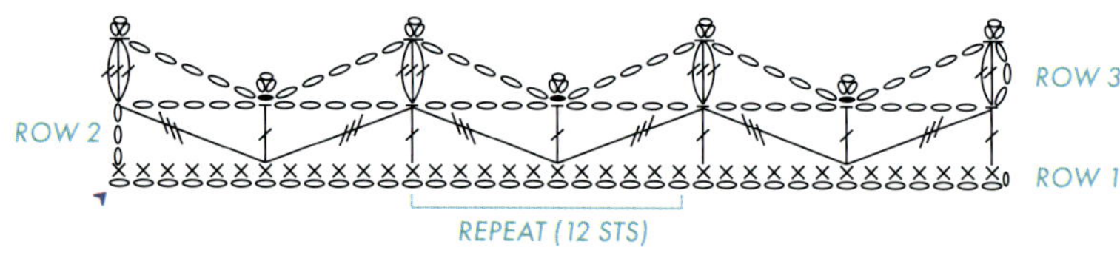

BORDER 84

DIFFICULTY **

COLOR: Black

STITCHES USED: Slip stitch (sl st) • chain (ch) • single crochet (sc) • half double crochet (hdc) • double crochet (dc) • treble crochet (tr) • ch-3 picot (pic)

This edging is crocheted back and forth in rows.

Chain a multiple of 12 + 1.

Row 1: Ch 2 (to replace first hdc), hdc across.

Row 2: Ch 1 to turn, sc in first st, *ch 4, skip 5 hdc, 5 dc in next, ch 4, skip 5 hdc, (sc, pic) in next*. Repeat from * to *. End with sc in last.

Row 3: Ch 1 to turn, sc in first st, ch 4, skip 4 chs, *dc in 5 dc of dc-group, ch 3, 2 tr closed together (with the first in the same st as last dc, and the second is first dc of next dc-group), ch 3*. Repeat from * to *. End with ch 4, sc in last st. Turn.

Row 4: Sl st in first ch, ch 4, *sc in next dc, ch 4, 3 tr closed together, pic, ch 4, sc in next dc, ch 3, skip 3 chs, sl st in next tr-group, ch 3, skip 3 chs*. Repeat from * to *. End with ch 4, sl st in last st. Fasten off.

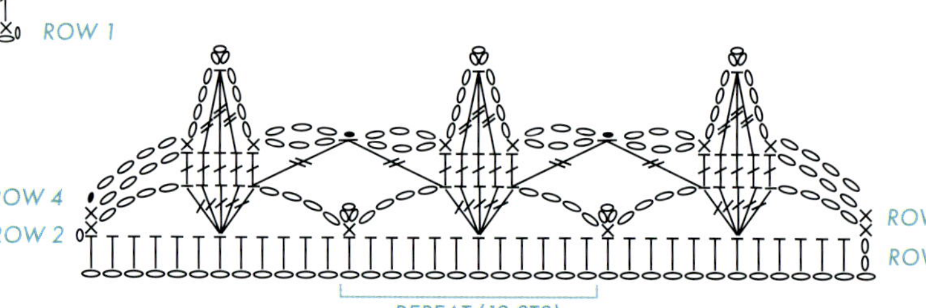

BORDER 85

DIFFICULTY **

COLOR: Black

STITCHES USED: Slip stitch (sl st) • chain (ch) • single crochet (sc) • double crochet (dc) • ch-3 picot (pic)

This corner edging can be crocheted back and forth in rows. It can also be crocheted in the round, in which case rnds will be closed with one or more sl sts, beginning the next rnd with the required number of starting chs for height. Instructions are given to crochet in the rnd.

Chain a multiple of 7 + 1.

Rnd 1: Sc across sides, 3 sc in corner st, sl st in first st.

Rnd 2: Ch 3 (to replace first dc), 4 dc in same st, *ch 2, skip 6 sc, 5 dc in next st*. Repeat from * to * on sides. In the corner, ch 2, skip 7 sc, 9 dc in next st, skip 7 sc. End with sl st in first st.

Rnd 3: Sl st in first 2 dc from previous row, ch 3 (to replace first dc), (2 dc, ch 1, 3 dc) in middle dc of dc-group, *skip (2 dc, ch 2, 2 dc), (3 dc, ch 1, 3 dc) in next dc*. Repeat from * to * on the sides. In the corner, skip (ch 2, 2 dc), (3 dc, ch 1, 3 dc) in next dc, skip 2 dc, (3 dc, ch 1, 3 dc) in next dc, skip (2 dc, ch 2, 2 dc). End with sl st in first st.

Rnd 4: *Ch 3, skip 3 dc, 3 dc closed together in ch from previous row, ch 3, skip 3 dc, sc between dc-groups*. Repeat from * to * on sides. In the corner, sc between dc-groups, ch 4, skip 3 dc, 3 dc closed together in next ch, ch 5, skip 3 dc, 3 dc closed together between dc-groups, ch 5, skip 3 dc, 3 dc closed together in next ch, ch 4, skip 3 dc, sc between dc-groups. End with sl st.

Rnd 5: *4 sc in first ch-3 space, pic, 4 sc in next ch-space*. Repeat from * to * on sides. In the corner, in the first ch-4 space make 5 sc, pic. In the next two ch-5 spaces, make 3 sc, pic, 3 sc, pic. In the next ch-4 space, make 5 sc. End with sl st. Fasten off.

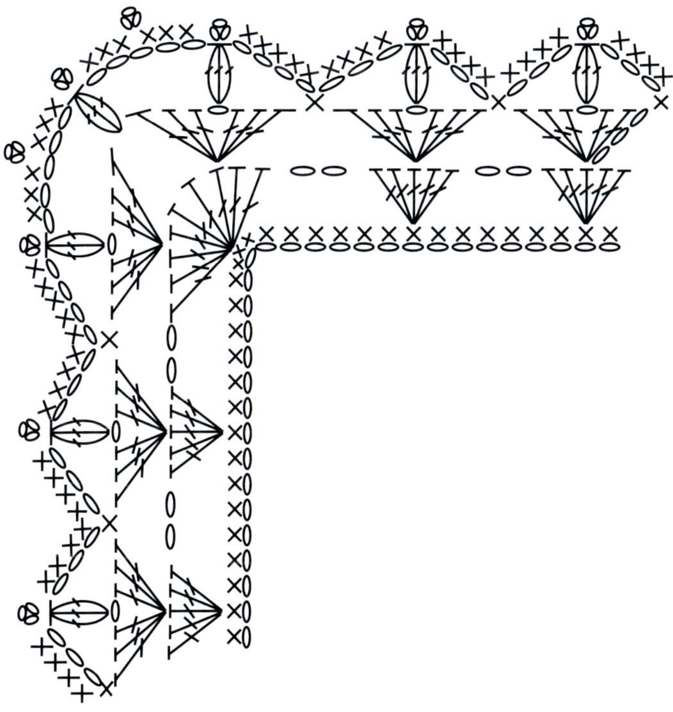

BORDER 86

DIFFICULTY **

COLOR: Black

STITCHES USED: Slip stitch (sl st) • chain (ch) • single crochet (sc) • double crochet (dc) • ch-3 picot (pic)

This corner edging is crocheted back and forth in rows. It can also be crocheted in the round, in which case rnds will be closed with one or more sl sts, beginning the next rnd with the required number of starting chs for height.

Chain a multiple of 8 + 1; add 3 chs for corner.

Row 1: Ch 3 (to replace first dc), *ch 1, skip 1, dc in next*. Repeat from * to * on sides. In the corner, ch 1, skip 1, 4 dc in next st.

Row 2: Ch 1 to turn, sc in first st, *ch 4, skip 3, 3 dc closed together in next st, ch 4, skip 3, sc in next st*. Repeat from * to * on sides. In the corner, ch 4, skip 2, 3 dc closed together in next dc, ch 3, 3 dc closed together between corner dc, ch 3, 3 dc closed together in next dc, ch 4, skip 2, sc in next st. End with sc. Turn.

Row 3: Sl st in first 2 chs, ch 3 (to replace first dc), ch 3, *sc in next dc-group, ch 3, 2 dc closed together in second ch of first ch-4 space and in third ch of next ch-space, ch 3*. Repeat from * to * on sides. In corner, sc in first dc-group, ch 3, sc in second dc-group, ch 3, sc in third dc-group. End with ch 3, dc in second ch of last ch-space.

Row 4: Ch 1 to turn, sc in first dc from previous row, *ch 3, 2 dc closed together in second ch of first ch-space and second ch of next ch-space, pic, ch 3, sc in next dc-group*. Repeat from * to * on sides. In corner, ch 3, skip 3 chs, 3 dc closed together in next sc, pic, ch 3, skip 3 chs, [(3 dc closed together, pic, ch 4) twice, 3 dc closed together, pic] in next sc, ch 3, skip 3 chs, 3 dc closed together in next sc, pic. End with sc in middle of last ch-space. Fasten off.

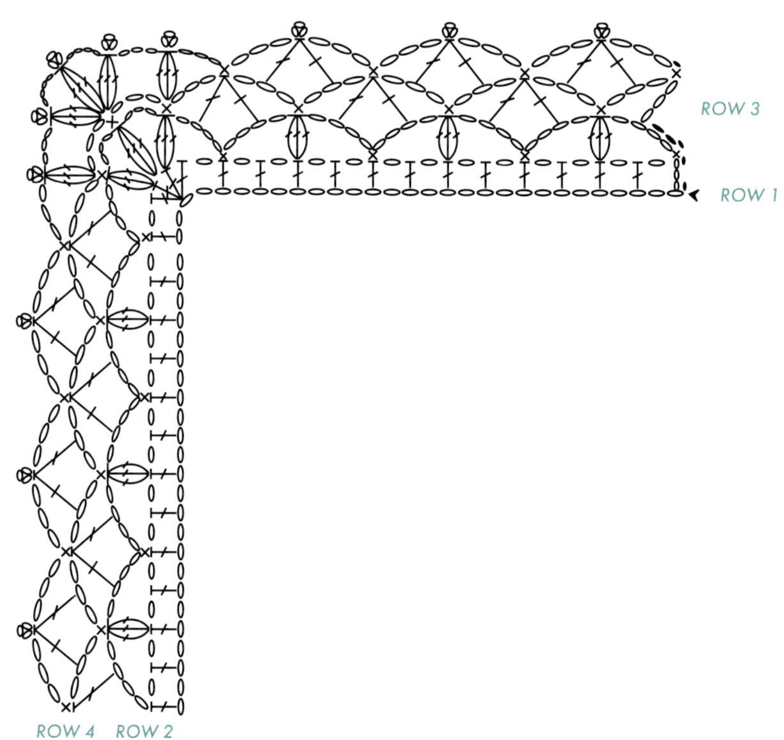

BORDER 87

DIFFICULTY **

COLORS: (A) Variegated; (B) Golden Ochre

STITCHES USED: Chain (ch) • single crochet (sc) • treble crochet (tr)

With A, chain a multiple of 6 + 1.

Row 1 (A): Ch 4 (to replace first tr), tr across. Fasten off.

Row 2 (B): Working on opposite side of starting chain, *sc, ch 5, skip 2, 3 tr in next st, skip 2, ch 5*. Repeat from * to *. End with sc in last. Fasten off.

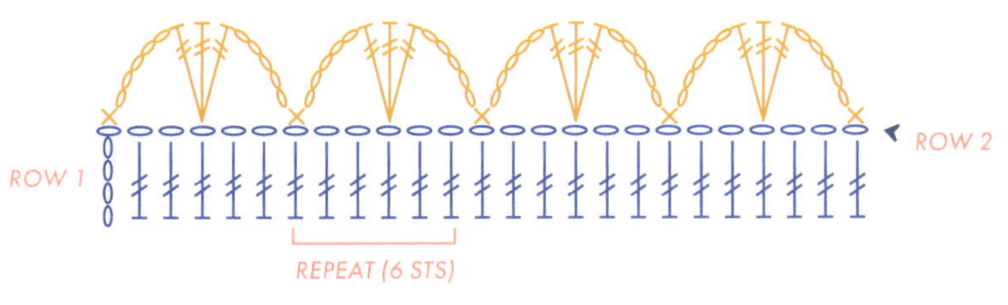

BORDER 88

DIFFICULTY **

COLORS: (A) Variegated; (B) Lake

STITCHES USED: Chain (ch) • single crochet (sc) • half double crochet (hdc)

With B, chain a multiple of 8 + 2.

Rows 1–4 (B): Ch 1 to turn, sc across.

Row 5 (A): Ch 1 to turn, *sc in next 2, ch 2, 3 hdc in last st made, skip 2, sc in next st, skip 2, 3 long sc in same st 2 rows below, skip 1*. Repeat from * to *. End with sc in last 2. Fasten off.

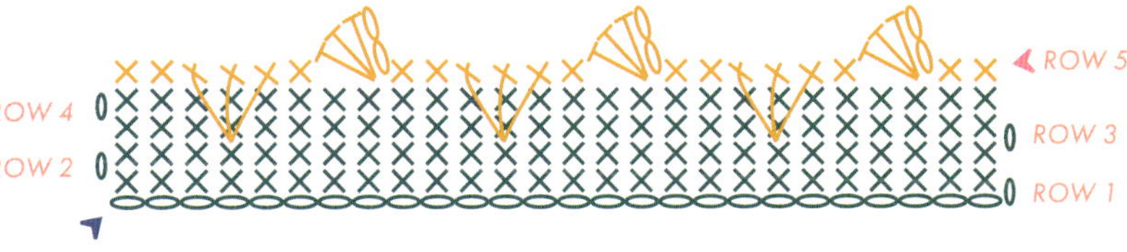

BORDER 89

DIFFICULTY **

COLORS: (A) Variegated; (B) Red; (C) Golden Ochre

STITCHES USED: Chain (ch) • single crochet (sc) • treble crochet (tr)

With A, chain a multiple of 12 + 1.

Row 1 (A): Ch 4 (to replace first tr), tr across. Fasten off.

Row 2 (B): Working in opposite side of starting ch, insert hook in first st and pull up a loop, sc in first st, *skip 2, 12 tr in next st, skip 2, sc in next, [ch 3, skip 2, sc in next] twice*. Repeat from * to *. Fasten off.

Resume work on Row 1, working behind the shells made in Row 2.

Row 3 (C): Sc in sc after first shell from previous row, *skip 3 chs, 12 tr in next sc, skip 3 chs, sc in the next sc, working behind next shell: ch 3, sc behind shell in the tr below it, ch 3, sc in next sc*. Repeat from * to *. End with sc. Fasten off.

BORDER 90

DIFFICULTY **

COLORS: (A) Variegated; (B) Red; (C) Golden Ochre

STITCHES USED: Slip stitch (sl st) • chain (ch) • treble crochet (tr)

With A, chain a multiple of 8 + 1.

Row 1 (A): Ch 4 (to replace first tr), tr across. Fasten off.

Row 2 (B): Working on the opposite side of the starting chain, make circles to be joined to the edging with sl sts and their right side facing; ch 8, sl st to close the ring, ch 3 to replace first tr, 10 tr in ring, sl st in third starting ch, 15 tr in ring, sl st in top of starting chain to close circle. Fasten off.

With C, ch 7, sl st to close the ring, ch 3 to replace first tr, 10 tr in ring, sl st in fourth st after sl st attaching previous circle to edging, 4 tr in ring, skip 3 edging sts, sl st in next st to join the circle to the edging, complete the ring (24 tr total). Fasten off.

Repeat, alternating circles made with colors B and C, joining them with a sl st to every fourth edging stitch.

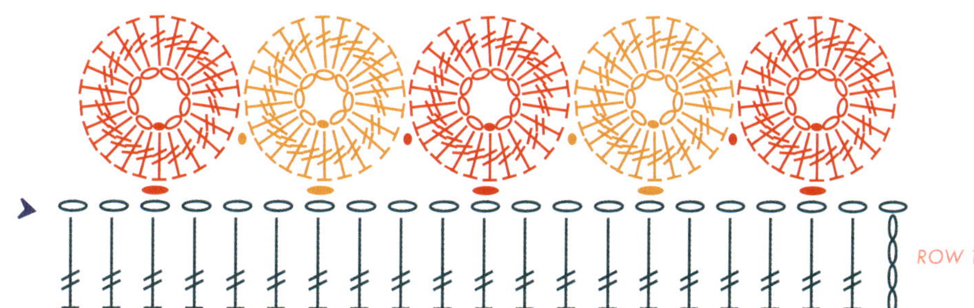

BORDER 91

DIFFICULTY ***

COLORS: (A) Variegated; (B) Lake

STITCHES USED: Chain (ch) • single crochet (sc) • double crochet (dc) • treble crochet (tr) • ch-3 picot (pic)

With B, chain a multiple of 3 + 2.

Rows 1–3: Ch 1 to turn, sc across. Fasten off.

Rows 4–5 (A): Ch 1 to turn, sc across. Fasten off.

Row 6 (B): Insert hook in first st, ch 6, *make a Y-shaped dc [yarn over twice, insert hook in first st, yarn over and pull up a loop, yarn over and pull through 2 loops, yarn over, skip 2 sts, insert hook in next st, yarn over and pull up a loop, yarn over and pull through 2 loops, yarn over and pull through 3 loops, yarn over and pull through 2 remaining loops], ch 2*. Repeat from * to *, inserting hook into same st as last Y-shaped dc made. End with tr in last st. Fasten off.

Row 7 (A): With right side facing, insert hook in fourth starting ch and pull up a loop, *working around next 2 chs, (sc, pic, sc) in ch-space, skip dc*. Repeat from * to *. End with sc in last st. Fasten off.

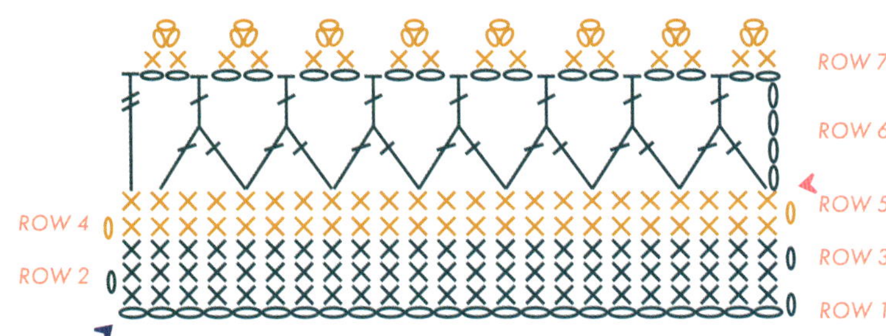

BORDER 92

DIFFICULTY ***

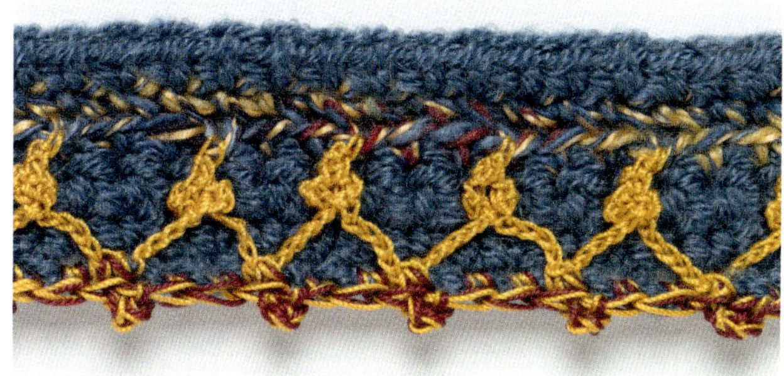

COLORS: (A) Variegated; (B) Lake; (C) Golden Ochre; (D) Red

STITCHES USED: Slip stitch (sl st) • chain (ch) • single crochet (sc) • ch-3 picot (pic)

With B, chain a multiple of 3 + 1.

Rows 1–3: Ch 1 to turn, sc across.

Row 4 (A): Ch 1 to turn, sc across.

Row 5: Ch 1 to turn, sc across.

Rows 6–7 (B): Ch 1 to turn, sc across. Fasten off.

Now working across starting chain. Make the motifs over the first 3 rows of sc, with right side facing.

Row 8 (C): Insert hook in first st and pull up a loop, sc in first 2 sts, *ch 4, make a series of pics as follows: ch 3, sc in first of 3 chs, ch 1, sc in third sc from Row 4 to attach the motif, ch 1, sc in first of 3 chs from pic just made, ch 3, sc in first of 3 chs, sl st in first pic made to join them, ch 4, skip 2 sts, sc in next.* Repeat from * to *. Pics attached to Row 4 have 2 sts between them. Fasten off.

Crochet the last row with C and D held together, on opposite side of starting ch.

Row 9: Insert hook in first st and pull up a loop, sc in first st, pic, *sc in next 2, sc in next, pic*. Repeat from * to *. Fasten off.

BORDER 93

DIFFICULTY ***

COLORS: (A) Black; (B) Red

STITCHES USED: Slip stitch (sl st) • chain (ch) • single crochet (sc) • half double crochet (hdc) • double crochet (dc) • treble crochet (tr) • ch-3 picot (pic)

This edging consists of a base of rings adorned with tassels.

Row 1 (A): *Ch 13, sl st in first ch to close the ring, ch 2, 11 hdc in ring, ch 5, 4 tr closed together in first of 5 chs just made*. Repeat from * to * to desired length. End with a 13-ch ring, sl st in first st to close rnd, ch 2, 11 hdc in ring. Fasten off.

Row 2 (B): Insert hook in first hdc from Row 1 and pull up a loop, (4 dc, tr, pic, tr, 4 dc) in ring, (sc, ch 6, sc) in middle of the post of the next tr*. Repeat from * to *. End with (4 dc, tr, pic, tr, 4 dc) in last ring. Fasten off.

To make the tassels, cut eight 4¾ inches (12 cm) lengths of A and fold them in half. With a small hook, pull the fold of tassel yarn through the 6-ch ring from Row 2 about ½ inch (1 cm), and pass the tassel ends through the loop to tighten.

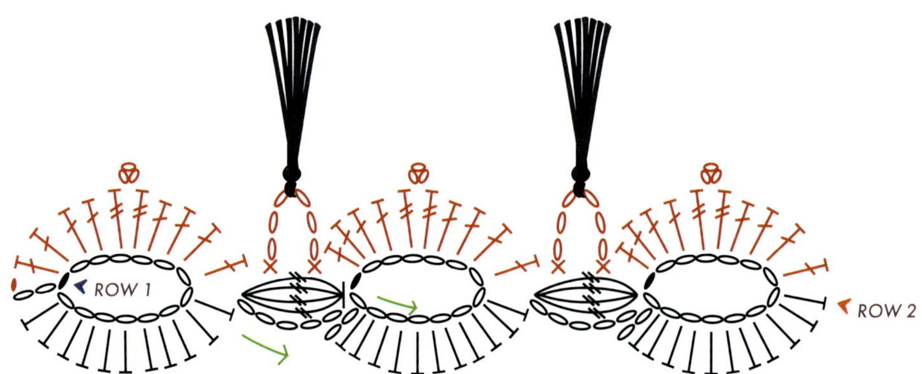

BORDER 94

DIFFICULTY ****

COLORS: (A) Black; (B) Red

STITCHES USED: Slip stitch (sl st) • chain (ch) • single crochet (sc) • double crochet (dc) • treble crochet (tr) • ch-3 picot (pic)

This edging consists of motifs adorned with embellishments.

With B, chain a multiple of 6 + 3.

Row 1: Ch 1 to turn, sc in next 2, *sc in next, ch 4, 3 tr closed together, pic, ch 4, sc in next 2*. Repeat from * to *. End with sc in last. Fasten off.

Row 2 (A): On the opposite side of the starting ch and with right side facing, insert hook in first st and pull up a loop, sc in first st, *make a tassel as follows: (sc, ch 3, 2 dc closed together, ch 3, sl st) in next st, sc in next, ch 3, skip 3 chs, sc in next, sc in next and make an embellishment as follows: [ch 9, 4 dc in fourth ch from hook, 4 dc in each of next 5 chs, sl st in sc at base of embellishment], sc in next st, ch 3, skip 3 chs, sc in next sc*. Repeat from * to *. End with tassel, sc in last st. Fasten off.

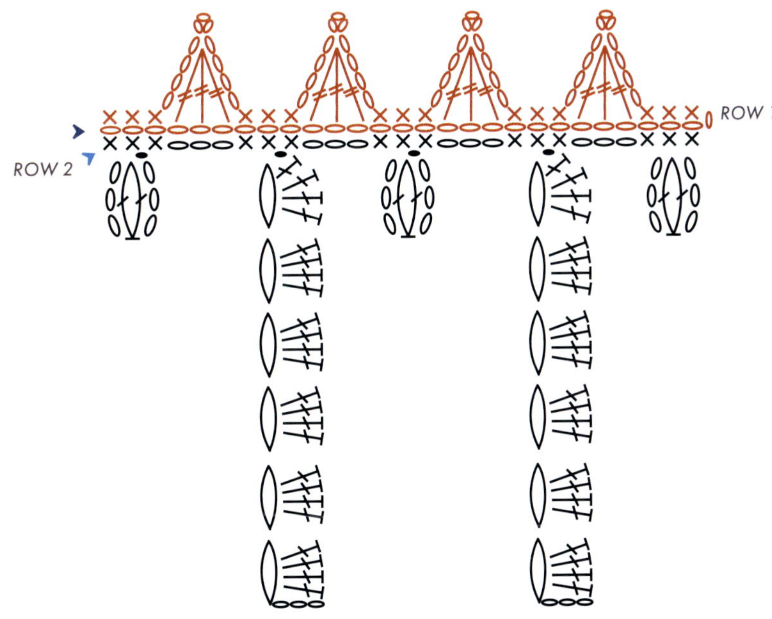

SHANGHAI

BORDER 95

DIFFICULTY ***

COLORS: (A) Black; (B) Red

STITCHES USED: Slip stitch (sl st) • chain (ch) • single crochet (sc) • half double crochet (hdc) • double crochet (dc) • treble crochet (tr)

This edging consists of motifs worked back and forth in rows.

With A, chain a multiple of 21 + 3.

Row 1 (A): Ch 1 to turn, *sc in next 2, ch 2, skip 2 chs, sc in next, ch 3, skip 3 chs, sc in next, ch 2, skip 2 chs, sc in next 3, hdc in next, dc in next, tr in next, dc in next, hdc in next, sc in next 2*. Repeat from * to *. End with sc in last 2.

Row 2: Ch 1 to turn, sc in next, *sc in next, ch 3, skip 3, dc in next st, ch 3, (dc, ch 3, dc, ch 3) in next st, dc in next st, ch 3, skip 3, sc in next st, ch 2, skip 2 chs, sc in next, ch 3, skip 3 chs, sc in next, ch 2, skip 2 chs, sc in next*. Repeat from * to *. End with sc in last st. Fasten off.

Row 3 (B): Insert hook in first st and pull up a loop, sc in first st, *sc in next, ch 4, skip 2 chs, 5 dc closed together, ch 4, skip 2 chs, sc in next, ch 2, 3 hdc closed together in ch-3 space, ch 2, sc in next st, [ch 3, 3 dc closed together in next ch-3 space, ch 3, sc in next st] 3x, ch 2, 3 hdc closed together in next ch-3 space, ch 2*. Repeat from * to *. End with sc in last 2. Fasten off.

From Row 4, work on opposite side of starting chain with the right side always facing.

Row 4 (A): Insert hook in first st and pull up a loop, sc across. Fasten off.

Row 5 (B): Insert hook in first st and pull up a loop, *sc in next 4, hdc in next, dc in next, tr in next, dc in next, hdc in next, sc in next 12*. Fasten off.

Row 6: Insert hook in first st and pull up a loop, sl st in back loop of each st across. Fasten off.

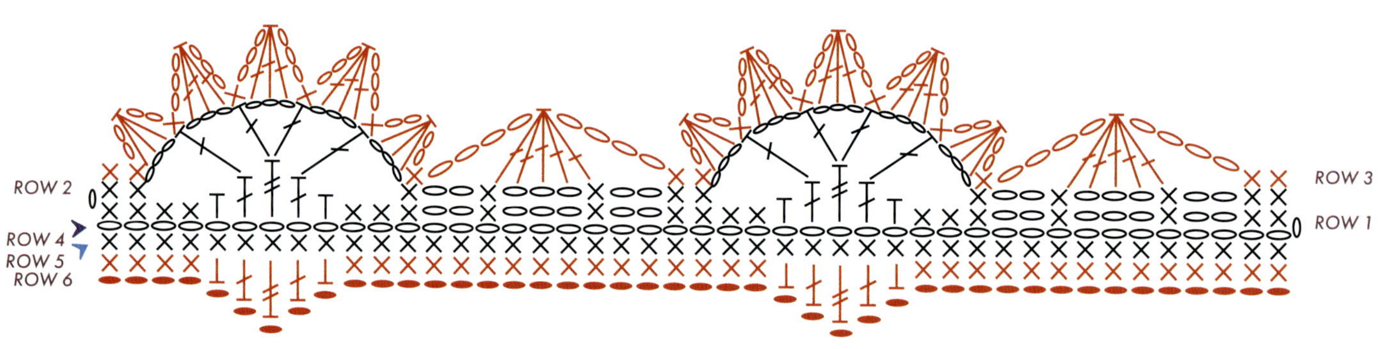

BORDER 96

DIFFICULTY **

COLORS: (A) Black; (B) Red

STITCHES USED: Slip stitch (sl st) • single crochet (sc) • half double crochet (hdc) • double crochet (dc)

This edging consists of interlocking rings.

Wrap A three times around your finger and work over this ring (make the first st over all 4 threads, then work over just 3 of them to avoid excess thickness which would deform the ring).

Continuing with A, insert hook in ring and pull up a loop, 5 sc, 5 hdc, 20 dc, 5 hdc, 5 sc. End with sl st in first st. Fasten off.

Work as established alternating between A and B to desired length, joining the motifs to each other with a sl st after the tenth dc into the sl st closing the previous ring.

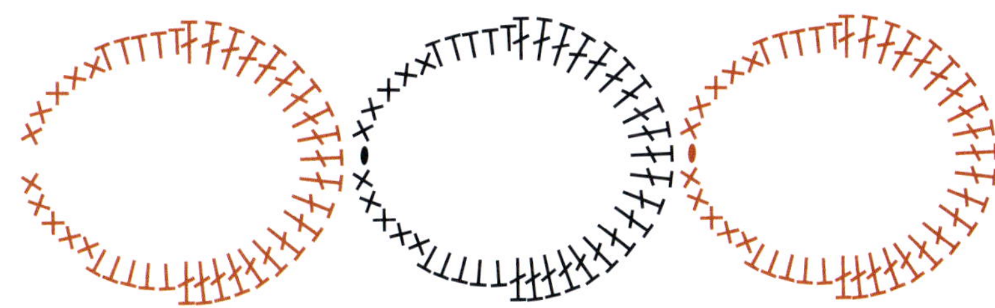

BORDER 97

DIFFICULTY ***

COLORS: (A) Black; (B) Red

STITCHES USED: Slip stitch (sl st) • chain (ch) • single crochet (sc) • half double crochet (hdc)

This edging consists of tassels which are then joined to a supporting edging.

Make a Tassel with A and B: Wrap threads 20x around a 3½-inch (9 cm) template and cut them. Pass a long length of B under the wraps with a yarn needle and tie a tight knot. Wrap this thread 4 or 5 more times and secure with 3 knots. Fold entire length in two: The loop at the top is the tassel's head.

Insert the needle into the thickness and pull it out ½ inch (1 cm) below. Wrap thread once around all the strands to tighten and define the head. Tie a knot, wrap thread 4 or 5 more times to tighten. Tie 3 knots and slip the needle under the wraps around the head of the tassel. Insert the needle through the thickness to conceal the thread and cut it to the length of the fringe, evening everything out.

Rnd 1 (B): Insert hook under the wraps around the tassel's head and pull up a loop, ch 12 working around tassel, sl st in first ch.

Rnd 2: Ch 2 (to replace first hdc), *2 hdc in next, hdc in next*. Repeat from * to *. End with 2 hdc in last st, sl st in first st. Fasten off.

Rnd 3 (A): Insert hook in first st and pull up a loop, *sc, ch 2, skip 1, sc in next st*. Repeat from * to *. End with ch 2, skip 1, sl st to close.

Rnd 4: Sl st in first ch, sc in first ch-2 space, *ch 3, sc in next ch-space*. Repeat from * to *. End with ch 3, sl st in first sc.

Rnd 5: Sl st in first ch, sc into center of first ch-3 space, *ch 4, sc in next ch-space*. Repeat from * to *. End with ch 4, sl st in first sc.

Rnd 6: Sl st in first ch, sc into center of first ch-4 space, *ch 5, sc in next ch-space*. Repeat from * to *. End with ch 5, sl st in first sc.

Finishing: With B, make a 6-ch ring at the top of the head of the tassel as follows: insert hook under tightening threads and pull up a loop, ch 6, sl st at base. Knot the ends and hide them in the thickness, then even out the lengths.

With A and B held together, ch 15, *attach a tassel with sc in ch-6 ring, ch 18*. Repeat from * to *. End with 15 chs.

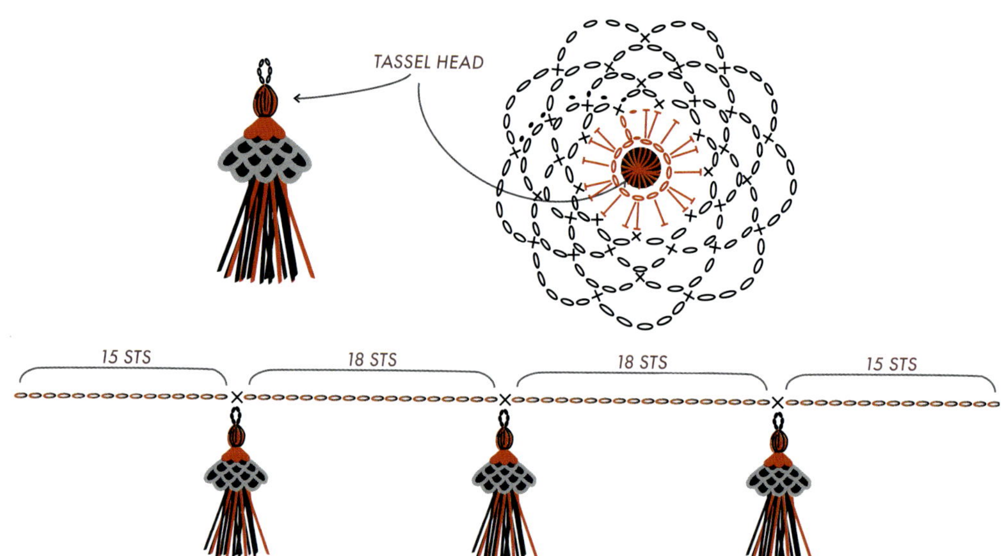

BORDER 98

DIFFICULTY ****

COLORS: (A) Black; (B) Red

STITCHES USED: Slip stitch (sl st) • chain (ch) • single crochet (sc) • double crochet (dc)

Make a Tassel with A and B: Wrap threads 20x around a 3½-inch (9 cm) template and cut them. Pass a long length of B under the wraps with a yarn needle and tie a tight knot. Wrap this thread 4 or 5 more times and secure with 3 knots. Fold entire length in two: The loop at the top is the tassel's head.

Insert the needle into the thickness and pull it out ½ inch (1 cm) below. Wrap thread once around all the strands to tighten and define the head. Tie a knot, wrap thread 4 or 5 more times to tighten. Tie 3 knots and slip the needle under the wraps around the head of the tassel. Insert the needle through the thickness to conceal the thread and cut it to the length of the fringe, evening everything out.

With B, ch 6, sl st to close the ring.

Rnd 1: Ch 1, 12 sc in ring, sl st to close; continue working in the round as follows: *sc in next 3, 2 sc in next*. Repeat from * to * until there are 30 sc around ring. Fasten off.

Rnd 2 (A): To crochet the finishing rnd, insert hook in a st on edge and pull up a loop, *sc in next 2, pic*. Repeat from * to *. End with sl st. Fasten off.

Make the Fringe: with wrong side facing. Insert hook in first sc of Rnd 1 and pull up a loop, *ch 19, pic, ch 19, sc in next sc*. Repeat from * to *. You have 11 fringes. Fasten off.

With A, insert hook in center of Rnd 1 and pull up a loop, ch 3, 2 dc closed together, ch 6, sl st in top of dc-group. Fasten off.

Create the support strip:

With A, ch 20, *join 1 tassel with sc in ch-6 ring, ch 25*. Repeat from * to * to desired length, ending with 20 chs. Fasten off.

With A, ch 20, *sc in next sc, ch 25*. Repeat from * to * to desired length, ending with 20 chs. Fasten off.

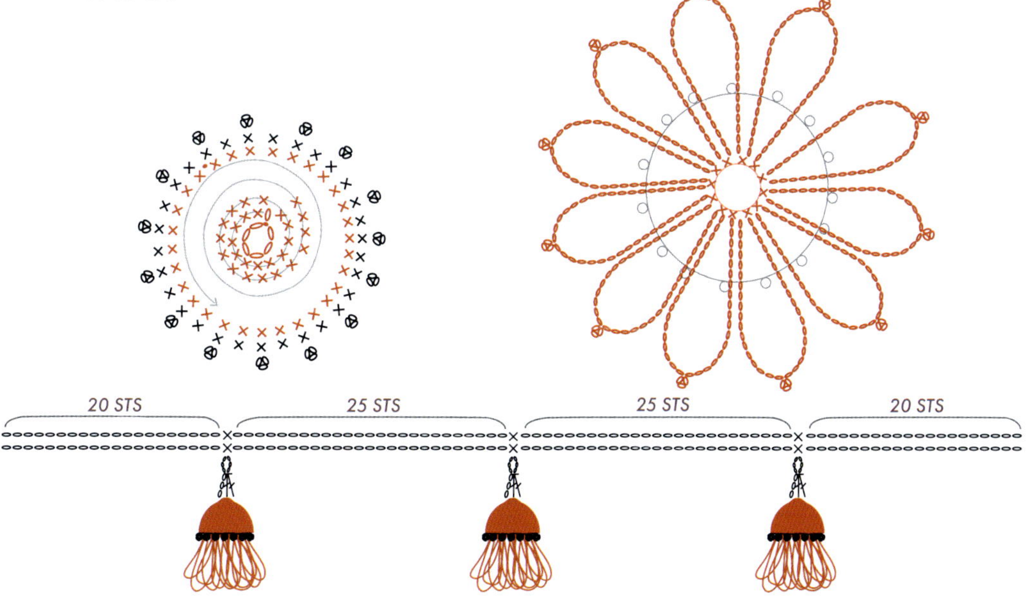

BORDER 99

DIFFICULTY **

COLORS: (A) Buff; (B) Red Currant; (C) Blue; (D) Orange; (E) Green

STITCHES USED: Slip stitch (sl st) • chain (ch) • double crochet (dc) • treble crochet (tr)

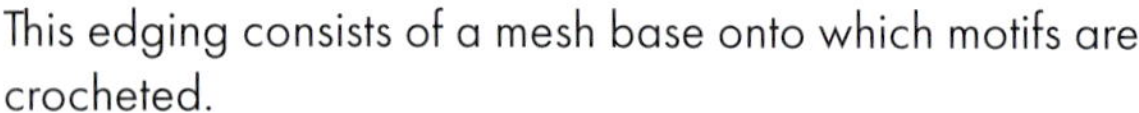

This edging consists of a mesh base onto which motifs are crocheted.

Mesh is worked over 11 rows, progressively increasing and decreasing to form the base of the work.

Row 1 (A): Ch 3 (to replace first dc), ch 2, dc in first ch. Turn.

Row 2: Ch 3 (to replace first dc), ch 2, dc in first st, ch 2, skip 2 chs, (dc, ch 2, dc) in last st. Turn.

Row 3: Ch 3 (to replace first dc), ch 2, dc in first st, [ch 2, skip 2 chs, dc in next] 3x, ch 2, dc in same st as last dc. Turn.

Row 4: Ch 3 (to replace first dc), ch 2, dc in first st, [ch 2, skip 2 chs, dc in next] 5x, ch 2, dc in same st as last dc. Turn.

Rows 5–7: Ch 3 (to replace first dc), [ch 2, skip 2 chs, dc in next] 7x. Turn.

Row 8: Ch 3, skip 2 chs, dc in next, [ch 2, skip 2 chs, dc in next] 4x, ch 2, skip 2 chs, 2 dc closed together in last 2 dc. Turn.

Row 9: Ch 3, skip 2 chs, dc in next, [ch 2, skip 2 chs, dc in next] 2x, ch 2, skip 2, 2 dc closed together in last 2 dc. Turn.

ROW 1 ROW 2 ROW 3 ROW 4 ROW 5 ROW 6 ROW 7 ROW 8 ROW 9 ROW 10 ROW 11

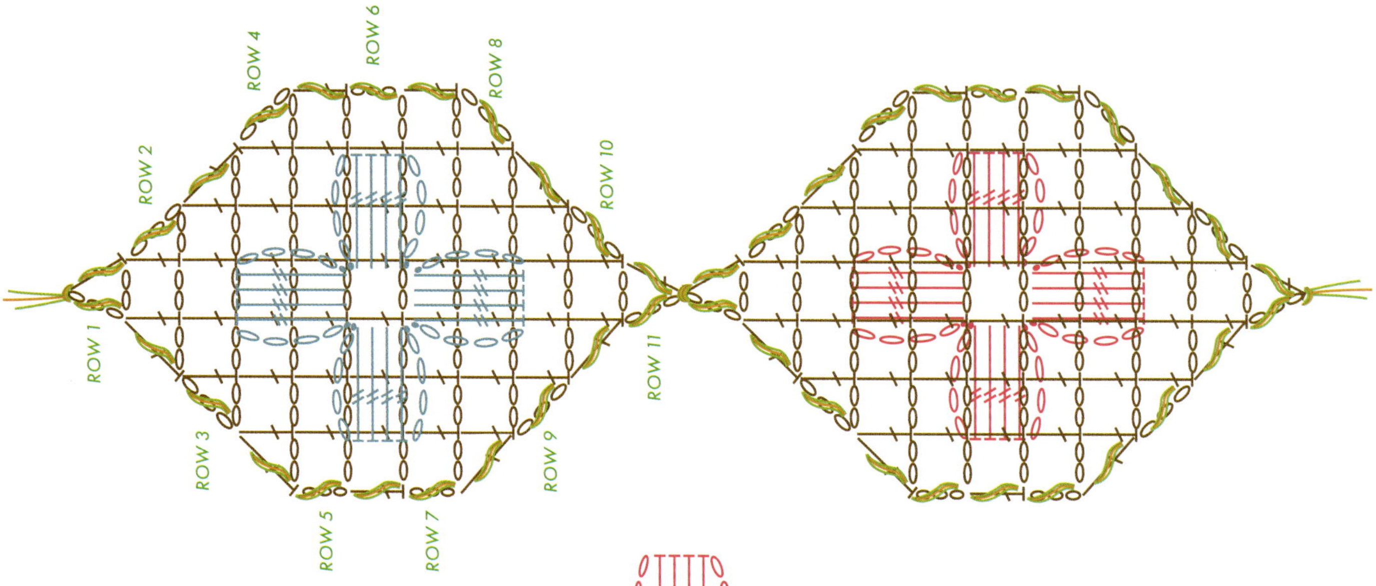

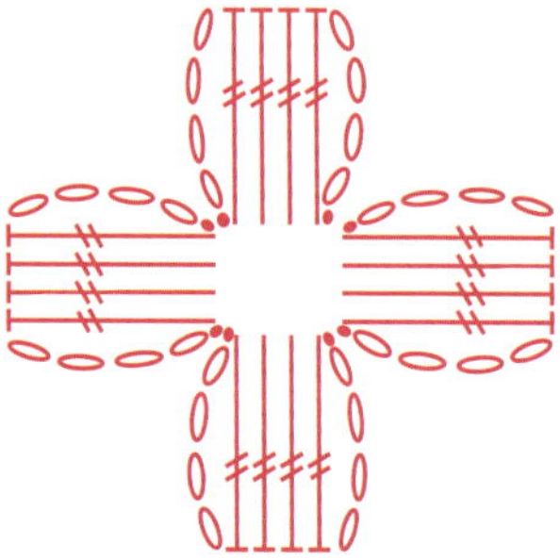

FLOWER TO CROCHET ONTO THE MESH

Row 10: Ch 3, skip 2 chs, dc in next, ch 2, skip 2, 2 dc closed together in last 2 dc. Turn.

Row 11: Ch 3, skip 2, dc in last st. Turn.

Repeat these 11 rows to desired length. Fasten off.

With B, make the flower by crocheting around the central square of the mesh. Insert hook in top of mesh dc and pull up a loop, *ch 4, 4 tr, ch 4, end petal with sl st at bottom of same mesh dc*. Create the second petal on the next side of the square, starting with a sl st and repeating from * to *. Make 2 more petals as established. Fasten off leaving approximately 8 inches (20 cm) aside to attach the petals.

Make a flower centered on each section of mesh, alternating between B and C. Secure the petal ends with the length of thread.

Finishing: With 2 very long lengths of D and E held together in a yarn needle, weave yarn around the sections of mesh, along top edge of one section and bottom edge of the next. Return in the other direction, completing the weave. Threads should cross between each section, wrapping lengths twice around this thin part of the edging.

BORDER 100

DIFFICULTY ***

COLORS: (A) Maroon; (B) Buff; (C) Green; (D) Violet; (E) Orange mohair; (F) Green mohair

STITCHES USED: Slip stitch (sl st) • chain (ch) • single crochet (sc) • double crochet (dc) • treble crochet (tr) • ch-3 picot (pic) • straight weave

This edging consists of alternating mesh and floral motifs. Motif is worked over 11 rows, progressively increasing and decreasing the mesh to form the base of the work.

With A, chain a multiple of 35 + 2.

Row 1: Ch 3 (to replace first dc), ch 2, dc in ninth ch from hook, *ch 2, skip 2 chs, dc in next*. Repeat from * to *. Fasten off.

Row 2 (B): Insert hook at beginning of row and pull up a loop, ch 3 (to replace first dc), skip 2 chs, dc in next, [ch 2, skip 2, dc] 3x, ch 2, skip 2 chs, 2 dc closed together spaced by 2 chs. Turn.

Row 3: Ch 3 (to replace first dc), skip 2 chs, dc in next, ch 2, skip 2 chs, dc in next, ch 2, skip 2 chs, 2 dc closed together spaced by 2 chs. Turn.

Row 4: Ch 3 (to replace first dc), skip 2 chs, 2 dc closed together spaced by 2 chs. End with 8 chs, sl st in tip of motif just made.

CONTINUED ON NEXT PAGE

PERTH

Repeat as established, skipping 6 squares from the central mesh strip.

Begin floral motif with C.

Row 1: Working between triangles, skip 3 mesh squares, insert hook in next dc and pull up a loop, ch 4, skip 2 squares on the right, sc in next dc, [ch 1, tr in starting dc] 6x. End by skipping 2 squares after the starting dc, sc in next dc. Fasten off.

Row 2 (D): With right side facing, insert hook in st at edge of half-circle just made and pull up a loop, [ch 3, 2 tr closed together around next ch, ch 3, sl st in next tr] 6x. End with sl st in dc on mesh. Fasten off.

Now working on opposite side of starting ch, with right side facing.

Last Row (A): Insert hook in st at edge and pull up a loop, *sc in mesh square, pic, sc in same mesh square, skip dc*. Repeat from * to * in all mesh squares. Fasten off.

With yarn needle weave mohair (2 E and 2 F as long as the border) over and under the dc from Row 1. Weave ends in at edges.

To make the fringe, cut two 5½-inch (14 cm) lengths of C and two 5½-inch (14 cm) lengths of D. Fold in half and attach to 8-ch ring at the ends of the triangles.

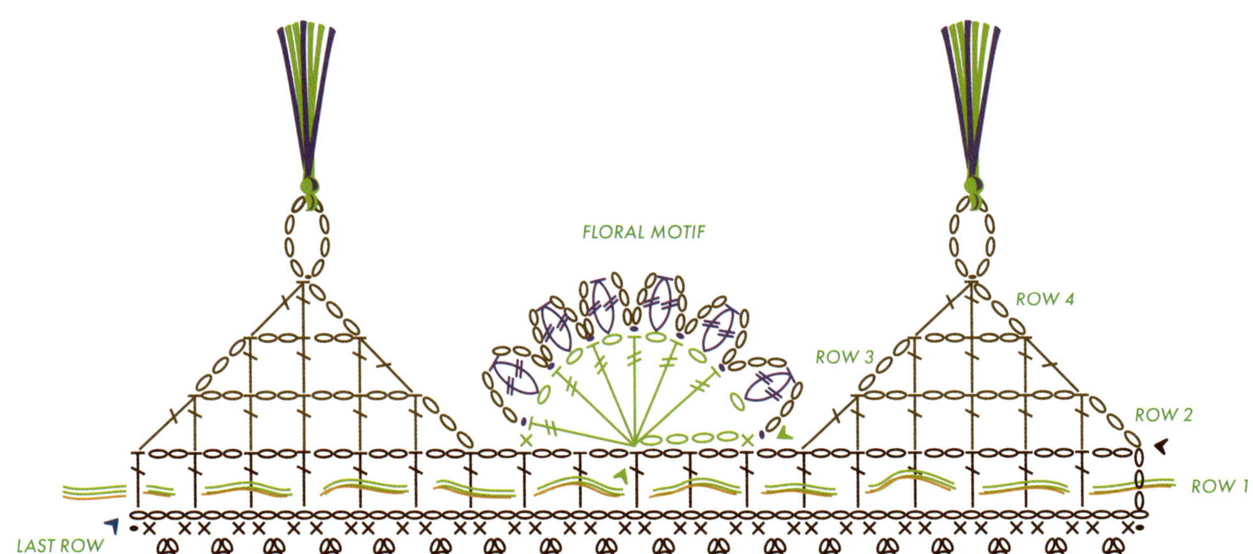

BORDER 101

DIFFICULTY ****

COLORS: (A) Orange; (B) Green; (C) Grey; (D) Khaki; (E) Violet; (F) Dark Maroon

HOOKS: 2 sizes, such as 2 mm and 3 mm

STITCHES USED: Slip stitch (sl st) • chain (ch) • single crochet (sc) • half double crochet (hdc) • double crochet (dc) • treble crochet (tr) • ch-3 picot (pic) • crab stitch

This edging consists of circle motifs linked together by edge trims.

Begin Motif A with A and B and the larger hook: ch 6, sl st to close the ring.

Rnd 1: Ch 2 (to replace first hdc), 2 dc, 2 tr, 2 dc, 3 hdc, 2 dc, 2 tr, 2 dc, 2 hdc in ring. End with sl st in second starting ch. Fasten off.

Rnd 2 (C, smaller hook): Ch 3 (to replace first dc), [ch 2, dc in next] 17x, ch 2, sl st in third starting ch. Fasten off.

Make Motif B with A and B at Rnd 1, and D at Rnd 2. Crochet the required number of motifs, alternating the colors.

Make the two finishing rows, working progressively on the top half of the first motif and the bottom half of the next motif, to link them together. Work alternately from right to left and from left to right for the crab stitch.

Row 1 (E, larger hook): On Motif A (with right side facing and beginning on the same side as the central tr), working right to left, insert hook in dc and pull up a loop. Working in ch-2 spaces [sc, pic, sc] 9x. Turn Motif A to position the work just done at the bottom. Now working on Motif B, with right side facing and beginning at the tr on the left side of the Motif, insert hook in dc and pull up a loop, sc in same st, then work in crab stitch (from left to right): 2 sts in 9 ch-2 spaces. Work as established, progressively joining the Motifs at each stitch change. Fasten off.

Row 2 (F): On Motif A (with right side facing), starting on the left, insert hook in dc at edge (last st of finishing Row 1) and pull up a loop, sc, then work in crab stitch (from left to right): 2 sts in 9 ch-2 spaces. Sc in last dc, pass the hook and thread under finishing Row 1 while turning the motif. Insert hook in first dc of next Motif and sc in same st. [Sc, pic, sc] 9x in ch-2 spaces. Repeat this operation, always passing the hook and thread under finishing Row 1. End with sc in last dc, sl st in st at edge of finishing Row 1. Fasten off.

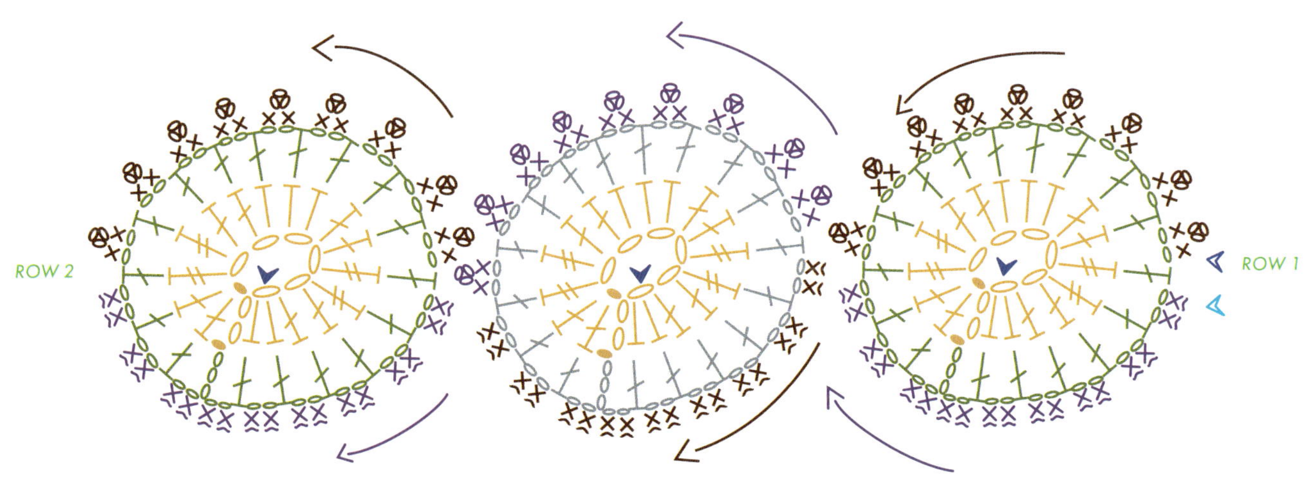

BORDER 102

DIFFICULTY **

COLORS: (A) Orange mohair; (B) Green mohair; (C) Beige; (D) Buff; (E) Dark Maroon; (F) Red Currant; (G) Grey; (H) Green

STITCHES USED: Slip stitch (sl st) • chain (ch) • double crochet (dc) • treble crochet (tr) • tassel • straight and diagonal weaving

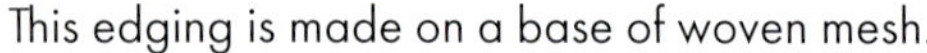

This edging is made on a base of woven mesh.

To begin mesh with C, chain a multiple of 18 + 1.

Row 1: Ch 3 (to replace first dc), *ch 2, skip 2, dc in next*. Repeat from * to *. Fasten off.

Row 2 (D): With right side of Row 1 facing and starting on the right, insert hook in first st and pull up a loop, Repeat Row 1. Fasten off.

Row 3 (E): With right side of Rows 1 and 2 facing and starting on the right, insert hook in first st and pull up a loop, Repeat Row 1. Fasten off.

To begin the tassel with C, insert hook at base of third dc and pull up a loop, ch 4, 2 tr, ch 4, sl st in base st.

Make a tassel as established with F in the fifth dc of Row 1.

Make a tassel as established with H in ninth dc of Row 1.

Make a tassel as established with G in eleventh dc of Row 1. Repeat tassels as established.

First weave: Loosely measure the border, then with yarn needle and mohair (2 lengths of A and 2 lengths of B) weave under and over dc from Row 2. Weave in ends at both ends.

Second weave: Multiply the length of the edging by three and cut lengths of F, G, and H. Weave diagonally as shown on diagram (work relatively loosely). Weave in ends at both ends.

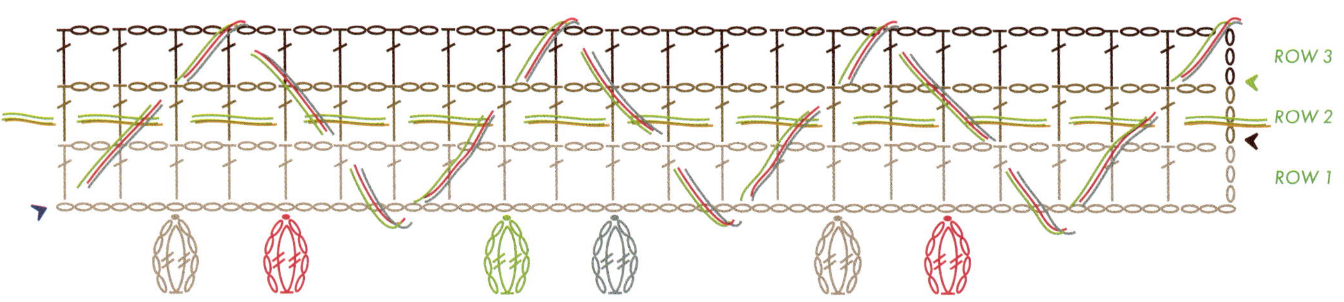

BORDER 103

DIFFICULTY ***

COLORS: (A) Green; (B) Blue; (C) Red Currant; (D) Violet; (E) Dark Maroon; (F) Orange mohair; (G) Green mohair

STITCHES USED: Slip stitch (sl st) • chain (ch) • single crochet (sc) • double crochet (dc) • treble crochet (tr) • ch-3 picot (pic)

This edging consists of sections of mesh alternating with flowers.

To begin a flower with A, ch 6, sl st to close the ring.

Rnd 1 (A or B): 9 sc in ring, sl st to close.

Rnd 2 (A or B): Working in the front loop of the sts, pic in each st. End with sl st to close. Fasten off.

Rnd 3 (C or D): Working in the back loop of the same sts (behind pics just made), insert hook and pull up a loop, sc in next 9, sl st to close.

Rnd 4 (C or D): To make the petals, [(sc, ch 4, tr, 2 dc, tr, ch 4, sc) in next st, sl st in next] 5x. End with sl st to close. Fasten off.

Crochet the required number of flowers and mesh section for the length of the border.

Mesh sections attached to the flowers will be worked back and forth in rows.

Row 1 (E): Insert hook behind work, between 2 dc on a petal, and pull up a loop, sl st, ch 3 (to replace first dc), ch 2, dc in first st. Turn.

Row 2: Ch 3 (to replace first dc), ch 2, dc in first st, ch 2, skip 2 chs, dc in next, ch 2, dc in same st as last dc. Turn.

Row 3: Ch 3 (to replace first dc), ch 2, dc in first st, [ch 2, skip 2 chs, dc in next] 3x, ch 2, dc in same st as last dc. Turn.

Row 4: Ch 3 (to replace first dc), [ch 2, skip 2 chs, dc in next] 5x. Turn.

Row 5: Ch 3, skip 2 chs, dc in next st, [ch 2, skip 2 chs, dc] twice, ch 2, skip 2 chs, 2 dc closed together skipping last ch-2 space. Turn.

Row 6: Ch 3, skip 2 chs, dc in next st, ch 2, skip 2 chs, 2 dc closed together skipping last ch-2 space. Turn.

Row 7: Ch 3, insert hook between dc on petal to be joined and pull up a loop, sl st, skip 2, dc in next st on mesh. Fasten off.

CONTINUED ON NEXT PAGE

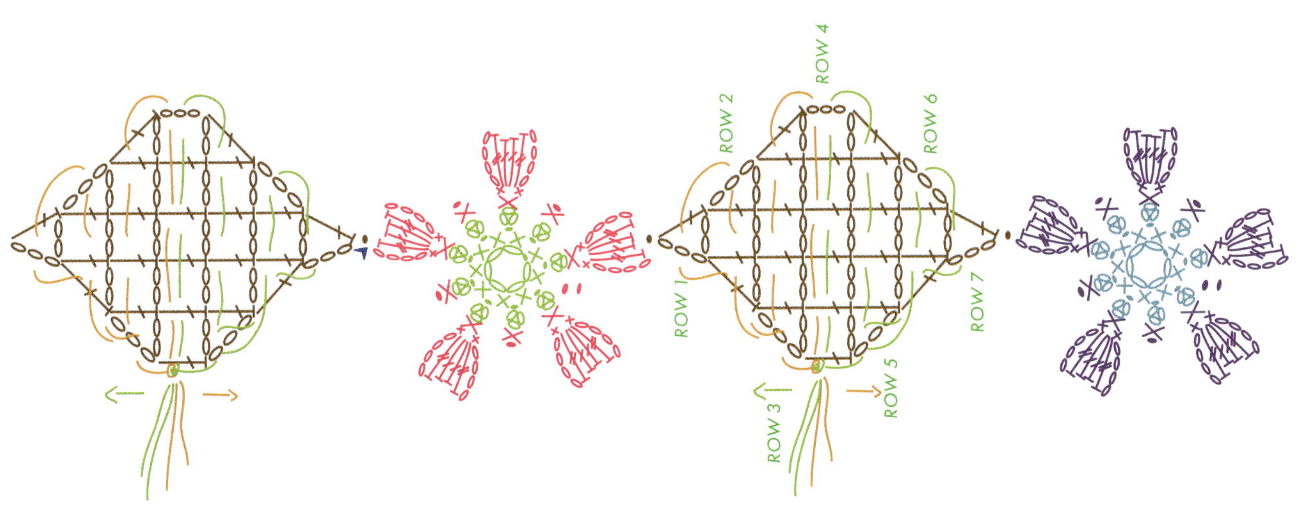

Repeat these 7 rows between each flower while alternating col. Weave ends in on wrong side.

Both motifs (flowers and mesh) can be used at ends.

Weaving: Prepare 19¾-inch (50 cm) lengths of yarn: 2x (2 of F and 2 of G). Pass them through the central bottom square of a section of mesh with a yarn needle, even them out and tie a simple knot. Now, work with 4 lengths (2 lengths of F and 2 lengths of G), leaving the others on standby. Weave from center bottom to right tip as shown on the diagram, return to the center by overlocking the bottom edge of the mesh section and passing the needle through the knot from right to left. Leave on standby. Repeat this operation in the other direction with the lengths previously left on hold. Finish by passing the needle through the knot from left to right. Tie the 8 lengths together, bringing the knot back over the initial knot. Even out the lengths. Repeat on all mesh sections, always starting at the bottom.

BORDER 104

DIFFICULTY ***

COLORS: (A) Beige; (B) Violet; (C) Red Currant; (D) Green; (E) Orange mohair; (F) Green mohair

STITCHES USED: Slip stitch (sl st) • chain (ch) • single crochet (sc) • double crochet (dc) • treble crochet (tr)

This edging consists of woven squares adorned with tassels.

To begin the square with A, ch 13.

Row 1 (A or B): Ch 3 (to replace first dc), ch 2, dc in ninth ch from hook, [ch 2, skip 2 chs, dc in next st] 3x. Turn.

Rows 2–4: Ch 3 (to replace first dc), [ch 2, skip 2 chs, dc in next st] 4x. Fasten off.

Crochet the number of squares needed to obtain the desired length.

Weaving: Prepare 23¾-inch (60 cm) lengths of mohair (2 lengths of E and 2 lengths of F), fold them and attach them to the work on the wrong side. Following the diagram, weave through the outer edge of the squares twice and fasten off on the wrong side.

Make the tassels on the bottom of each square, with the right side of Row 1 facing. With B on a beige square and A on a violet square, insert hook at base of central dc and pull up a loop, ch 5, tassel: (ch 3, 2 dc closed together in same st, ch 3, sl st in same st), sl st in 5 starting chs. Fasten off.

With D and right side facing (tassel on the bottom), insert hook in st at top left corner of same square, ch 4, (tr, ch 4, sl st) in same st, 2 sc in each row end, sc in bottom corner, ch 4, (tr, ch 4, sl st) in same st, sc under dc from Row 1, ch 9, sl st in top of tassel, (ch 4, tr, ch 4, sl st) twice in same st, ch 9, sc under dc at next corner (on the right). Fasten off.

Work as established on next square, making a sl st after each tr on the side to join it to the corresponding st of the previous square. Join the squares while alternating colors.

With C, insert hook in bottom corner of a square (to work on same side as tassel) and pull up a loop, 2 sc in first ch-space, sc under next dc, ch 4, make the next ch slightly longer (in front of the stem of the next tassel), pass yarn behind tassel adjusting the length of the ch, ch 4, sc under third dc, 2 sc in next ch-space. Working along the height of the same square, 2 sc in first and second dc row ends, sc at base of next dc, (ch 4, tr in sc, sl st in corresponding sc on next square, ch 4, sl st) in same st. Continue working on the same side of the square, making 2 sc in next 2 dc row ends. End with sc in st at top corner. Fasten off.

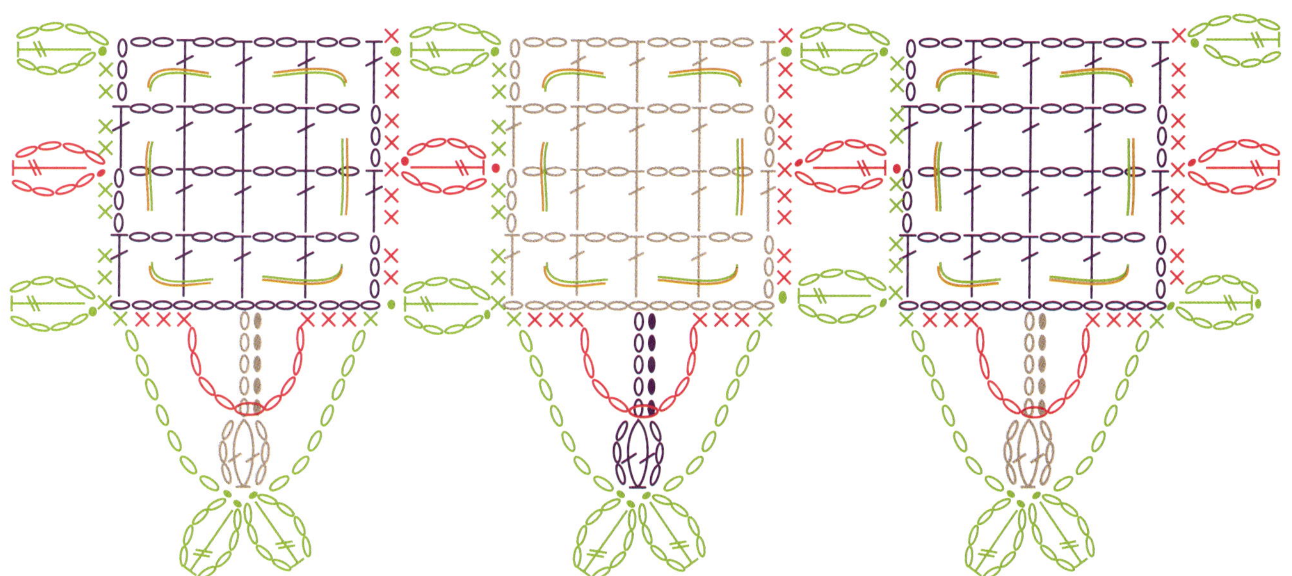

BORDER 105

DIFFICULTY **

COLORS: (A) Muted Violet; (B) Yellow Green; (C) Grey; (D) Smoked Brown

STITCHES USED: Slip stitch (sl st) • chain (ch) • single crochet (sc) • half double crochet (hdc) • double crochet (dc) • treble crochet (tr)

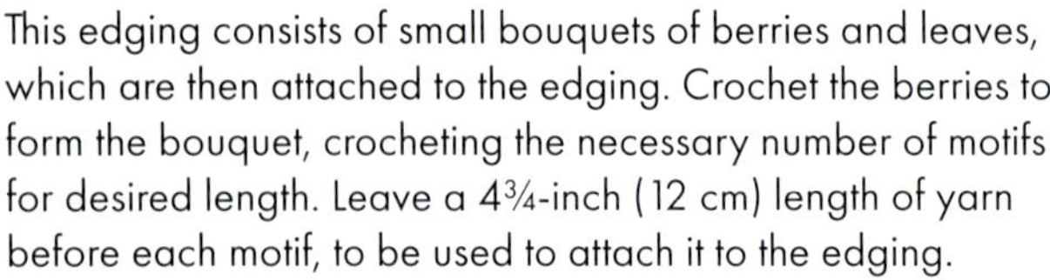

This edging consists of small bouquets of berries and leaves, which are then attached to the edging. Crochet the berries to form the bouquet, crocheting the necessary number of motifs for desired length. Leave a 4¾-inch (12 cm) length of yarn before each motif, to be used to attach it to the edging.

Motif 1 (A): Ch 13, make the berry as follows: [ch 6, 3 tr closed together in sixth ch from hook] twice. Fold the second tr-group made over the first, sl st in first 2 chs of ch-13. Fasten off.

Motif 2 (B): Insert hook in first ch from Motif 1 and pull up a loop, [ch 6, make a grain as follows: ch 3, yarn over, insert hook in first of 3 chs and pull up a loop, yarn over, insert hook in same ch and pull up a loop, pull through 5 loops on hook, sl st in same ch] twice. End with sl st in ch before last grain. Fasten off.

Motif 3 (B): Insert hook in first ch from Motif 1 and pull up a loop, ch 9, [ch 5, sc in first of 5 chs, ch 5] 3x. End with ch 5, sc in first of 5 chs, sl st in previous ch. Fasten off.

Motif 4 (B): Insert hook in first ch from Motif 1 and pull up a loop, ch 18, ch 5, 4 dc closed together in fifth ch from hook, ch 1 to close the st, ch 5. End with sl st in first ch before the motif. Fasten off.

To begin the support strip with D, chain a multiple of 16 + 1.

Row 1: Ch 1 to turn, *sc in next 3, hdc in next 2, dc in next, hdc in next 2*. Repeat from * to *. End with sc in last 3. Fasten off.

Row 2 (C): Working on opposite side of starting chain, sc in next 3, *ch 12, make a leaf as follows: ch 10, working over these 10 chs, ch 1 to turn, sc in next 2, hdc in next, dc in next 2, tr in next, dc in next 2, hdc in next, sc in next, sl st in next, ch 12, skip 13 chs, sc in next 3*. Repeat from * to *. Fasten off.

To assemble the edging, take the small bouquet of berries (Motifs 1, 2, 3, and 4), even out the lengths of thread set aside at the start and use the yarn needle to pass these threads from bottom to top in the second st of the support strip, secure the motif by tying a knot with all the threads just above the border. Finish by evening out the strands.

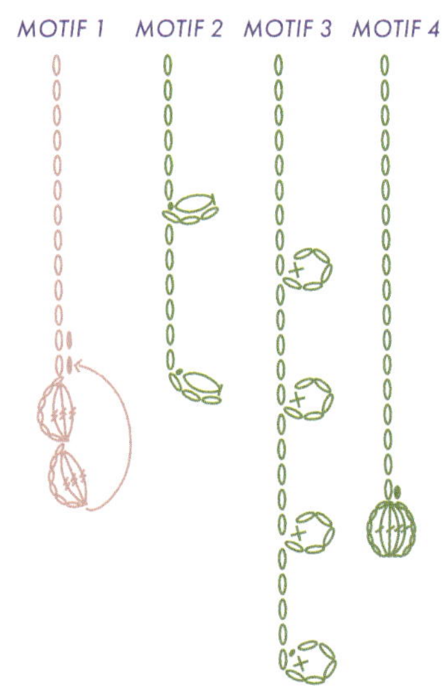

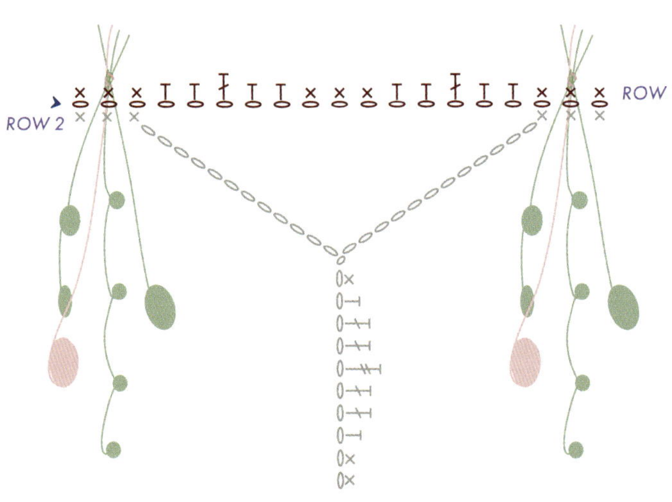

BORDER 106

DIFFICULTY ***

COLORS: (A) Lagoon; (B) Rock

STITCHES USED: Slip stitch (sl st) • chain (ch) • single crochet (sc) • half double crochet (hdc) • double crochet (dc)

This edging consists of flowers attached to a support strip.

Make a rosette with A.

Rnd 1: Ch 3, (ch 2, dc in first ch) 9x, ch 2, sl st in third starting ch.

Rnd 2: Insert hook in next ch-2 space, (sc, ch 3, sc) in 10 ch-spaces, sl st in first st. Fasten off.

To begin the support strip, with B crochet the starting ch joining the rosettes as follows:

Row 1: Ch 12, *ch 4, sl st in sl st on a rosette, ch 4, sl st in eighth ch from hook, ch 15*. Repeat from * to *. End with ch 12. Turn.

Row 2: Ch 3 (to replace first dc), dc in fourth ch from hook, *ch 3, skip 3 chs, 3 dc closed together in next ch, ch 3, skip 3 chs, dc in next ch, ch 3, skip 3 chs, sc in next sl st, ch 3, skip 3 chs, dc in next st*. Repeat from * to *. End with ch 3, skip 3 chs, 3 dc closed together in next ch, ch 3, skip 3 chs, 2 dc in last. Fasten off.

Working with right side facing.

Row 3: Ch 3 (to replace first dc), dc in next dc, *ch 3, skip 3 chs, dc in next st, ch 3, skip 3 chs, 3 dc closed together in next st, ch 3, skip 3 chs, hdc in next sc, ch 3, skip 3 chs, 3 dc closed together in next st*. Repeat from * to *. End with ch 3, skip 3 chs, dc in next st, ch 3, skip 3 chs, 2 dc in last. Fasten off.

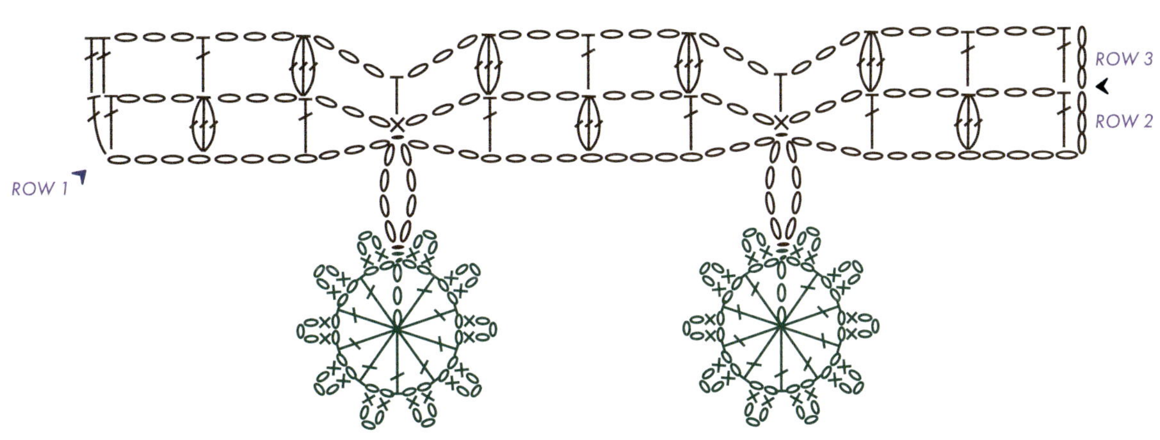

BORDER 107

DIFFICULTY *

COLOR: Variegated

STITCHES USED: Slip stitch (sl st) • chain (ch) • treble crochet (tr) • ch-3 picot (pic)

This edging consists of flowers created as an extension of the border. Crochet the number of motifs required for desired length.

Row 1: *[Ch 5, pic] 4x, ch 5, make the flower as an extension of the work: ch 5, sl st to close, working in ring: (ch 4, 2 tr closed together, ch 4, sl st) 6x*. Repeat from * to *. End with [ch 5, pic] twice, ch 4. Fasten off.

BORDER 108

DIFFICULTY **

COLORS: (A) Red – Variegated; (B) Pink – Variegated

STITCHES USED: Slip stitch (sl st) • chain (ch) • single crochet (sc) • double treble crochet (dtr)

This edging consists of flowers joined together by a petal.

With A, ch 6, sl st to close the ring.

Rnd 1: 8 sc in ring.

Rnd 2: [Sl st, ch 6, dtr, ch 6, sl st] in each sc. Fasten off.

Make another flower with B. Assemble the flowers with a sl st after the dtr made into the end of a petal of the previous flower. Make and join flowers together while alternating colors until desired length.

BORDER 109

DIFFICULTY ***

COLORS: (A) Light Green – Variegated; (B) Pink – Variegated; (C) Ebony – Variegated

STITCHES USED: Slip stitch (sl st) • chain (ch) • single crochet (sc) • half double crochet (hdc) • double crochet (dc) • treble crochet (tr)

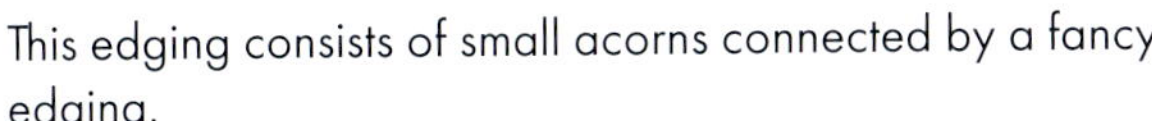

This edging consists of small acorns connected by a fancy edging.

To begin the top of the acorn with A, ch 5, 7 tr in first ch, ch 4, sl st in same ch. Fasten off. Now, crochet the acorn with B.

Row 1: Insert hook in back loop to work across tr, 8 sc, ch 1 to turn (starting from the next row, work under both loops).

Row 2: Sc in next 3, 2 sc closed together, sc in last 3, ch 1 to turn.

Row 3: Sc in next 7, ch 1 to turn.

Row 4: Sc in next 3, 2 sc closed together, sc in last 2, ch 1 to turn.

Row 5: Sc in next 6, ch 1 to turn.

Row 6: Skip 1, sc in next 3, 2 sc closed together, ch 1 to turn.

Row 7: Skip 1, sc in next 3, ch 1 to turn.

Row 8: Skip 1, 2 sc closed together. Fasten off.

Make a support ring at the top of the acorn as follows: Insert hook in ch at bottom of tr-group and pull up a loop, ch 6, sl st at base to close.

Crochet the number of acorns needed for desired length.

With C, crochet the support strip.

Row 1: *Ch 7, begin a dc in fourth ch from hook, insert hook in third ch before dc just made, yarn over and pull through 3 loops on hook, ch 8, join 1 acorn: sc in top ring, ch 8*. Repeat from * to *. End with ch 7, begin a dc in fourth ch from hook, insert hook in third ch before dc just made, yarn over and pull through 3 loops on hook.

Row 2: Ch 2 to turn (and replace first hdc), hdc in first st, *ch 4, skip 4 chs, 2 hdc closed together in next, ch 4, skip 3 chs, hdc in next st*. Repeat from * to *. Fasten off.

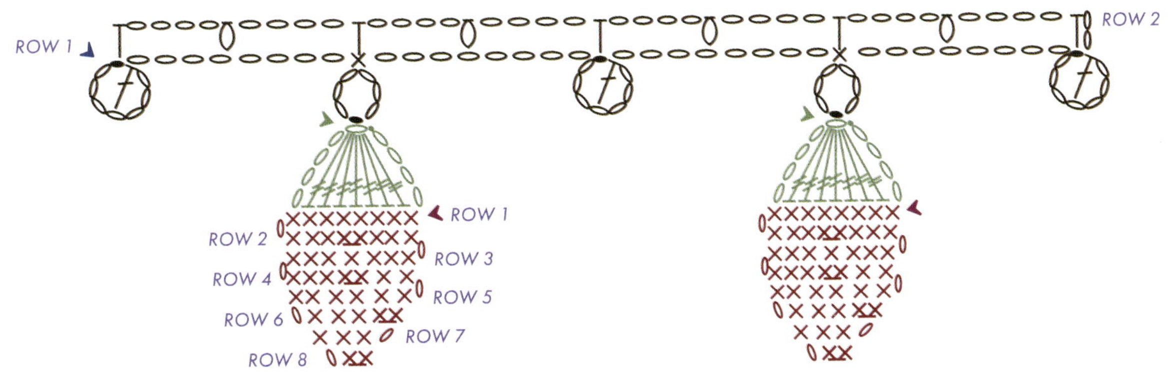

BORDER 110

DIFFICULTY **

COLORS: (A) Light Pink – Variegated; (B) Yellow – Variegated; (C) Beige – Variegated; (D) Chestnut – Variegated

STITCHES USED: Slip stitch (sl st) • chain (ch) • single crochet (sc) • treble crochet (tr) • ch-3 picot (pic)

This edging consists of small bouquets linked by a fancy edging.

To make the flowers for the bouquet, begin with A. Before first ch, leave a length of 4¾-inch (12 cm). Ch 15, the fifteenth ch becomes the support for each petal. To make first petal, *ch 6, sl st in support ch*. Make 5 more petals. Fasten off and weave ends inside the heart of the flower.

With B, insert hook in first ch and pull up a loop, ch 22, make 6 petals with the twenty-second ch as the supporting ch.

With C, insert hook in first ch and pull up a loop and pull up a loop, ch 18, make 6 petals with the eighteenth ch as the supporting ch.

To finish the bouquet, braid the three lengths of thread before each motif over ½ inch (1 cm), tie a knot at the end and cut ½ inch (1 cm) after the knot. Crochet the number of bouquets needed for desired length.

Crochet the support strip with D.

Row 1: Ch 12, *sl st under knot on a bouquet, ch 15*. Repeat from * to *. End with 12 chs.

Row 2: Ch 1 to turn, *sc in next 2, ch 3, skip 1 ch, 3 tr closed together, pic, ch 3, skip 1 ch, sc in next 2, pic, sc in next 2, sl st in next, pass the thread loosely behind the knot, sl st in next, sc in next 2, pic*. Repeat from * to *. End with sc in next 2, ch 3, skip 1 ch, 3 tr closed together, pic, ch 3, skip 1 ch, sc in next 2.

BORDER 111

DIFFICULTY ***

COLORS: (A) Maroon – Variegated; (B) Fir Green – Variegated

STITCHES USED: Slip stitch (sl st) • chain (ch) • single crochet (sc) • double crochet (dc) • treble crochet (tr)

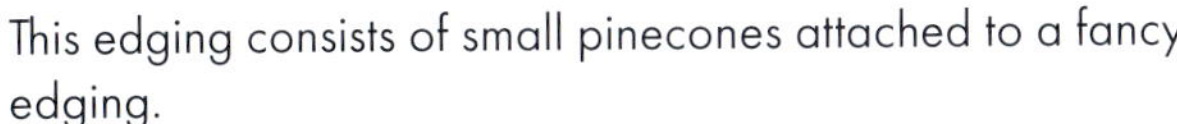

This edging consists of small pinecones attached to a fancy edging.

To begin a pinecone, ch 7 with A.

Row 1: Starting in fifth ch from hook, 4 dc closed together, sl st to close dc-group, ch 3, make a grain in first ch as follows: (5 dc closed together in same st, ch 1 to close).

Row 2: Ch 5, 4 dc closed together in first ch, ch 3, grain in second of next 3 chs, ch 3, grain in last grain of previous row.

Row 3: Ch 5, 4 dc closed together in first ch, [ch 3, grain in second of next 3 chs] twice, ch 3, grain in last grain of previous row.

Row 4: Ch 5, 4 dc closed together in ch after first grain, ch 3, grain in ch after next grain, ch 3, skip 1 ch, grain in next ch, ch 3, grain in ch before last grain.

Row 5: Sl st in first grain, ch 5, 4 dc closed together in ch after first grain, grain in second of next 3 chs, grain in ch before last grain.

Row 6: Sl st in first grain, ch 5, 4 dc closed together in ch after first grain, ch 2, grain in ch before last grain.

Row 7: Skip grain, sl st in first of 2 chs, ch 4, tr in next ch. Fasten off.

Crochet the number of pinecones needed for desired length.

Begin the support strip with A.

Row 8: Ch 14, with right side of motif facing, *sc in tr on pinecone, ch 7, tassel: (ch 4, 2 tr in first ch, ch 4, sl st in same st) ch 7*. Repeat from * to *. End with 14 chs.

Row 9: Ch 1 to turn, ch 1, skip 1, sc in next st, *ch 2, skip 2, sc in next st*. Repeat from * to *. End with 2 sc. Fasten off.

Row 10 (B): With right side facing, insert hook in first st and pull up a loop, sc in first, *ch 12, sl st in same st, sc in next 4, ch 20, sl st in same st, sc in next 4*. Repeat from * to *. Fasten off.

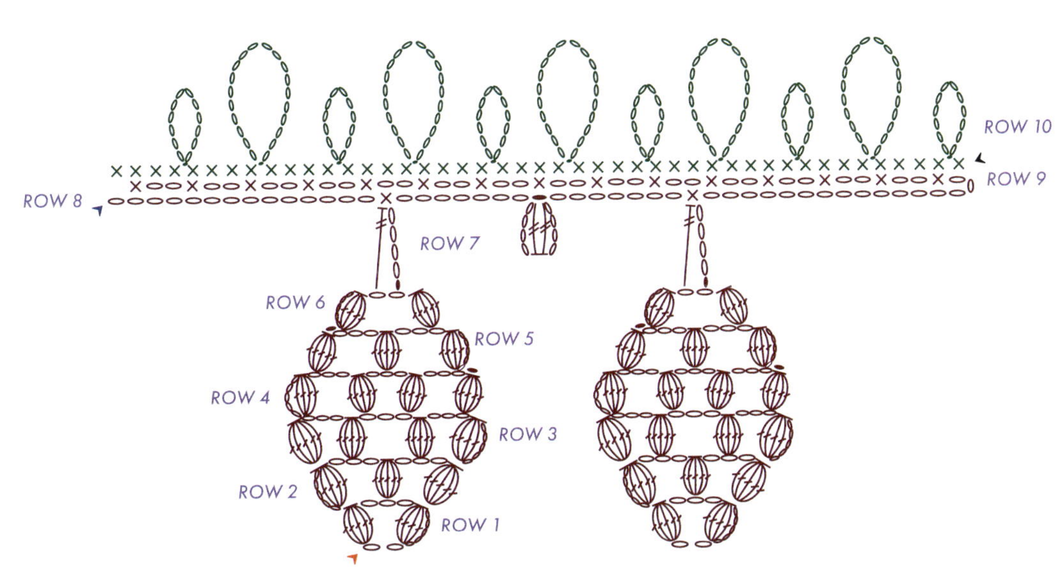

BORDER 112

DIFFICULTY ***

COLORS: (A) Opaline – Variegated; (B) Ombre Brown – Variegated

STITCHES USED: Slip stitch (sl st) • chain (ch) • single crochet (sc) • double crochet (dc) • treble crochet (tr) • ch-3picot (pic)

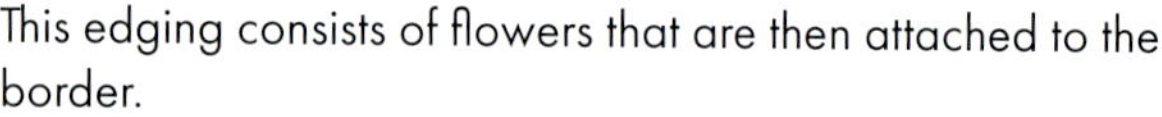

This edging consists of flowers that are then attached to the border.

Begin the flower with A: ch 9, (ch 4, 2 dc, ch 4, sl st) in last ch made, [sl st in next, (sl st in next, ch 5, 2 tr, ch 5, sl st in same)] 3x, sl st in next, (ch 4, 2 dc, ch 4, sl st) in next, ch 4, dc in first of 9 chs made, ch 12, sl st in dc just made. Fasten off.

Crochet the number of flowers needed for desired length.

Crochet the support strip with B.

Row 1: Ch 9, *sl st in top of 12-ch ring of flower, ch 7, pic, ch 7*. Repeat from * to *. End with 9 chs, omitting last pic.

Row 2: Ch 1 to turn, 2 sc, *ch 4, skip 3 chs, 3 dc closed together in next, ch 4, skip 3 chs, (sc, pic) in next*. Repeat from * to *, end with sc in last 2. Fasten off.

BORDER 113

DIFFICULTY **

COLORS: (A) Yellow; (B) Turquoise; (C) Red; (D) Apricot

STITCHES USED: Chain (ch) • single crochet (sc) • half double crochet (hdc) • double crochet (dc) • ch-3 picot (pic) • puff (yarn over 3x, insert hook in st and pull up a loop, yarn over and pull through 7 loops on hook, ch 1 to close)

This edging consists of very colorful rows worked mainly on the right side.

With A, chain a multiple of 6 + 1.

Row 1: Ch 3, in fourth ch *puff, ch 1, skip 2 chs, (2 dc, ch 2, dc) in next, ch 1, skip 2*. Repeat from * to *. End with puff in last ch. Fasten off.

Row 2 (B): With right side facing, starting on the right, insert hook and pull up a loop, sc in first st, pic, *ch 3, skip 3, sc in next ch-2 space, ch 3, skip 3, (sc, pic) in next puff*. Repeat from * to *. Fasten off.

Row 3 (C): With right side facing, starting on the right, insert hook and pull up a loop, sc in first st, *ch 3, skip 3, (sc, pic) in next st, ch 3, skip 3, sc in next st*. Repeat from * to *. Fasten off.

Row 4 (D): With right side facing, starting on the right, insert hook and pull up a loop, sc in first st, pic, *ch 3, skip 3, sc in next pic, ch 3, skip 3, (sc, pic) in next*. Repeat from * to *. Fasten off.

Row 5 (B): With wrong side facing, starting on the right, insert hook in pic and pull up a loop, sc in pic, *ch 2, skip 3, hdc in next st, ch 2, skip 3, sc in next pic*. Repeat from * to *. Turn.

Row 6: With right side facing, ch 3, puff in first st, *ch 1, skip 2, (dc, ch 2, 2 dc, ch 1) in next hdc, skip 2, puff in next st*. Repeat from * to *. Fasten off.

Row 7 (A): Repeat Row 2, making sc in ch-2 spaces and (sc, pic) in puffs. Fasten off.

Row 8 (C): Repeat Row 3.

Row 9 (C): Repeat Row 4. Fasten off.

Row 10 (D): Working on opposite side of starting chain, sc across. Fasten off.

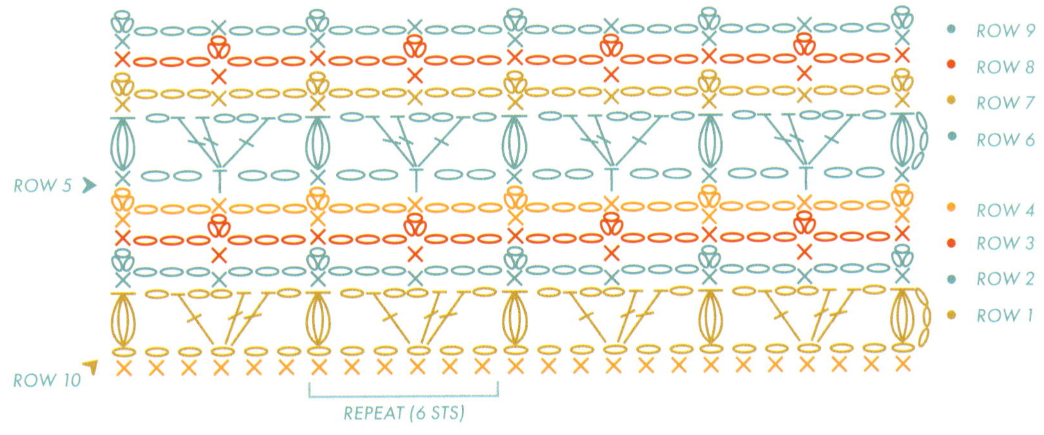

BORDER 114

DIFFICULTY **

COLORS: (A) Rust; (B) Yellow; (C) Pink; (D) Green

STITCHES USED: Chain (ch) • single crochet (sc) • half double crochet (hdc) • puff (yarn over 3x, insert hook in st and pull up a loop, yarn over and pull through 7 loops on hook, ch 1 to close)

This edging consists of very colorful rows worked mainly on the right side.

With A, chain a multiple of 4 + 1.

Row 1: Ch 1 to turn, sc in first st, *ch 2, skip 1 ch, puff in next, ch 2, skip 1 ch, sc in next st*. Repeat from * to *. Fasten off.

Row 2 (B): With right side facing, starting on the right, insert hook in first sc from Row 1 and pull up a loop, ch 2, *ch 3, skip 2 chs, puff in puff from previous row, ch 3, skip 2 chs, hdc in next sc*. Repeat from * to *. Fasten off.

Row 3 (C): With right side facing, starting on the right, insert hook in third ch from Row 1 and pull up a loop, sc in same st, *ch 3, skip 3 chs, puff in puff from previous row, ch 3, skip 3 chs, sc in next hdc*. Repeat from * to *. Fasten off.

Row 4 (D): With right side facing, starting on the right, insert hook in first sc and pull up a loop, ch 2, *ch 3, skip 3 chs, puff in puff from previous row, ch 3, skip 3 chs, hdc in next sc*. Repeat from * to *. Fasten off.

Row 5 (D): Now working on opposite side of starting ch, insert hook in first st and pull up a loop, ch 2 (to replace first hdc), *ch 2, skip 2, hdc in next st*. Repeat from * to *. Fasten off.

Row 6 (D): Now working from beginning of previous row, insert hook in second starting ch and pull up a loop, sc in same st, *sc around next ch, ch 2, skip 2, hdc in next st on starting ch, ch 2, skip 2*. Repeat from * to *. End with skip 1, sc in last st. Fasten off.

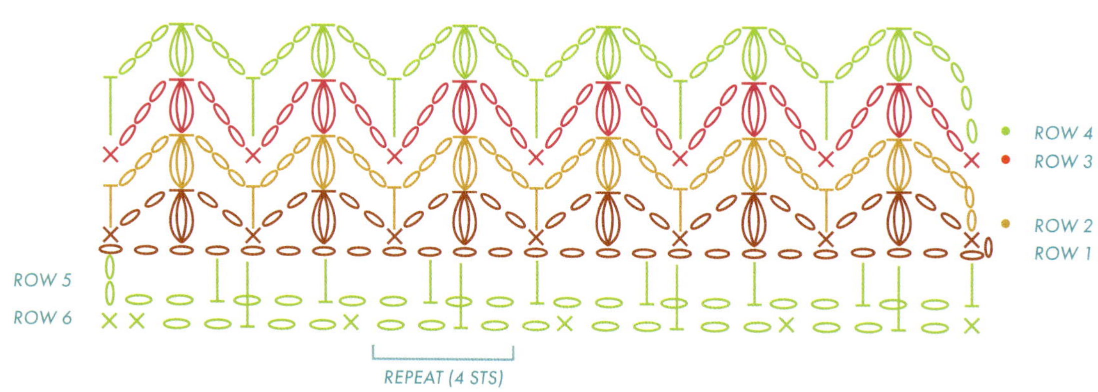

BORDER 115

DIFFICULTY ***

COLORS: (A) Almond Green; (B) Anise; (C) Verbena; (D) Yellow; (E) Olive; (F) Rust

STITCHES USED: Chain (ch) • single crochet (sc) • double crochet (dc) • ch-3 picot (pic)

This edging consists of very colorful rows worked with right side always facing and starting on the same side.

With A, chain a multiple of 6 + 1.

Row 1: Ch 3 to turn, dc in fourth ch from hook, *skip 2, (2 dc, ch 3, 2 dc) in next, skip 2, dc in next st*. Repeat from * to *. Fasten off.

Row 2 (B): Insert hook in first st from Row 1 and pull up a loop, ch 3 (to replace first dc), *skip 3, (2 dc, ch 3, 2 dc) in next, skip 3, front post dc in next st*. Repeat from * to *. Fasten off.

Rows 3–4 (C): Repeat Row 2. Fasten off.

Row 5 (E): Repeat Row 2. Fasten off.

Row 6 (E): Insert hook in first st, ch 3, 2 dc in same st, skip 2 dc, (sc, pic, sc) in next ch-3 space, skip 2 dc, 4 dc in next dc*. Repeat from * to *. End with (sc, pic, sc) in ch-space, 3 dc in last dc. Fasten off.

Row 7 (D): Now working on opposite side of starting chain with right side facing, insert hook in first st and pull up a loop, sc in same st, *ch 3, skip 2, sc in next st, ch 3, skip 2, sc in next st*. Repeat from * to *. Fasten off.

Row 8 (F): With right side facing, insert hook in first st and pull up a loop, sc in same st, ch 1, *sc around next ch-space, ch 3*. Repeat from * to *. End with ch 1, sc in last st. Fasten off.

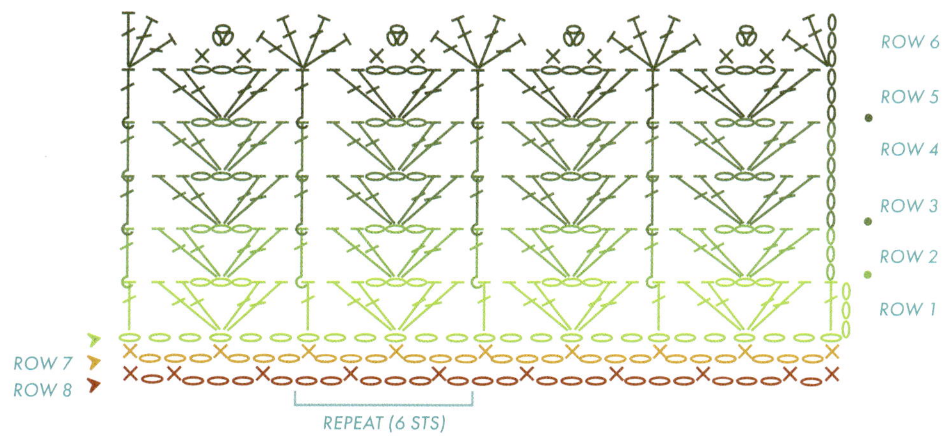

BORDER 116

DIFFICULTY *

COLORS: (A) Lime Green; (B) Fuchsia; (C) Powder Pink; (D) Hot Pink

STITCHES USED: Slip stitch (sl st) • chain (ch) • single crochet (sc) • half double crochet (hdc) • double crochet (dc)

This edging consists of very colorful rows worked with right side always facing and starting on the same side. Change to next color by making the last yarn over with the next color.

With A, chain a multiple of 11.

Row 1: Ch 3, hdc across. Fasten off.

Row 2 (B, C, and D): Carry yarn across work when unused; with right side facing, insert hook and pull up a loop, sc in third ch from previous row, *skip 3, in next st make (3 dc with B, 3 dc with C, 3 dc with D), skip 3, sc in next 2 with D, sc in next 2 with B*. Repeat from * to *, ending with sc in last st. Fasten off.

Row 3 (B): Now working on opposite side of starting ch with right side facing, insert hook in first st and pull up a loop, *sl st in next, dc in next st*. Repeat from * to *, ending with sl st in last st. Fasten off.

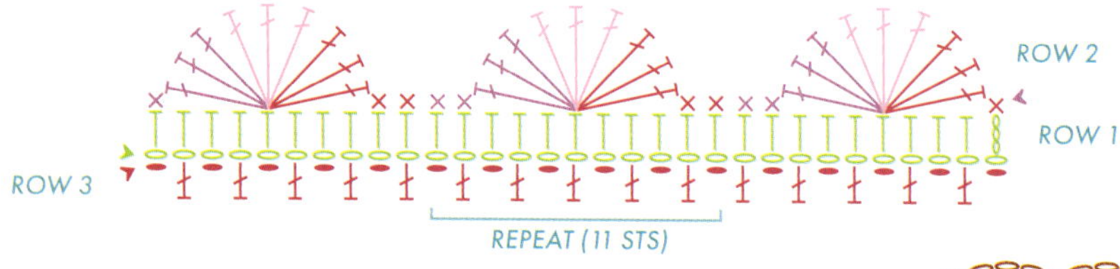

BORDER 117

DIFFICULTY **

COLORS: (A) Lime Green; (B) Orange; (C) Yellow

STITCHES USED: Slip stitch (sl st) • chain (ch) • single crochet (sc) • double crochet (dc)

This edging consists of very colorful rows worked with right side always facing and starting on the same side.

With A, chain a multiple of 4 + 3.

Row 1: Ch 1, sc across. Fasten off.

Row 2 (B): With right side facing, insert hook in first st and pull up a loop, ch 3, dc in next st, skip 3, dc in next st, *ch 3, dc in third st before last dc made, skip 2, dc in next st*. Repeat from * to *. End with ch 3, dc in third st before last dc made, dc in last st. Fasten off.

Row 3 (C): With right side facing and working on opposite side of starting ch, insert hook and pull up a loop, sl st in next 3, *(sl st, ch 3, sl st) in next, sl st in next 2*. Repeat from * to *. Fasten off.

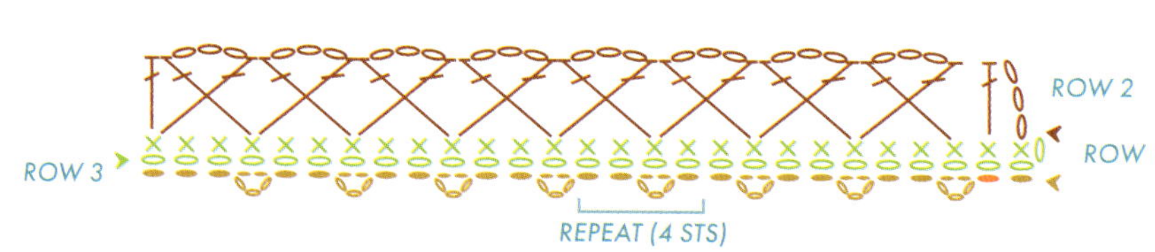

BORDER 118

DIFFICULTY **

COLORS: (A) Teal; (B) Orange; (C) Fuchsia; (D) Yellow

STITCHES USED: Slip stitch (sl st) • chain (ch) • single crochet (sc) • half double crochet (hdc) • double crochet (dc) • treble crochet (tr)

This edging consists of very colorful rows worked with right side always facing and starting on the same side.

With A, chain a multiple of 15 + 1.

Row 1: Ch 1 (to replace first sc), dc in first st, *skip 1, (sc, dc) in next st*. Repeat from * to *. End with sc in last. Fasten off.

Row 2 (B): With right side facing, insert hook in first ch and pull up a loop, *sc in next dc, ch 3, skip 3*. Repeat from * to *. End with sc in last 2 sc. Fasten off.

Row 3 (B): With right side facing, insert hook in first st and pull up a loop, sc in same st, *hdc in next ch, dc in next 2 chs, 3 tr in next sc, dc in next 2 chs, hdc in next ch, sc in next sc*. Repeat from * to *. End with sc in last. Fasten off.

Row 4 (C): With right side facing, insert hook in first st and pull up a loop, sc in same st, *working in back loops, sl in next 9 sts, long sc in sc from Row 2*. Repeat from * to *. End with sc in last. Fasten off.

Work on the opposite side of the starting ch, shifting the pattern. With right side of edging facing, begin working across the starting chain.

Row 5 (C): Repeat Row 1, ending with sc, dc in last st. Fasten off.

Row 6 (D): With right side facing, sc in first st, *ch 3, sc in next*. Repeat from * to *. Fasten off.

Row 7 (D): With right side facing, insert hook in first st and pull up a loop, ch 4 (to replace first tr), tr in same st, dc in next 2, hdc in next, sc in next sc, *hdc in next, dc in next 2, 3 tr in next, dc in next 2, hdc in next, sc in next*. Repeat from * to *. End with hdc in next, dc in next 2, 2 tr in last. Fasten off.

Row 8 (A): With right side facing, insert hook in first st and pull up a loop, sl st in first 5, *long sc in sc from Row 6, sl st in next 9*. Repeat from * to *. End with 5 sl sts rather than 9. Fasten off.

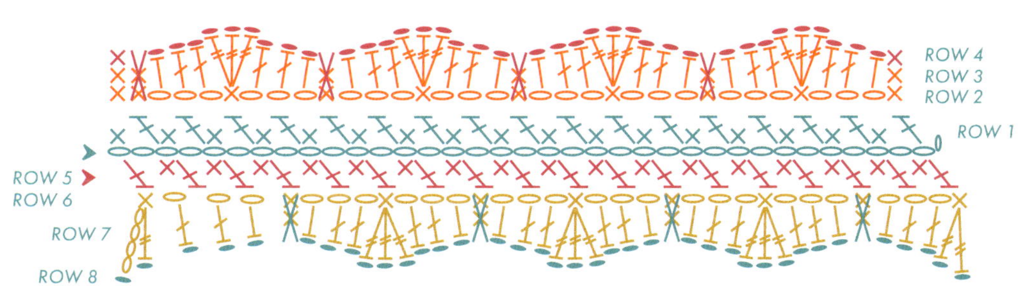

BORDER 119

DIFFICULTY *

COLORS: (A) White; (B) Navy Blue

STITCHES USED: Slip stitch (sl st) • chain (ch) • single crochet (sc) • half double crochet (hdc) • double crochet (dc) • treble crochet (tr)

This edging consists of different motifs joined together.

Begin Motif 1 (small circle) with A, ch 5, sl st to close the ring.

Rnd 1: Ch 1, 11 sc in ring, sl st to close.

As an extension of the circle, begin the base for the fish: with A, ch 22.

Row 1: Ch 1 to turn, sc in next 18 chs, 4 sl sts. Fasten off.

Row 2 (B): Working on opposite side of starting chain, insert hook in first st after circle and pull up a loop, sl st in first st, sc in next 2, hdc in next 2, dc in next 4, tr in next 4, dc in next 4, hdc in next 2, sc in next 2, sl st in last. For the tail, ch 4 in same space as last sl st, then make (2 tr, dc, 2 tr) in Row 1 first ch, ch 4, sl st in first st of Row 1; you will work the next row across Row 1.

Row 3: Sc in next 2, hdc in next 2, dc in next 4, tr in next 4, dc in next 4, hdc in next 2, sc in next 2, sl st in last. Fasten off.

With B, make a large circle: ch 6, sl st to close the ring.

Rnd 1: Ch 2, 6 hdc in ring, sl st in sixth sc of small circle, 6 hdc in ring. End with sl st to close. Fasten off.

Make another motif and join them together by making a second small circle: with A, ch 5, sl st to close the ring.

Rnd 1: Ch 1, 5 sc in ring, sl st in dc of previous fish tail, 6 sc in ring, sl st in sixth hdc of large circle (starting at the sl st joining first 2 circles), sl st to close.

Crochet the number of motifs required for desired length. The ends of the border consist of a small circle and a large circle joined with sl sts.

BORDER 120

DIFFICULTY **

COLORS: (A) White; (B) Navy Blue

STITCHES USED: Slip stitch (sl st) • chain (ch) • single crochet (sc) • double crochet (dc) • treble crochet (tr)

This edging consists of a fancy support strip on which small fish are attached.

First, begin the support strip with B: Chain a multiple of 12 + 2.

Row 1: Ch 1 to turn, sc in first ch, *sc in next, skip 2, (dc, ch 1) 4x in next, dc in same st, skip 2, sc in next st, sc in next 5*. Repeat from * to *. End with sc in last 2. Fasten off.

Now working on opposite side of starting chain with right side facing, make the same motifs—but shifted.

Row 2 (A): Insert hook in first st and pull up a loop, sc in same st, *sc in next 7, skip 2, (dc, ch 1) 4x in next, dc in same, skip 2*. Repeat from * to *, ending with sc in last 8. Fasten off.

To begin the fish with A, ch 25 and fasten off.

Rnd 1 (B): Insert hook in first st and pull up a loop, sc in next 12, 3 sc in next, sc in next 12, sl st in first st, ch 3, sl st in fifth sc at the beginning of Row 2, ch 3, sl st in first ch made. Fasten off.

Make the fish tail with B. Insert hook in second of 3 sc in same st and pull up a loop, ch 4, (tr, ch 1, dc, ch 1, tr, ch 4, sl st) in same st. Fasten off.

Make the number of fish needed to fill the entire length of the edging, attaching them to the fourth sc of each group of 7 sc.

BORDER 121

DIFFICULTY **

COLORS: (A) White; (B) Navy Blue

STITCHES USED: Slip stitch (sl st) • chain (ch) • single crochet (sc) • half double crochet (hdc) • double crochet (dc) • treble crochet (tr)

This edging consists of small fish joined together.

To begin a fish with A or B, ch 9.

Row 1: Ch 1 to turn, sc in first ch, hdc in next 2, dc in next 3, tr in next 3, ch 4, sl st in same st as last tr.

Row 2: With right side facing and on opposite side of starting ch, ch 4, tr in first ch, tr in next 2, dc in next 3, hdc in next 2, sc in last. End with sl st in ch at beginning of Row 1.

To make the fish tail, keep working in the same ch from Row 1: (ch 3, 5 dc, ch 3, sl st) in same ch. Fasten off.

To make the head and fins, work in the back loops: Insert hook in third dc of Row 1 and pull up a loop, ch 2, hdc in next 2, sc in next, then working in 8 chs: sc in next, hdc in next, dc in next, tr in next, tr in next sl st, tr in next ch, dc in next 2, hdc in last, sc in next tr, sl st in next, ch 3, hdc in same st. Fasten off.

Make the necessary number of motifs for desired length, while alternating col. To join the motifs, sl st in third dc on tail after first tr of head. Embroider the eye with a knot stitch in contrasting col on first tr on head, tying a knot on the wrong side.

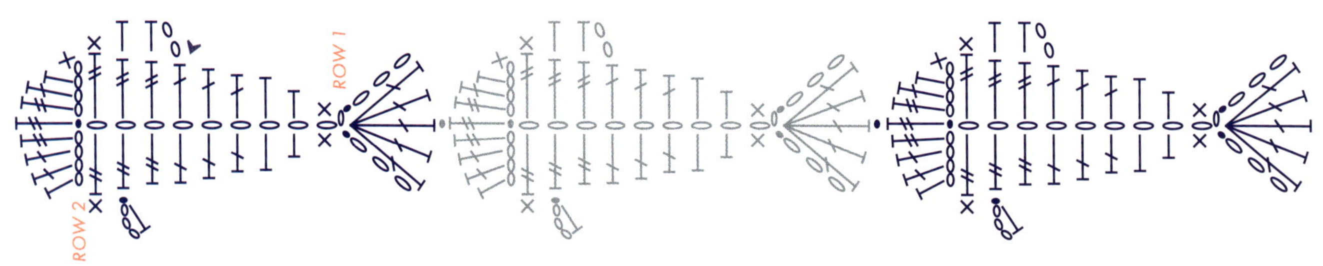

BORDER 122

DIFFICULTY **

COLORS: (A) White; (B) Navy Blue

STITCHES USED: Chain (ch) • single crochet (sc) • double crochet (dc) • treble crochet (tr)

This edging consists of motifs created one after the other and then attached to a support strip. To change to the next color as you make the fish, make the last yarn over with the next color.

Row 1 (B): Ch 2, 2 sc in first ch.

Row 2: Ch 1 to turn, [2 sc in next] twice.

Row 3: Ch 1 to turn, sc in next, [2 sc in next] twice, sc in last.

Row 4: Ch 1 to turn, 2 sc in same st, sc in next 4, 2 sc in last. Fasten off.

Row 5 (A): Crochet across previous row without turning work. Insert hook in first st and pull up a loop, sc in 8 sts working in the back loop.

Row 6: Crocheting normally, ch 1 to turn, sc in next 8, change to next col at last yarn over.

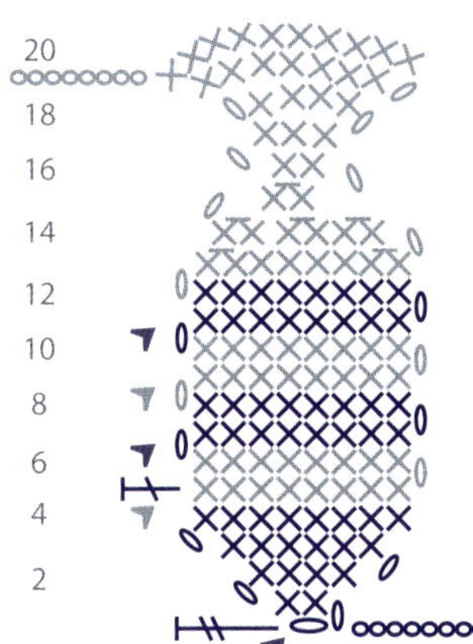

Row 7 (B): Ch 1 to turn, sc in next 8.

Row 8: Ch 1 to turn, sc in next 8, change to next col at last yarn over.

Rows 9–12: Repeat Rows 5–8, alternating col.

Row 13 (A): 2 sc closed together, sc in next 4, 2 sc closed together.

Row 14: Ch 1 to turn, [2 sc closed together] 3x.

Row 15: Ch 1 to turn, skip 1, 2 sc closed together.

Row 16: Ch 1 to turn, 2 sc in same st.

Row 17: Ch 1 to turn, sc in first, 2 sc in next.

Row 18: Ch 1 to turn, sc in first, 2 sc in next, sc in last.

Row 19: Ch 1 to turn, sc in first, [2 sc in next st] 3x.

Row 20: Ch 1 to turn, 2 sc in first, [2 sc in next, sc in next] twice, 2 sc in last, ch 8.

To make the next motif, repeat Rows 1–20 while alternating colors and beginning with B. Crochet the number of motifs required for desired length.

Make the support strip with B.

Row 1: After last motif, ch 9, ch 1 to turn, *ch 12, dc in first st from Row 5, ch 6, tr in ch ending next motif*. Repeat from * to *. End with 12 chs.

Row 2: Ch 1 to turn, *sc, ch 3, skip 3*. Repeat from * to *. End with sc in last.

Row 3: Ch 1 to turn, sc in first, ch 1, skip 1, *sc in next, ch 3, skip 3*. Repeat from * to *. End with sc, ch 1, skip 1, sc in last. Fasten off.

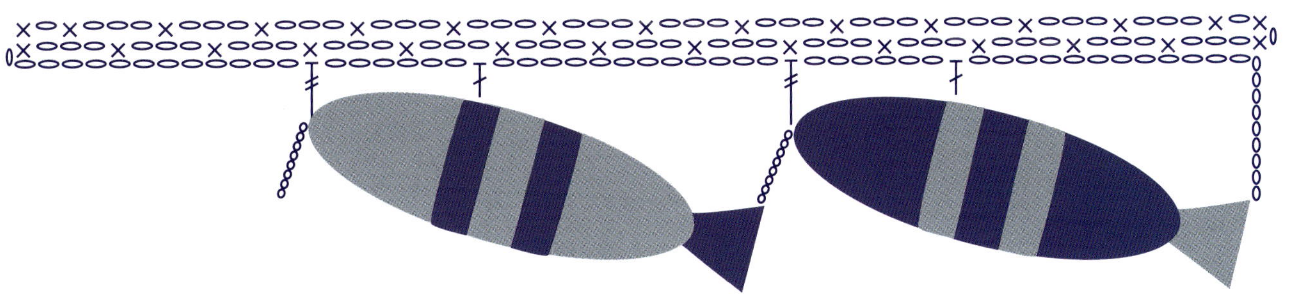

BORDER 123

DIFFICULTY **

COLORS: (A) White; (B) Navy Blue

STITCHES USED: Slip stitch (sl st) • chain (ch) • single crochet (sc) • half double crochet (hdc) • double crochet (dc) • treble crochet (tr)

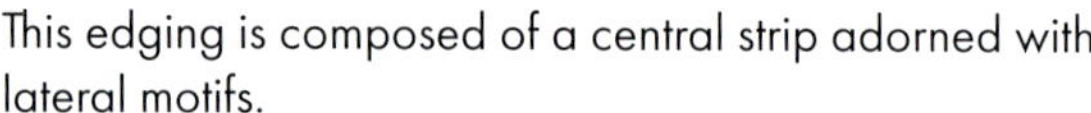

This edging is composed of a central strip adorned with lateral motifs.

To begin the central strip with A, chain a multiple of 28 + 1.

Row 1: Alternate col, keeping strands behind work, *sc in next 2 with A, sc in next 2 with B*. Repeat from * to *. Fasten off.

Row 2: With right side facing, working on opposite side of starting ch, alternate col, keeping strands behind work, *sc in next 2 with B, sc in next 2 with A*. Repeat from * to *. Fasten off.

Row 3: With A, insert hook in second st from Row 1 and pull up a loop, *sc, skip 2, (2 dc, ch 3) in next, sl st in next, sc in next, hdc in next, dc in next, tr in next 3, dc in next, hdc in next, sc in next, sl st in next*. Fasten off. Skip 13 sc, Repeat from * to * with B. Alternate until the end of the strip.

Row 4: With right side facing, now working on opposite side of edging with B, insert hook in sixteenth st and pull up a loop, *sc, skip 2, (2 dc, ch 3) in next, sl st in next, sc in next, hdc in next, dc in next, tr in next 3, dc in next, hdc in next, sc in next, sl st in next*. Fasten off. Skip 13 sc, Repeat from * to * with A. Alternate until the end of the strip.

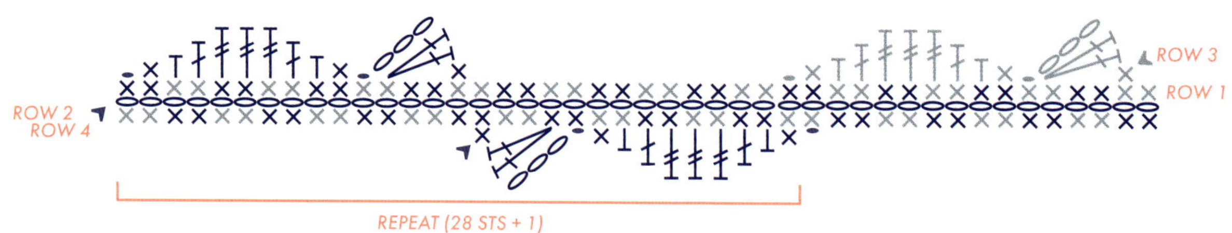

BORDER 124

DIFFICULTY **

COLORS: (A) White; (B) Navy Blue

STITCHES USED: Slip stitch (sl st) • chain (ch) • single crochet (sc) • half double crochet (hdc) • double crochet (dc) • treble crochet (tr)

This edging consists of interlinked motifs.

To begin the fish with A, ch 15.

Row 1: Ch 1 to turn, sc in next 2, hdc in next 3, dc in next 2, tr in next 7, ch 3, sl st in first ch. Pivot to work on other side of starting chain.

Row 2: Ch 3, 4 dc in same ch, tr in next 6, dc in next 3, hdc in next 3, sc in next 2. To make the fish tail, ch 5, (tr, ch 1, 3 dc, ch 1, tr, ch 4, sl st) in starting ch. Fasten off.

Row 3 (B): With right side facing, make the ring by inserting hook in first tr from Row 1 and pulling up a loop, ch 19, sl st in first dc from Row 2, ch 13, sl st in fourth tr from Row 2.

Row 4: In chs just made and to join the motifs, sl st in next 15, sl st in last tr of previous fish tail (for first motif, sl st in ch from previous row), sl st in next 17 chs. Fasten off.

Crochet the number of motifs required for desired length.

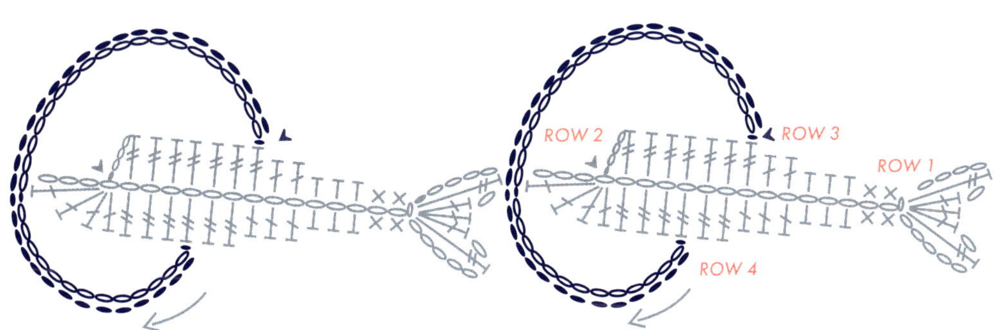

BORDER 125

DIFFICULTY ***

COLORS: (A) Black; (B) Pink

STITCHES USED: Slip stitch (sl st) • chain (ch) • single crochet (sc) • double crochet (dc) • ch-3 picot (pic)

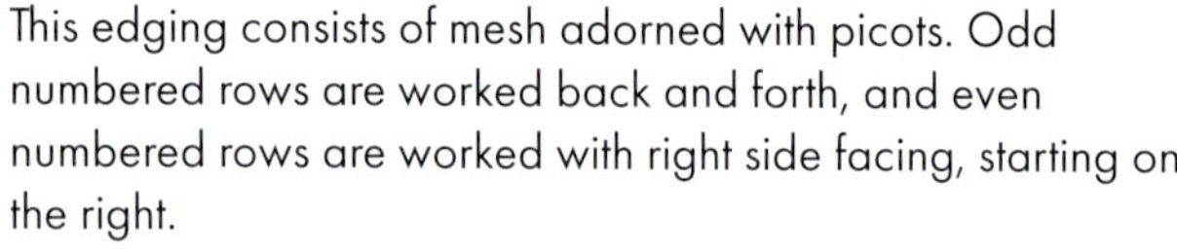

This edging consists of mesh adorned with picots. Odd numbered rows are worked back and forth, and even numbered rows are worked with right side facing, starting on the right.

With A, chain a multiple of 3 + 1.

Row 1: Ch 3 (to replace first dc), *ch 2, skip 2 chs, dc in next st*. Repeat from * to *. Set thread aside.

Rows 2, 4, 6, and 8 (B): With right side facing, working in ch-2 spaces (between dc). Insert hook in second ch from previous row and pull up a loop, *(sc, pic) in ch, sc in next ch, ch 1, skip 1 working behind dc from previous row*. Repeat from * to *. Fasten off.

Rows 3, 5, and 7 (A): Ch 3 (to turn and replace first dc), *ch 2, skip 2 chs, dc in next st*. Repeat from * to *.

Row 9: Ch 1 to turn, sc across. Fasten off.

Row 10: Working on opposite side of starting chain with right side facing, insert hook in first ch (see diagram) and pull up a loop, pic in first st, *sl st in next 2, pic*. Repeat from * to *. Fasten off.

BORDER 126

DIFFICULTY ****

COLORS: (A) Black; (B) Pink

STITCHES USED: Slip stitch (sl st) • chain (ch) • single crochet (sc) • half double crochet (hdc) • double crochet (dc) • treble crochet (tr) • double treble crochet (dtr) • ch-3 picot (pic)

This edging consists of rosettes adorned with picots, then assembled on a fancy edging.

With A, ch 7, sl st to close the ring.

Rnd 1: Ch 2 (to replace first hdc), ch 1, 15 hdc in ring, sl st in third starting ch.

Rnd 2 (B): Ch 3 (to replace first dc), ch 1, *dc in next hdc, ch 1*. Repeat from * to *. End with sl st in third starting ch.

Rnd 3: [Sc, pic] 13x, [sc in next, (sc, pic) in next] 3x, sc in next ch, 2 sc in next dc, [sc in next, (sc, pic) in next] 4x, [sc, pic] 3x, sl st to close. Fasten off.

Crochet the number of rosettes required for desired length. With A, make the edging assembling them. Use the diagram to visualize the work, and work with right side of rosettes facing.

Row 1: *In the last of the series of 13 pics, sl st, ch 5, 3 tr closed together in sl st, ch 8, skip 3 pics, 4 tr between next 2 sc, ch 8, skip 3 pics, 4 tr closed together in first pic of 13, close with ch 1*. Repeat from * to * beginning with 4 tr closed together in last of 13 pics on next rosette. Fasten off.

Row 2 (A): With right side facing and starting on the right, sl st in tr-group, ch 5, skip 4 chs, dc in next st, ch 6, skip 3 chs, *3 tr closed together in next tr, ch 6, skip 2 tr, 3 tr closed together in next tr, ch 7, skip 8 chs, dtr between tr-groups, ch 7, skip 8 chs*. Repeat from * to *. End with ch 6, skip 3 chs, dc in next st, ch 5, skip 4 chs, sl st in last tr-group. Fasten off.

Now with right side facing and A, starting on the right.

Row 3: Sl st in first sl st, sl st in next 5, (sc, pic) in next dc, sl st in next 6, *(sc, pic) in next tr-group, sl st in next 6, (sc, pic) in next tr-group, sl st in next 7, (sc, pic) in next dtr, sl st in next 7*. End with sl st in next 6, (sc, pic) in next tr-group, sl st in next 6, (sc, pic) in next dc, sl st in last 6. Fasten off.

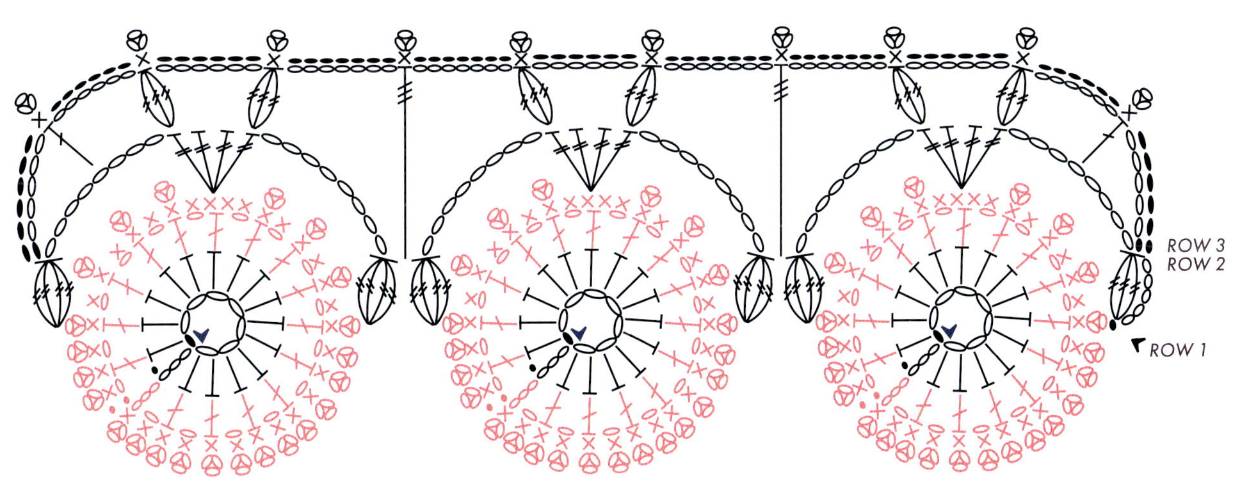

BORDER 127

DIFFICULTY ***

COLORS: (A) Black; (B) Pink

STITCHES USED: Slip stitch (sl st) • chain (ch) • single crochet (sc) • double crochet (dc) • treble crochet (tr) • ch-3 picot (pic)

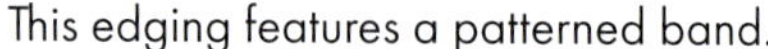

This edging features a patterned band.

With A, chain a multiple of 16 + 14 for border.

Row 1: Work over col when not in use; ch 3 (to replace first dc), *with A dc in next 4, change to next col at last yarn over, with B dc in next 4*. Repeat from * to *, ending with dc in last 5. Fasten off.

Row 2 (A): With right side facing, insert hook in first st and pull up a loop, sc in first st, *ch 3, pic, ch 2, pic, ch 4, tassel: (ch 5, 3 tr closed together in first ch, ch 5, sl st in first ch), ch 4, pic, ch 2, pic, ch 3, skip 12 dc, sc in next 4*. Repeat from * to *. End by skipping 12 dc, sc in last dc. Fasten off.

Row 3 (B): With right side facing, insert hook in tassel and pull up a loop, ch 5, ch 2, inserting hook in tassel each time: (tr, ch 2) 7x, tr in same st, ch 1, *in next tassel: (tr, ch 2) 8x, tr in same st, ch 1*. Repeat from * to *. Fasten off.

Row 4 (B): With right side facing, insert hook in fifth starting ch from Row 3 and pull up a loop, sc in same st, *[2 sc in ch-2 space, skip tr] 7x, 2 sc in first ch-2 space, sc in last tr, ch 1, sc in first tr on next motif*. Repeat from * to * on all motifs.

Row 5 (A): With right side facing, insert hook in first sc of previous row and pull up a loop, sc in first, ch 3, sc in next, [long sc under next 2 sc, inserting hook in ch-space between 2 tr, sc in next, ch 3, sc in next] 7x, 3 long sc with the first in the next ch-2 space, the second under the sl st and the third in the ch-2 space of the next motif. Work as established across. End with sc in sc before last st, ch 3, sc in last st of last motif. Fasten off.

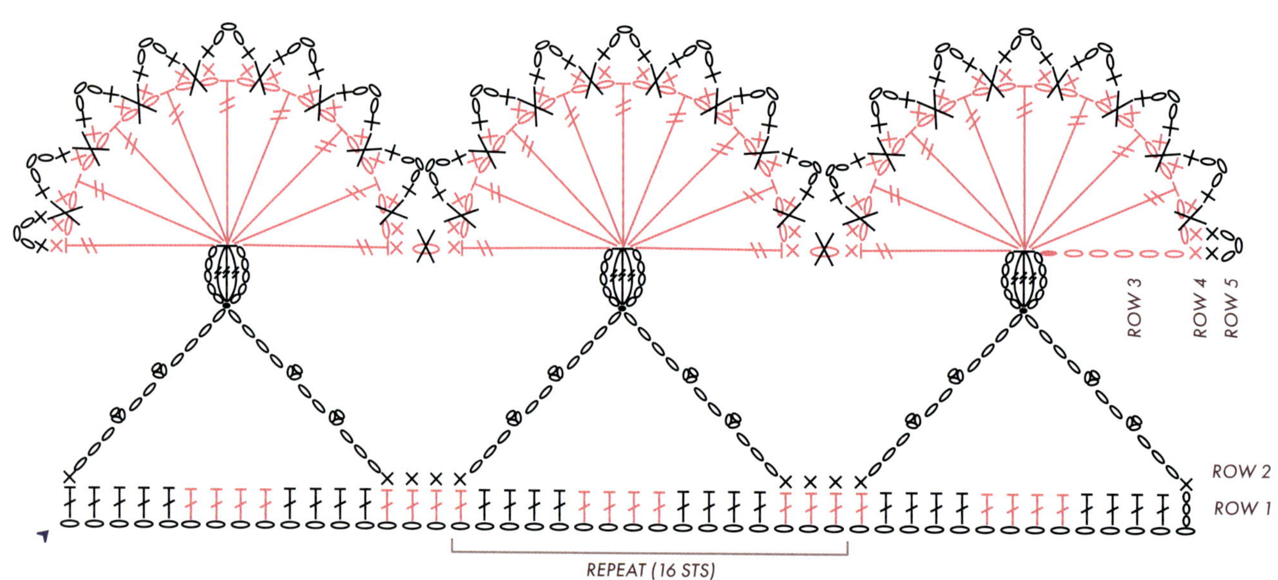

BORDER 128

DIFFICULTY *****

COLORS: (A) Black; (B) Pink

STITCHES USED: Slip stitch (sl st) • chain (ch) • single crochet (sc) • half double crochet (hdc) • double crochet (dc) • treble crochet (tr) • ch-3 picot (pic)

This edging consists of motifs attached to a support strip.

Begin with A.

Row 1: Ch 4, 3 tr in fourth ch from hook. Turn.

Row 2: Ch 3 (to replace first dc), ch 1, skip 1, 2 dc between 2 dc from previous row, ch 1, dc in last. Turn.

Row 3: Ch 3 (to replace first dc), ch 1, skip (ch 1 and dc), dc in next st, ch 1, dc in previous st, ch 1, skip 1, dc in last. Turn.

Row 4: Ch 3 (to replace first dc), [dc in next, ch 1, skip 1] twice, dc in last 2.

Row 5: Ch 1 to turn, sc in next 7. Turn.

Row 6: Ch 3 (to replace first dc), skip 2, dc in next st, ch 1, dc at base of starting ch-3, ch 1, skip 2, dc in last st, ch 1, dc in fourth st of row, dc in last st.

Row 7: Ch 1 to turn, sc in next 9. Turn.

Row 8: Ch 3 (to replace first dc), ch 1, [dc in next, ch 1, skip 1] 4x, dc in last. Turn.

Row 9: Ch 4 (to replace first tr), skip 2, tr in next, ch 2, tr at base of starting ch, ch 1, skip 1, tr in next ch, ch 1, skip 1, tr in last st, ch 2, tr in third st before last, tr in last. Turn.

Row 10: Ch 3 (to replace first dc), ch 1, [dc in next, ch 1, skip 1] 5x, dc in last.

Row 11: Ch 2 to turn, hdc in next 13. Turn.

Row 12: Ch 3 (to replace first dc), skip 3, dc in next st, ch 2, dc in second st, ch 1, dc in next, ch 1, skip 1, dc in next, ch 1, dc in st before last, ch 2, dc in st after the second dc in the middle of the row, dc in last. Turn.

Row 13: Ch 3 (to replace first dc), skip 3, dc in next st, ch 2, dc in second st, dc in next, skip 1, (dc, ch 2, dc) in next, skip 1, dc in next, dc in st before last, ch 2, dc in st after last straight dc, dc in last.

Row 14: Ch 2 to turn, hdc in same st, hdc in last 14, 2 hdc in last st.

Row 15: Ch 1 to turn, sc in next 18. Turn.

Row 16: Ch 3 (to replace first dc), ch 1, skip 1, [dc in next st, ch 1, skip 1] 3x, dc in next, (dc, ch 2, dc) in next st, dc in next, [ch 1, skip 1, dc in next] 4x. Turn.

Row 17: Ch 3 (to replace first hdc), ch 1, skip 1, dc in next st, ch 1, skip 2, (dc, ch 2, dc) in next st, ch 1, skip 2, dc in next 2, ch 2, sc in each of next 2 chs, ch 2, dc in next 2, ch 1, skip 2, (dc, ch 2, dc) in next st, ch 1, skip 2, dc in next, ch 1, skip 1, dc in last. Turn.

Row 18: Ch 3 (to replace first dc), dc in next ch, ch 1, skip 1, dc in next, ch 1, skip 1, (dc, ch 2, dc) in next st, ch 1, skip 2, dc in next 2, ch 5, skip (dc, ch 2, 2 sc, ch 2, dc), dc in next 2, ch 1, skip 2, (dc, ch 2, dc) in next st, [ch 1, skip 1, dc in next] twice, dc in last.

Row 19: Ch 1 to turn, sc in next 29. Turn.

Row 20: Ch 3 (to replace first dc), dc in next, skip 1, (dc, ch 2, dc) in next st, skip 1, dc in next, [ch 1, skip 1, dc in next] 9x, skip 1, (dc, ch 2, dc) in next st, ch 1, skip 1, dc in last 2. Turn.

Row 21: Ch 3 (to replace first dc), dc in next, skip 4, dc in next, ch 2, crossed dc in same st as second dc, dc in next 2, ch 1, skip 1, hdc in next, ch 2, skip 2, sc in next 5, ch 2, skip 2, hdc in next, ch 1, skip 1, dc in next 2, skip 5, dc in next st, ch 2, dc crossed in same st as last straight dc made, dc in last 2. Turn.

From next row, finish one side then the other.

Row 22, First Half: Ch 3 (to replace first dc), dc in next, skip 1, dc in next, ch 3, dc in next, skip 1, dc in next 2, ch 1, skip 1, dc in next, skip 2, dc in sc. Turn.

Row 23: Ch 3 (to replace first dc), dc in same st, dc in next, [ch 1, skip 1, dc in next] 4x, dc in last 2. Turn.

Row 24: Ch 3 (to replace first dc), dc in same st, dc across. Fasten off.

CONTINUED ON NEXT PAGE

Make the next part symmetrically.

Row 22, Second Half: With wrong side of Row 20 at the top, insert hook in last sc from Row 20, ch 3 (to replace first dc), skip 2, dc in next, ch 1, skip 1, dc in next 2, skip 1, dc in next, ch 3, dc in next, skip 1, dc in last 2. Turn.

Row 23, Second Half: Ch 3 (to replace first dc), dc in next 2, [ch 1, skip 1, dc in next] 4x, 2 dc in last st. Turn.

Row 24, Second Half: Ch 3 (to replace first dc), dc across. End with 2 dc in last st. Fasten off.

Sl st in each st and row end around motif. Crochet the desired number of motifs for the border.

Begin the rosette with B, ch 9, sl st to close the ring.

Rnd 1: 9 sc in ring, sl st to close.

Rnd 2: In front loops of starting chs, [sc, pic] 9x, sl st to close. Turn.

Crochet as many rosettes as required, then join them to the motifs by sewing them with matching thread.

Make the support strip with B.

Row 1: Ch 17, *sc in st at top of motif, ch 32*. Repeat from * to *. End with 17 chs.

Row 2: Ch 1 to turn, sc across. Turn.

Row 3: Ch 4 (to replace first tr), *tr in next st, ch 1, skip 1*. Repeat from * to *. End with 2 tr.

Row 4: Ch 1 to turn, sc across. Fasten off.

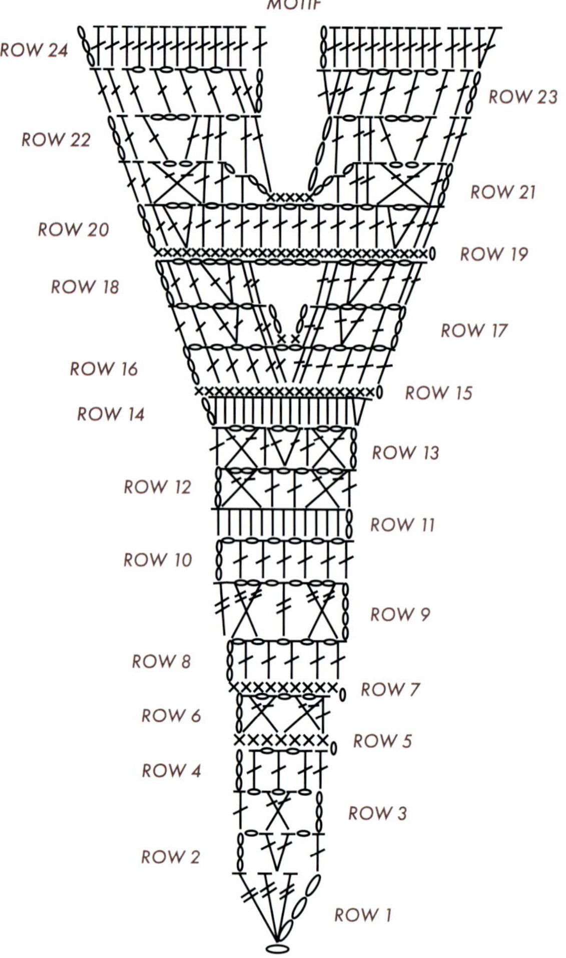

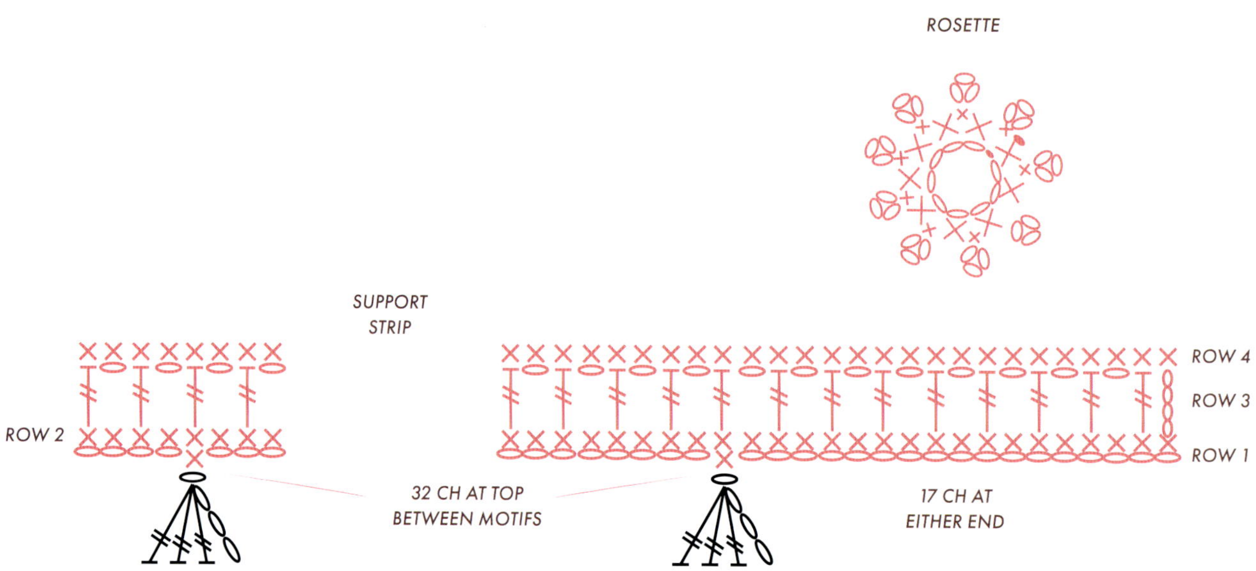

BORDER 129

DIFFICULTY ***

COLORS: (A) Black; (B) Pink

STITCHES USED: Slip stitch (sl st) • chain (ch) • single crochet (sc) • half double crochet (hdc) • double crochet (dc) • treble crochet (tr) • ch-3 picot (pic)

This edging features a patterned band.

To begin the motif with B, ch 6, sl st to close the ring.

Crochet a 4-tassel motif as follows: ch 5, 3 tr closed together in first ch, ch 1. Make three more tassels on top of the first one. Fasten off. Make the number of motifs required for desired length.

Begin the edging with A.

Row 1: *Tassel (ch 5, 2 tr in first ch, ch 5, sl st at base), ch 8, sc in top of tassel from 4-tassel motif; you will be working around the 4-tassel motif as follows: [ch 3, hdc in middle of outer st of first tassel, pic, ch 3, dc between first and second tassels] 3x—working as established across first 3 tassels, ch 4, dc in middle of outer st of fourth tassel, pic, ch 4, sc in top of ch-6 ring, pic, ch 4, dc in third ch on side of fourth tassel, pic, ch 4, dc between fourth and third tassels, [ch 3, hdc in third ch on side of third tassel, pic, ch 3, dc between third and second tassels] repeat twice—working as established to complete work across all 4 tassels, ch 3, hdc in third ch on side of first tassel, pic, ch 3, sl st in sc at beginning of this section, ch 8*. Repeat from * to *. Turn.

Row 2: Ch 3 (to replace first dc), *ch 8, skip 8 chs, sc in next sc, ch 8, skip 8 chs, dc in sl st closing the tassel*. Repeat from * to *. Fasten off.

Row 3 (B): With right side facing, insert hook in first st and pull up a loop, sc in third ch, pic, *ch 8, skip 8 chs, (2 dc closed together and pic) in next sc, ch 8, skip 8 chs, (sc and pic) in next dc*. Repeat from * to *. Fasten off.

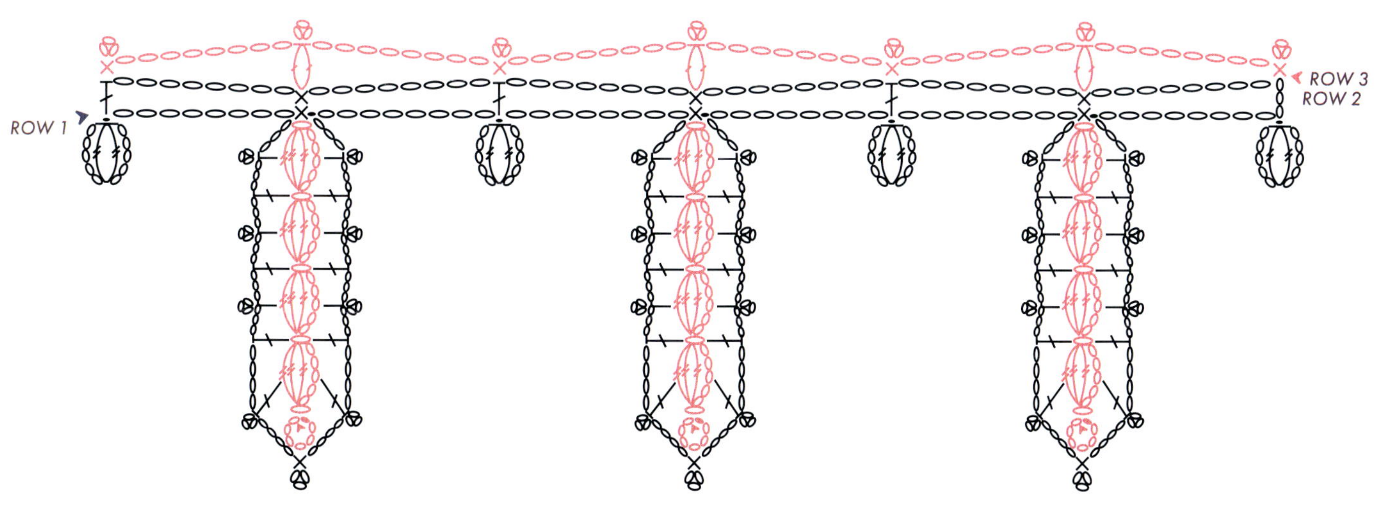

BORDER 130

DIFFICULTY ****

COLORS: (A) Black; (B) Pink

STITCHES USED: Slip stitch (sl st) • chain (ch) • single crochet (sc) • treble crochet (tr) • double treble crochet (dtr) • ch-3 picot (pic)

This edging consists of repeating motifs worked with right side always facing.

With A, chain a multiple of 7 + 1.

Row 1: Ch 1, sc in next 4, *ch 3, sc in next 7*. Repeat from * to *. End with sc in last 4. Fasten off.

Row 2 (B): Insert hook in first st and pull up a loop, ch 5, skip 3, *3 tr closed together in next ch, ch 1 to close, ch 5, sl st in next ch, sl st in next ch, ch 5, 3 tr closed together in next ch, ch 1 to close, skip 7 sc*. Repeat from * to *. End with tr in last st. Fasten off.

Row 3 (A): Insert hook in sl st between 2 tr-groups and pull up a loop, ch 6 (to replace first dtr), ch 4, sl st in fifth ch from hook, *ch 9, dtr in sl st between next 2 tr-groups, ch 4, sl st in top of tr*. Repeat from * to *. Fasten off.

Row 4 (B): Insert hook in top of from Row 2 starting ch, ch 6, dtr in same st, (tr, pic) 6x in ch-4 ring, tr in same ring, *skip 4 chs, sc in next ch, skip 4 chs, (tr, pic) 6x in next ch-4 ring, tr in same ring*. Repeat from * to *. End with 2 dtr in last st. Fasten off.

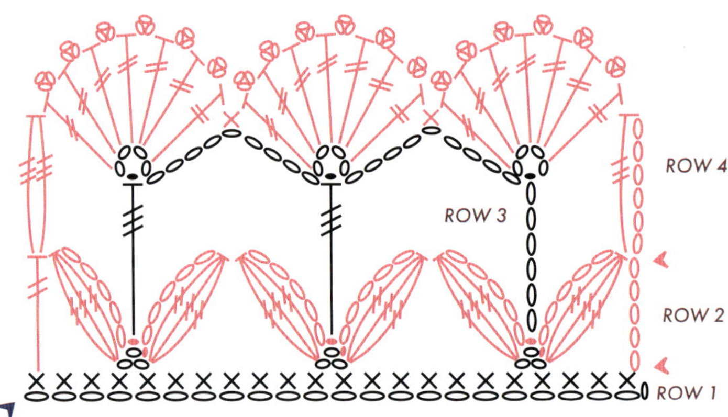

BORDER 131

DIFFICULTY *****

COLORS: (A) Yellow; (B) Green; (C) Blue; (D) Pink

STITCHES USED: Slip stitch (sl st) • chain (ch) • single crochet (sc) • half double crochet (hdc) • double crochet (dc) • treble crochet (tr)

This edging consists of different patterns assembled together. It is imperative to follow the diagram as you work.

To begin the parrot with A, ch 6, sl st to close the ring.

Row 1: With right side facing, ch 3 (to replace first dc), 12 dc in ring.

Row 2: Ch 23.

Row 3: With right side facing (working in Row 2 chs), (dc, ch 2) in sixth ch from hook, [2 dc closed together with first in same st as previous dc, skip 2 chs, and second in next st, ch 2] 5x, dc in same st as previous st, skip 1, dc in next st, sc in second of 3 chs made at beginning of Row 1, sl st in next 3 dc, sc in next 7, ch 2, skip 3 dc, now working on opposite side of 23 chs, dc in next, ch 1, skip 1, (dc, ch 2, dc) in next st, skip 2, dc in next st, skip 2, (dc, ch 2, dc) in next st, skip 2, ch 2, hdc in next, ch 2, skip 2, hdc in next, ch 2, skip 2, sc in next 2, sl st in next 2, (2 sc, hdc) in next, 2 dc in next st. Fasten off.

Row 4 (B): With right side facing, make the beak (start at A on diagram) by inserting the hook in the back loop of the sc after 3 sl sts (see diagram) and pulling up a loop, hdc in same st, sc in next, 2 sc in next st, sc in next, 2 sc in next, sc in next 5, 2 sc in next, sc in next 20. Fasten off.

Row 5 (C): With right side facing, make the top of the head and the left side of the parrot (Start B on diagram) by inserting the hook in the back loop of the st and pulling up a loop, sc in next 3, hdc in next 2, [2 dc in next] twice, dc in next 3, tr in next 4, 2 tr in next, tr in next 2, (tr, dc) in next, dc in next 3, (dc, hdc) in next, hdc in next 2, sc in next 7. End with ch 12, sl st in last st made. Fasten off.

Row 6: Work back and forth to make the right wing (start at C on diagram), inserting the hook in the top of the sc before 3 sl sts from Row 3 and pulling up a loop, ch 3, sl st in dc-group from Row 3 to attach, 2 dc in same st as starting chs. Fasten off.

Row 7: Ch 3, dc in same st, dc in next, 2 dc in last, sl st in dc-group from Row 3 to attach. Turn.

Row 8: Ch 3, sl st in dc-group from Row 3 to attach, dc in next 3, 2 dc in last. Turn.

Row 9: Ch 3, dc in same st, dc in next 4, sl st in dc-group from Row 3 to attach. Turn.

Row 10: Ch 3, sl st in dc-group from Row 3 to attach, dc in next 3, 2 dc closed together. Turn.

Row 11: Ch 3, 2 dc closed together, dc in next, sl st in dc from Row 3 to attach. Turn.

Row 12: Ch 3, sl st in dc at edge of Row 3 to attach, dc in dc-group. Fasten off.

To make the feathers and tail with B, insert hook in first yellow sc and pull up a loop, (sc, ch 24, sc) in next st, 3 sl sts, ch 20, sl st in same st, sl st in next st. Fasten off. With A, make the last feather: Insert hook in first sl st between feathers just made, ch 30, sl st in next st. Fasten off.

Make the eye with B: Make a knot st in the center of Row 1. Fasten off.

Make the flower with A, ch 6, sl st to close the ring.

Rnd 1: 11 sc in ring, sl st in first st to close.

Rnd 2: [Sc in next, ch 3] 11x, sl st in first st to close. Fasten off.

Row 1 (D): On wrong side of flower heart, insert hook in second ch of a ch-3 space, sc in same st, [ch 4, skip next ch-3 space, sc in next] 3x. Turn.

Row 2: With right side facing, ch 3 (to replace first dc), dc in first of 4 chs, 2 dc in next ch, dc in next 2, ch 2, skip sc, dc in next ch, [2 dc in next ch] twice, dc in next ch, ch 2, skip sc, dc in next ch, [2 dc in next ch] 3x. Turn.

CONTINUED ON NEXT PAGE

Row 3—First Petal: Ch 3 (to replace first dc), 2 dc closed together with first one at base of ch 3, dc in next 2, 3 dc closed together. Turn.

Row 4—Finish First Petal: Ch 3, 3 dc closed together. Fasten off.

Row 3—Second Petal: On wrong side, insert hook in dc from Row 2, ch 3 (to replace first dc), 2 dc in next, dc in next, 2 dc in next, dc in next, 2 dc in last st. Turn.

Row 4—Finish Second Petal: Ch 3 (to replace first dc), skip dc, 5 dc closed together. Fasten off.

Row 3—Third Petal: On wrong side, insert hook in dc from Row 2, ch 3 (to replace first dc), dc in next 2, 2 dc closed together. Turn.

Row 4—Finish Third Petal: Ch 3 (to replace first dc), 3 dc closed together. Fasten off.

To crochet the support strip, start at 1 on diagram. As you crochet this row, only the hearts of the flowers are joined to the edging with sl sts.

With B, crochet the row decorated with leaves to which the previously crocheted motifs will be attached. Read the diagram starting from the left.

To create the first hanging leaf on the left side of the diagram, ch 8, ch 1 to turn, sc in next, hdc in next 2, dc in next 2, hdc in next, sc in next 2, sl st in last ch, ch 8.

Crochet a Second Leaf: Ch 6, ch 1 to turn, sc in next, hdc in next, dc in next 2, hdc in next, sc in next, sl st in last ch (turn the hook counterclockwise following the arrows on the diagram: the leaf turns to the left and falls downward), *ch 9, ch 1 (insert a st marker in this ch).

Crochet the Length of the Support Strip: Ch 8, attach flower with sl st in corresponding ch-space (see diagram), ch 1, sl st in next ch-space on same flower, ch 13, ch 1 (insert a st marker in this ch), ch 5.

Crochet the first leaf hanging above the parrot: ch 5, ch 1 to turn, sc in next, hdc in next, dc in next, hdc in next, sc in next, sl st in next ch, ch 6.

Crochet the Second Hanging Leaf Attached to the Parrot: Ch 5, sl st in second sc at the top of the head of the parrot (in blue on the diagram), work across 5 chs: sc in next, hdc in next 2, sc in next 2, sl st in next ch, ch 8.

Crochet the Third Leaf Hanging Above the Parrot: Ch 7, ch 1 to turn, sc in next, hdc in next 2, dc in next 2, hdc in next, sc in next, sl st in next ch, ch 6, ch 1 (insert a st marker in this ch), ch 13, attach flower with sl st in ch-space (see diagram), ch 1, sl st in next ch-space on same flower, ch 10, ch 1 (insert a st marker in this ch), ch 8.

Crochet the Leaf Attached to a Petal on the Right-Hand Side of the Diagram: Ch 5, ch 1 to turn, sc in next, hdc in next, dc in next, hdc in next, sc in next, sl st in next st, ch 8.

Crochet the Last Leaf on the Right-Hand Side: Ch 8, ch 1 to turn, sc in next, hdc in next 2, dc in next 2, hdc in next, sc in next 2, sl st in next ch. Fasten off.* Repeat from * to * for a longer edging. Fasten off.

Make the top edging starting at 2 on diagram and working with right side always facing.

Row 1 (B): Insert hook in marked ch (8 sts after leaf before last on support strip) and pull up a loop, sc in each ch and sl st to last marked st. Fasten off.

Row 2 (A): Begin on the right in the first sc of the previous row, sc in next 2, *ch 3, skip 3, sc in next 2*. Repeat from * to *. Fasten off.

Row 3 (C): Begin on the right in the first sc of the previous row, sc in same st, ch 2, skip 2, *sc in next st, ch 4, skip 4*. Repeat from * to *. End with ch 3, sc in last st. Fasten off.

Row 4 (D): Begin on the right in the first sc of the previous row, sc in next 2, *ch 3, skip 3, sc in next 2*. Repeat from * to *. Fasten off.

Make the perch, starting at 3 on diagram.

With B, insert hook in marked st after first flower on the left and pull up a loop, ch 8, crochet the first leaf of the perch, which will be attached to a petal later: ch 5, ch 1 to turn, sc in next, hdc in next, dc in next, hdc in next, sc in next, sl st in next, ch 5.

Crochet a Leaf Attached to the Parrot, the Second on the Perch: Ch 6, sl st in corresponding tr (left side of the parrot, see diagram), now working in chs: sc in next, hdc in next, dc in next 2, hdc in next, sc in next, sl st in next, ch 6.

Crochet the Third Leaf of the Perch: Ch 6, ch 1 to turn, sc in next, hdc in next, dc in next 2, hdc in next, sc in next, sl st in next, ch 6.

Crochet the Fourth Leaf of the Perch: Ch 8, ch 1 to turn, sc in next, hdc in next 2, dc in next 2, hdc in next, sc in next 2, sl st in next, ch 9. End with sl st in third dc before first feather on parrot's tail (see diagram). Fasten off.

Make the other side of the perch starting at 4 on the diagram.

Insert hook in corresponding marked st after the parrot and pull up a loop, ch 8, crochet the fifth leaf of the perch to be joined to a petal later: ch 6, ch 1 to turn, sc in next, hdc in next, dc in next 2, hdc in next, sc in next, sl st in next, ch 6.

Crochet the Sixth Leaf of the Perch: Ch 6, ch 1 to turn, sc in next, hdc in next, dc in next 2, hdc in next, sc in next, pass thread under the chs and ch 1 tightly to position the leaf on the same side as the previous one, ch 6.

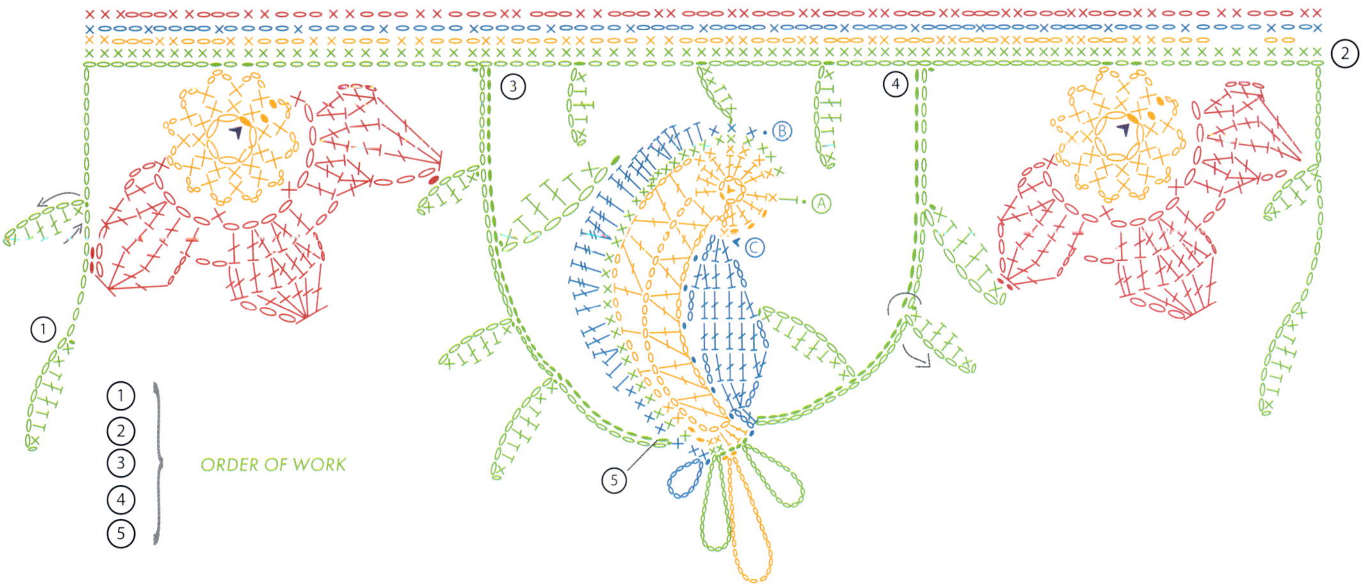

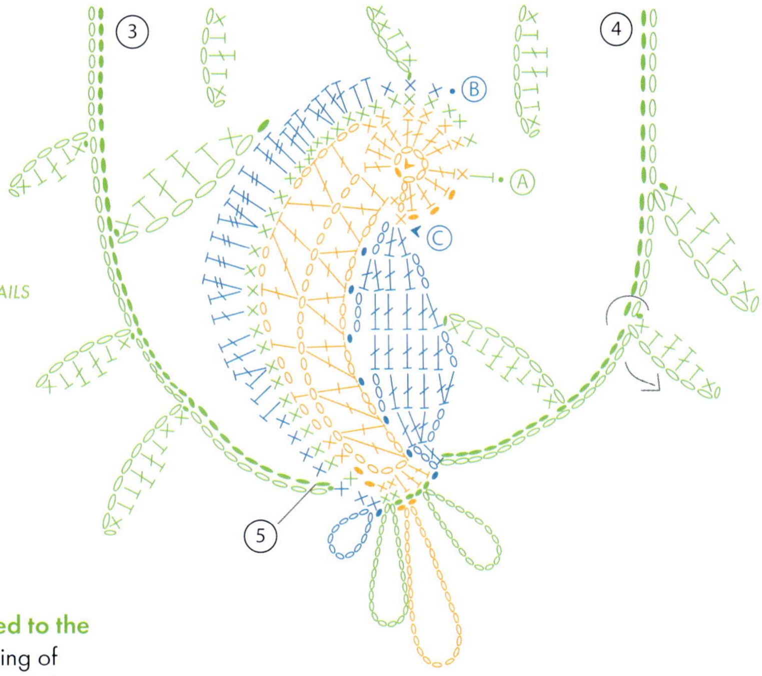

ORDER OF WORK

PARROT DETAILS

Crochet the Seventh Leaf of the Perch, Attached to the Parrot: Ch 8, sl st in corresponding dc (on right wing of parrot, see diagram), now working in chs: sc in next, hdc in next 2, dc in next 2, hdc in next, sc in next 2, sl st in next, ch 9. End with sl st at base of right wing. Fasten off.

Crochet a supporting row of sl sts across: Begin at 4 and sl st in each ch on perch, working on the inside of the chs. Then, begin at 5 on the diagram and sl st in each ch on perch, working on the inside of these chs. Fasten off.

Attach petals as shown with the same color thread over 1 or 2 sts (see diagram).

Fasten off and weave all ends in. Place the edging on a flat surface and shape it using the steam from an iron.

BORDER 132

DIFFICULTY **

COLORS: (A) Red; (B) Yellow; (C) Turquoise; (D) Green

STITCHES USED: Slip stitch (sl st) • chain (ch) • single crochet (sc) • half double crochet (hdc) • double crochet (dc) • treble crochet (tr)

This edging consists of identical motifs joined together.

To begin the leaves with C, ch 17 + 1 turning chain.

Row 1: Sc in next 2, hdc in next 2, dc in next 3, tr in next, ch 4, sc in next, ch 4, tr in next, 2 dc in next, hdc in next 3, sc in next 2, sl st in last st. Fasten off.

Alternate between C and D for each motif. To join a leaf, begin with a sl st in the edge of the previous leaf.

To begin the heart of the flower with B, ch 5, sl st to close.

Rnd 1: Ch 4, 3 tr in ring, sl st in third of 4 chs of leaf motif (see diagram), 3 dc in ring, sl st in first of 4 chs after tr from leaf motif (see diagram), 3 dc in ring, 6 hdc in ring, sl st in third starting ch. Fasten off.

Rnd 2 (A): Working in back loops, insert hook in dc after 4 chs from Row 1 (see diagram) and pull up a loop, ch 4, tr in same st, 3 tr in next, 2 dc in next, 2 hdc in next, sc in next, ch 2, (dc, 2 tr) in next, 3 tr in next, (2 dc, hdc) in next, (sc, dc) in next, [2 tr in next st] twice, 2 dc in next, hdc in next, sl st in last of 4 chs. Fasten off.

Make another flower alternating A and B.

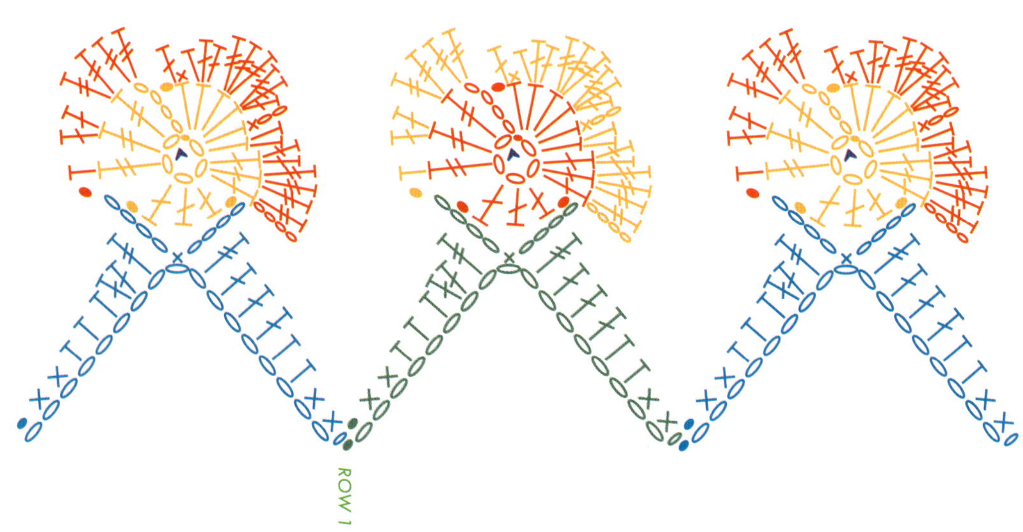

BORDER 133

DIFFICULTY **

COLORS: (A) Yellow; (B) Pink; (C) Red; (D) Green

STITCHES USED: Slip stitch (sl st) • chain (ch) • single crochet (sc) • half double crochet (hdc) • double crochet (dc) • treble crochet (tr)

This edging consists of identical motifs joined together. The motifs are joined together as you work (you can also crochet the motifs and join them after by sewing them with an invisible stitch on the wrong side of the work).

To begin the flower with A, ch 4, sl st to close the ring.

Rnd 1: (2 sc, 3 hdc, 3 dc, tr) in ring, changing to next color at last yarn over; with B, (2 dc, 2 tr) in ring.

Rnd 2: Working in back loops, 4 dc in next, 2 dc in next, dc in next 2, 2 hdc in next, sc, changing to next color at yarn over; with C, (sc, ch 2, dc) in next, [3 dc in next st] twice, dc in next, sc in next.

Rnd 3: Ch 2, (hdc, dc) in next, (2 dc, tr) in next, tr in next, 2 dc in next, 2 hdc in next, sc in next, ch 2, 2 dc in next, 3 dc in next, 2 dc in next, (dc, tr) in next, 3 tr in next, 2 dc in next, hdc in next, ch 2, sl st in same st. Fasten off.

Crochet the required number of flowers, alternating colors, until you reach the desired length.

To begin the leaf with D, ch 11.

Rnd 1: Ch 1 to turn, sc in next, hdc in next 2, dc in next, 2 dc in next, 2 tr in next, dc in next 3, hdc in next, sc in last, sl st in dc on flower (see diagram), then, on the other side of the leaf: sc in next, hdc in next 2, (hdc, dc) in next, dc in next 2, (dc, tr) in next, dc in next. Now, joining the next flower, [hdc in next ch, sl st in dc on next flower] twice, sc in last ch, sl st in next dc on flower. End leaf with sl st in starting ch. Fasten off. To join leaves and flowers, follow the diagram. To attach leaves at ends, use a yarn needle to join sts between motifs as shown on diagram.

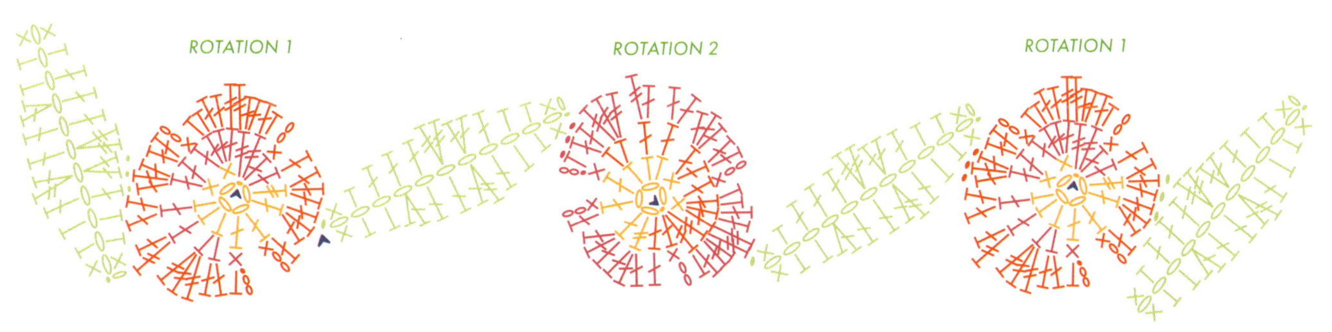

BORDER 134

DIFFICULTY **

COLORS: (A) Green; (B) Violet; (C) Faded Yellow; (D) Yellow; (E) Pink

STITCHES USED: Slip stitch (sl st) • chain (ch) • single crochet (sc) • half double crochet (hdc) • double crochet (dc) • treble crochet (tr)

This edging consists of identical motifs joined together.

To begin the leaf with A, ch 6.

Row 1: Ch 3 to turn, dc in fourth ch from hook, tr in next 2, 2 tr in next, tr in next, *6 dc in next, dc in next 3*. Fasten off. When joining leaves, repeat from * to * working as follows in same st: 2 dc, (dc, sl st in st on flower) twice (see diagram), 2 more dc in same st, dc in next 3. Fasten off.

Make the flower as follows:

With C or D, insert hook in first of 3 chs made at beginning of Row 1 of leaf and pull up a loop, sc in same st, ch 3, sc at base of last dc on leaf. Turn.

Row 1: Ch 2, 2 hdc in first ch, dc in next, 3 dc in next.

Row 2: Ch 3 to turn, dc in first, dc in next, 2 dc in next, dc in next, hdc in next, sc in next. Attach this row with a sl st in last dc on leaf. Fasten off.

Make the petals joining E to C, or B to D.

Row 3: Insert hook in last st of Row 2 and pull up a loop, ch 2, hdc in first, (2 dc, hdc) in next, hdc in next, sc in next, ch 2, dc in next, 2 dc in next, (dc, tr, dc) in next st; now working in starting chs from previous row and in dc row end below that: 2 hdc in next, hdc in next, sc in next 2, sl st. Fasten off.

Crochet the number of motifs needed to obtain the desired length, alternating the colors of the flowers.

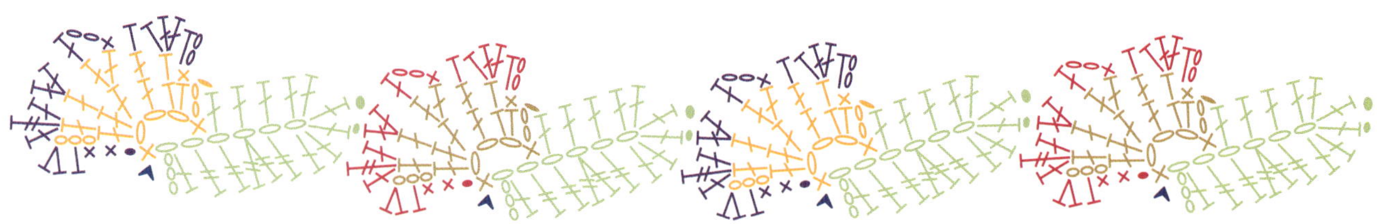

BORDER 135

DIFFICULTY **

COLORS: (A) Orange – Variegated; (B) Green – Variegated

STITCHES USED: Slip stitch (sl st) • chain (ch) • single crochet (sc) • half double crochet (hdc) • double crochet (dc)

This edging consists of identical motifs assembled to a support strip.

Crochet 4 circles for each motif, holding yarn double: With A and B, ch 6, sl st to close the ring.

Rnd 1: Ch 3 to turn, 12 hdc in ring, sl st to close. Fasten off.

To make the triangle, begin working on one of the circles with thread held double.

Row 1 (B): Insert hook in last st of a circle and pull up a loop, ch 4, 4 dc in same st.

Row 2: Ch 1 to turn, sc in next 5.

Row 3: Ch 3 to turn, dc in first st, dc in next, 2 dc in next st, dc in next, 2 dc in last.

Row 4: Ch 1 to turn, sc in next 8.

Row 5: Ch 3 to turn, dc in first st, dc in next 2, 2 dc in next, dc in next 3, 2 dc in last.

Row 6: Ch 1 to turn, sc in next 11.

Row 7: Ch 3 to turn, dc in first st, dc in next 9, 2 dc in last.

Row 8: Ch 1 to turn, sc in next 13.

Row 9: Ch 3 to turn, dc in first st, dc across, 2 dc in last.

Row 10: Ch 1 to turn, sc in next 15.

Assemble the 3 top circles on next row, with right sides facing.

Row 11: Ch 1 to turn, sc in next 2, sl st in hdc on circle, *sc in next 6, sl st in hdc on next circle*. Repeat from * to * to assemble third circle. End with sc in last. Fasten off.

Crochet the number of motifs needed for desired length.

To make the support strip, work on the wrong side of the motifs with A and B. Repeat is a multiple of 21 + 1.

Row 1: Ch 4, *sl st in top st of first circle, ch 5, sl st in top st of second circle, ch 5, sl st in top st of third circle, ch 8*. Repeat from * to *. End with 4 chs.

Row 2: Ch 3 to turn, dc across. Fasten off.

Row 3: With right side facing, insert hook in third ch from Row 2 and pull up a loop, sc across. Fasten off.

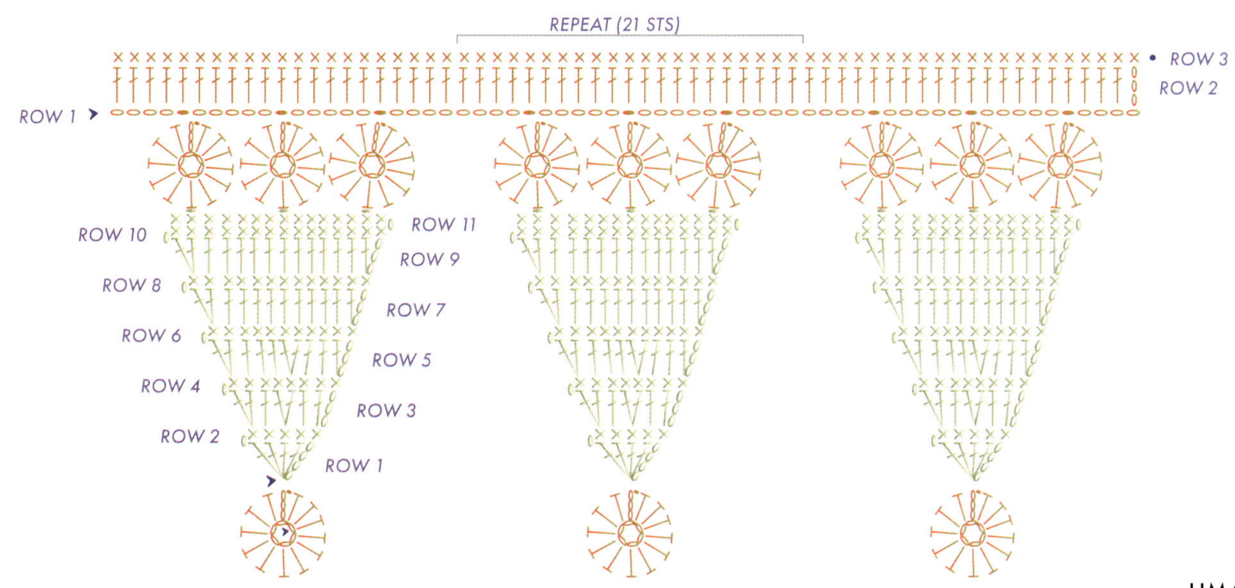

BORDER 136

DIFFICULTY ***

COLORS: (A) Black Currant – Variegated; (B) Raspberry – Variegated; (C) Ink

STITCHES USED: Slip stitch (sl st) • chain (ch) • single crochet (sc) • half double crochet (hdc) • double crochet (dc) • treble crochet (tr)

This edging consists of identical patterns assembled on a support strip.

To begin the central flower of the motif with A and B, ch 7, sl st to close the ring.

Rnd 1: 12 sc in ring, sl st in first st.

Rnd 2: 2 sc in each st (24 sts total), sl st in first st.

Rnd 3: Sc in next, *ch 2, dc in next, ch 2, sc in next*. Repeat from * to *. End with sl st in first st. Fasten off.

To create the base of the motif, use C.

Row 1: With right side facing, insert hook in dc on a petal and pull up a loop, sc in same st, [ch 2, sc in dc on next petal] 6x.

Row 2: Ch 1 to turn, sc in first st, *3 sc in next ch-2 space, sc in next st*. Repeat from * to *.

Row 3: Ch 1 to turn, 2 sc in first st, *sc in next 3, 2 sc in next*. Repeat from * to *. Fasten off.

Row 4 (B): With right side facing, insert hook in first sc and pull up a loop, ch 3 (to replace first dc), 3 dc closed together in same st, *ch 5, skip 5, 4 dc closed together in next st*. Repeat from * to *. Fasten off.

Row 5 (C): With right side facing, insert hook in first dc-group and pull up a loop, sc in same st, *8 sc in next ch-space, skip sc*. Repeat from * to *. End with sc in last dc-group. Do not fasten off.

To crochet the top of the motif, continue with C at 5 on diagram.

Row 6: Ch 6, [sc in top of next petal, ch 3] twice, sc in next petal, ch 4, 3 tr closed together in same st, ch 4, sl st in same st, [ch 3, sc in top of next petal] twice, ch 6, sl st in first sc of Row 5. Join this motif to the previous one with a sl st in the sc at the end of Row 5. Fasten off.

Crochet the number of motifs required for desired length.

To crochet the top strip and join the motifs, continue with C.

Row 7: With right side facing (in this row, make the dtr in the edge of the petal before or after the ch 6 from Row 6), ch 9, *dtr in sc of petal on motif to assemble (see diagram), ch 9, sc in dc-group, ch 9, dtr in sc of petal on motif to assemble (see diagram), skip (ch-6 space, 2 sc, ch-6 space)*. Repeat from * to *. End with 9 chs. Fasten off.

Row 8 (C): With right side facing, sc in first 2 chs, hdc in next 2, dc in next 3, tr in next 2, *tr in next dtr, tr in next, dc in next 3, hdc in next 2, sc in next 5, hdc in next 2, dc in next 3, tr in next, tr in next dtr, tr between 2 dtr*. Repeat from * to *. End with tr in next 2, dc in next 3, hdc in next 2, sc in last 2. Fasten off.

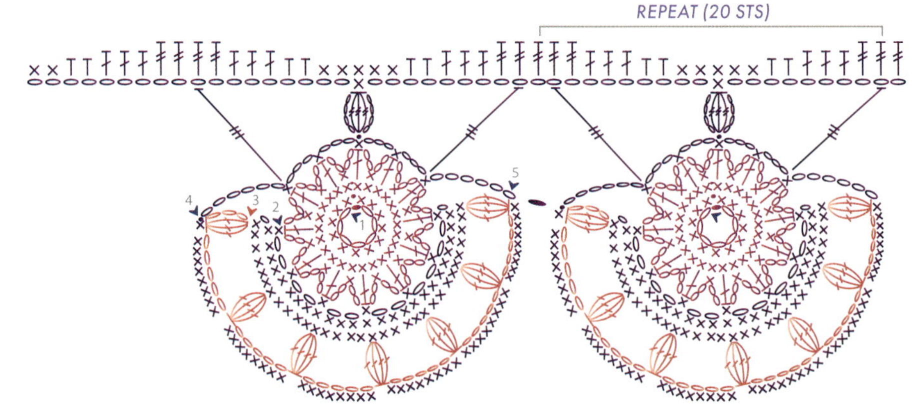

BORDER 137

DIFFICULTY ***

COLORS: (A) Green; (B) Wine – Variegated; (C) Olive; (D) Raspberry – Variegated

STITCHES USED: Slip stitch (sl st) • chain (ch) • single crochet (sc) • double crochet (dc) • treble crochet (tr) • ch-3 picot (pic)

This edging consists of identical patterns assembled on a support strip.

Alternate between A and B, or C and D.

With A or C, ch 12, sl st to close the ring.

Rnd 1: 24 sc in ring, sl st to close.

Rnd 2: Ch 3, 3 dc closed together with the first one at the base of the starting ch, ch 15, sl st in top of dc-group. Fasten off.

Rnd 3 (B or D): Insert hook at base of last dc and pull up a loop, sl st in next 5, ch 4 (to replace first tr), pic, [tr in next 2, pic] 6x, ch 4, sl st in next 5. Fasten off.

To assemble the motifs, sl st after ch 4 (to replace first tr) inserted at base of pic of previous motif. Crochet the number of motifs required for desired length.

To crochet the top of the motif, work in the 15-ch ring, associating D and A, or C and B.

Row 1 (B or D): Insert hook in seventh ch and pull up a loop, ch 4, tr in same, 3 tr in next, 2 tr in next. Fasten off.

Crochet the top of the edging with C, ch 11.

Row 1: *Now working on top of a motif, sc in fourth ch, sc in next 6 sts, ch 11*. Repeat from * to *.

Rows 2 and 4: Ch 1 to turn, sc in first st, *ch 5, skip 5, sc in next*. Repeat from * to *.

Row 3: Ch 1 to turn, sc in first st, ch 2, skip 2, *sc in next, ch 5, skip 5*. Repeat from * to *. End with ch 2, skip 2, sc in last.

Row 5: Ch 1 to turn, sc in first st, *5 sc in ch-5 space, skip sc*. Repeat from * to *. End with sc in last st. Fasten off.

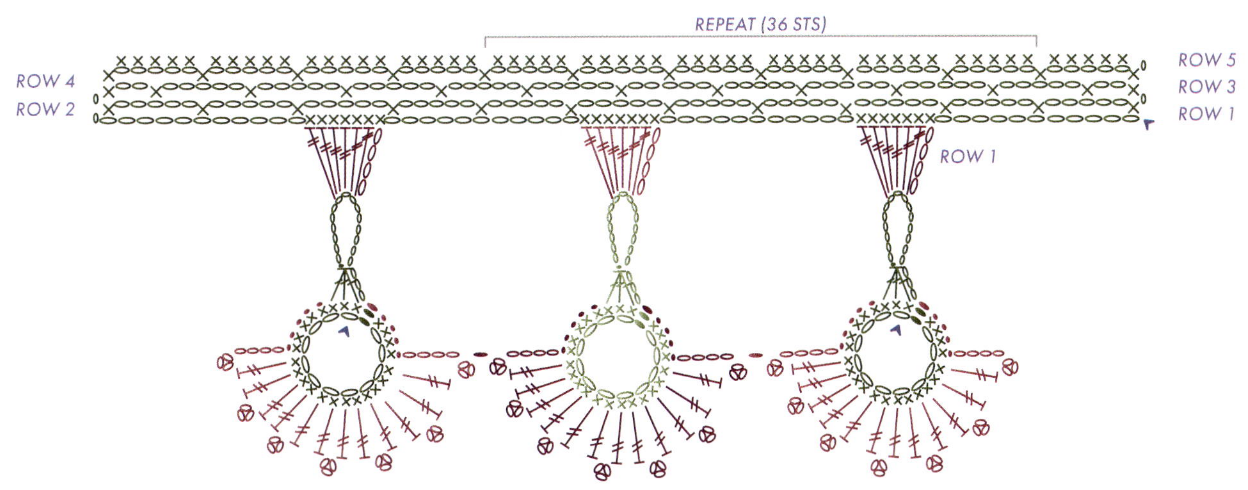

BORDER 138

DIFFICULTY ***

COLORS: (A) Green – Variegated; (B) Raspberry – Variegated; (C) Ink

STITCHES USED: Slip stitch (sl st) • chain (ch) • single crochet (sc) • half double crochet (hdc) • double crochet (dc) • treble crochet (tr)

This edging consists of identical patterns assembled on a support strip.

To make the large triangle (Motif 1), begin with A or B (holding 2 strands).

Row 1: Ch 4, 3 dc in same st.

Row 2: Ch 1 to turn, sc in next 4.

Row 3: Ch 3 to turn, dc in first st, dc in next 2, 2 dc in last st.

Row 4: Ch 1 to turn, sc in next 7.

Row 5: Ch 3 to turn, dc in first st, dc in next 5, 2 dc in last st.

Row 6: Ch 1 to turn, sc in next 9.

Row 7: Ch 3 to turn, dc in first st, dc in next 3, 2 dc in next, dc in next 3, 2 dc in last st.

Row 8: Ch 1 to turn, sc in next 12.

Row 9: Ch 3 to turn, dc in first st, dc in next 10, 2 dc in last st.

Row 10: Ch 1 to turn, sc in next 2, 2 sc in next, sc in next 8, 2 sc in next, sc in last 2.

Crochet as many large triangles as required for desired length, alternating between A and B, and join them together with a sl st after the last sc from Row 10 into the first sc of Row 10 on the previous motif. Make sure the right side is always facing.

On each large triangle made with A, make a small triangle (Motif 2) with B.

To make a small triangle, begin working on first large triangle made with B, inserting hook under fifth sc from Row 6 of Motif 1 (circled in red on the diagram) and pulling up a loop.

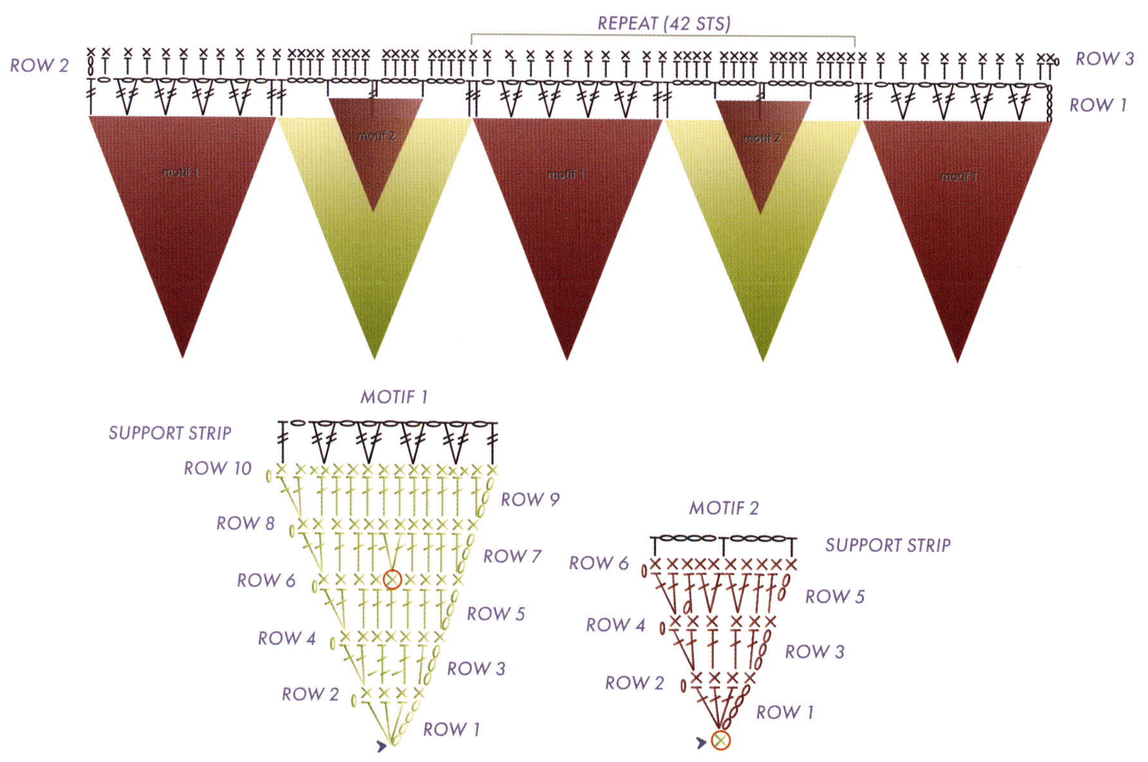

Row 1: Ch 4, 3 dc in same st.

Row 2: Ch 1 to turn, sc in next 4.

Row 3: Ch 3 to turn, dc in first st, dc in next 2, 2 dc in last st.

Row 4: Ch 1 to turn, sc in next 6.

Row 5: Ch 3 to turn, dc in first st, dc in next, [2 dc in next st] twice, dc in next, 2 dc in last st.

Row 6: Ch 1 to turn, sc in next 10. Fasten off.

To crochet the support strip and assemble the motifs, work with right side facing and C.

Row 1: Insert hook in sc at edge of a large motif and pull up a loop, ch 5 (to replace first tr), *[ch 1, skip 2, (tr, ch 1, tr) in next st] 4x, ch 1, skip 2, tr in last st of first motif, tr in next motif, ch 4, hdc in first sc of Motif 2, ch 4, skip 4, hdc between fourth and fifth sc of Motif 2; to join Motif 1, tr in central sc of Motif 1 working behind Motif 2, ch 4, skip 4, hdc in last st of Motif 2; ch 4, tr in last st of Motif 1, tr in first st of next Motif 1*. Repeat from * to * starting with tr in first sc of next Motif 1. End with tr in first sc of last motif, [ch 1, skip 2, (tr, ch 1, tr) in next st] 4x, ch 1, skip 2, tr in last st of last motif.

Row 2: Ch 2 (to turn and replace first hdc), *hdc in next ch, [skip 1, hdc in next ch] 8x, hdc between next 2 tr, [4 hdc in ch-4 space] 4x, hdc between next 2 tr*. Repeat from * to *. End with hdc in next ch, [skip 1, hdc in next ch] 8x, hdc in fifth sl st at beginning of Row 1.

Row 3: Ch 1 to turn, sc in each hdc. Fasten off.

BORDER 139

DIFFICULTY **

COLORS: (A) Violet – Variegated; (B) Currant – Variegated; (C) Olive – Variegated

STITCHES USED: Chain (ch) • single crochet (sc) • half double crochet (hdc) • double crochet (dc) • treble crochet (tr) • ch-3 picot (pic)

This edging consists of a strip decorated with different motifs.

With A, chain a multiple of 20 + 2.

Row 1: Ch 3 (to replace first dc), dc across. Fasten off.

Row 2 (B): Insert hook in first st and pull up a loop, sc in first st, *sc in next 13, 2 hdc in next, dc in next 2, 2 tr in next, dc in next 2, 2 hdc in next*. Repeat from * to *. End with sc in last. Fasten off.

Row 3 (C): *Insert hook in third sc and pull up a loop, sc in same st, skip 4 sc, (2 tr, pic, tr, ch 2, 2 tr, pic, 2 tr, ch 2, 2 tr, pic, tr) in next st, skip 4 sc, sc in next*. Fasten off. Repeat from * to * inserting hook in second sc after last 2 hdc of motif of previous row. Fasten off after each motif.

Row 4: Working on opposite side of starting chain with right side facing, sc across. Fasten off.

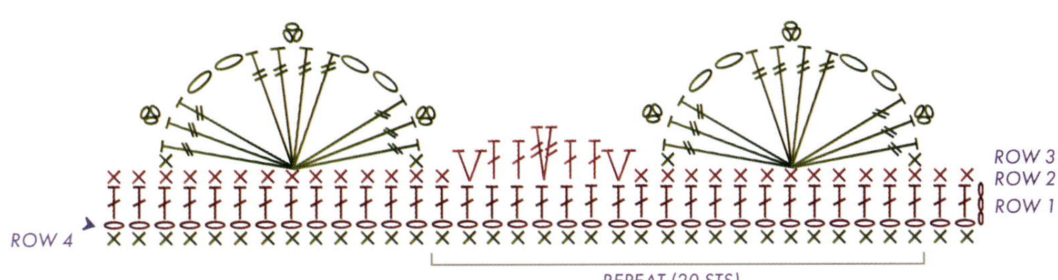

BORDER 140

DIFFICULTY *

COLORS: (A) Green; (B) Violet; (C) Olive; (D) Ink

STITCHES USED: Slip stitch (sl st) • chain (ch) • single crochet (sc) • double crochet (dc) • treble crochet (tr)

This edging consists of patterns joined to each other during work.

With A, ch 8, sl st to close the ring.

Rnd 1 (A or C): Ch 3 (to replace first dc), 21 dc in ring, sl st in third starting ch. Fasten off.

Rnd 2 (B or D): With right side facing, insert hook in a st and pull up a loop, sc in each dc. End with sl st in first st.

Now working back and forth in rows with the same col.

Row 1: Ch 5, 8 tr in same st.

Row 2: Ch 5, 8 tr closed together. Fasten off.

Continue, alternating col. (A with D, and C with B) to desired length. Join circle to previous diamond with a sl st in top of tr-group during Rnd 2.

CUSTOM BORDERS 141–BEYOND

DIFFICULTY *

COLORS: (A) White; (B) Yellow; (C) Red; (D) Blue; (E) Black; (F) Grey

STITCHES USED: Chain (ch) • single crochet (sc) • double crochet (dc)

EMBROIDERY STITCHED USED: Chain stitch

Note: To join the flags, with F, make a support strip: Crochet a starting chain based on the number of sts of the selected flags (between 9 and 12 sts), also count the intervals between motifs (6 or 7 sts) and double those for the ends. Add it all up to crochet the starting chain. Join each flag with 3 dc on the edge of the motif, 1 dc at each end and 1 dc in the center.

Each flag represents a letter in the International Code of Maritime Signals alphabet. You can combine them as you like to write a word or a first name.

FLAG A

With A, ch 9 (you will work widthwise).

Rows 1–6: Ch 1 to turn, sc in next 9. Fasten off after Row 6.

Rows 7–8 (D): Ch 1 to turn, sc in next 9.

Row 9: From here, work one side at a time. Ch 1 to turn, sc in next 4.

Row 10: Ch 1 to turn, skip 1, sc in next 3.

Row 11: Ch 1 to turn, sc in next 3.

Row 12: Ch 1 to turn, skip 1, sc in next 2.

Row 13: End with 2 sc closed together. Fasten off.

Make the second half of Rows 9–13 starting at Row 9.

Row 9: Insert hook in fifth st and pull up a loop, sc in next 4.

Row 10: Ch 1 to turn, sc in next 2, 2 sc closed together.

Row 11: Ch 1 to turn, sc in next 3.

Row 12: Ch 1 to turn, skip 1, sc in next 2.

Row 13: Ch 1 to turn, skip 1, sc in next. Fasten off.

FLAG B

With C, ch 9.

Work as per Flag A but without changing colors.

FLAG C

With A, ch 9 (you will be working height-wise).

Rows 1–4: Ch 1 to turn, 9 sc.

Row 5: Ch 1 to turn, skip 1, sc in next 6, 2 sc closed together.

Rows 6–8: Ch 1 to turn, sc in next 7.

Row 9: Ch 1 to turn, skip 1, sc in next 4, 2 sc closed together.

Rows 10–12: Ch 1 to turn, sc in next 5.

Row 13: Ch 1 to turn, skip 1, sc in next 2, 2 sc closed together.

Rows 14–15: Ch 1 to turn, sc in next 3.

Row 16: Ch 1 to turn, skip 1, sc in next 2.

Row 17: Ch 1, 2 sc closed together. Fasten off.

Create the circle: with C ch 5, sl st to close the ring.

Rnd 1: Ch 1, 9 sc in ring, sl st in first st. Fasten off.

Attach the circle to the width of the third row of sc.

FLAG D

With D, ch 9.

Work as per Flag C.

Make the circle motif with A and attach it as per Flag C.

FLAG E

With C, ch 9 (you will be working height-wise).

Rows 1–4: Ch 1 to turn, sc in next 9.

Row 5: Ch 1 to turn, skip 1, sc in next 6, 2 sc closed together. Fasten off.

Row 6 (A): Insert hook in first st and pull up a loop, sc in next 7.

Rows 7–8: Ch 1 to turn, sc in next 7.

Row 9: Ch 1 to turn, skip 1, sc in next 4, 2 sc closed together.

Rows 10–11: Ch 1 to turn, sc in next 5. Change to next col at last yarn over of last sc. Fasten off.

Row 12 (D): Ch 1 to turn, sc in next 5.

Row 13: Ch 1 to turn, skip 1, sc in next 2, 2 sc closed together.

Rows 14–15: Ch 1 to turn, sc in next 3.

Row 16: Ch 1 to turn, skip 1, sc in next 2.

Row 17: Ch 1 to turn, 2 sc closed together. Fasten off.

FLAG F

With C, ch 9 (you will be working height-wise).

Rows 1–4: Ch 1 to turn, sc in next 9.

Row 5: Ch 1 to turn, skip 1, sc in next 6, 2 sc closed together. Change to next col at last yarn over of last sc. Fasten off.

Rows 6–7 (A): Sc in next 7; at Row 7, change to next col at last yarn over of last sc. Fasten off.

Row 8 (C): Ch 1 to turn, sc in next 7.

Row 9: Ch 1 to turn, skip 1, sc in next 4, 2 sc closed together.

Row 10–12: Ch 1 to turn, sc in next 5.

Row 13: Ch 1 to turn, skip 1, sc in next 2, 2 sc closed together.

Row 14–15: Ch 1 to turn, sc in next 3.

Row 16: Ch 1 to turn, skip 1, sc in next 2.

Row 17: Ch 1, 2 sc closed together. Fasten off.

Finish by creating a white line along the entire height: Fold the flag just made in half along its height, press on the fold to highlight the corresponding sts. With A, crochet a row of sc in corresponding sc at fold, making 16 sc. Working on this row again, sc across, attach to surface with a st in same col. Fasten off.

FLAG G

With B, ch 9 (you will be working height-wise).

Rows 1–4: Ch 1 to turn, sc in next 9.

Row 5: Ch 1 to turn, skip 1, sc in next 6, 2 sc closed together.

Row 6: Ch 1 to turn, sc in next 7. Fasten off.

Row 7 (D): Insert hook and pull up a loop, ch 1 to turn, sc in next 7.

Row 8: Ch 1 to turn, sc in next 7.

Row 9: Ch 1 to turn, skip 1, sc in next 4, 2 sc closed together.

Row 10–12: Ch 1 to turn, sc in next 5.

Row 13: Ch 1 to turn, skip 1, sc in next 2, 2 sc closed together.

Rows 14–15: Ch 1 to turn, sc in next 3.

Row 16: Ch 1 to turn, skip 1, sc in next 2.

Row 17: Ch 1, 2 sc closed together. Fasten off.

FLAG H

With A, ch 9 (you will be working widthwise).

Rows 1–6: Ch 1 to turn, sc in next 9. Fasten off.

Rows 7–12 (C): Ch 1 to turn, sc in next 9. Fasten off.

FLAG I

With B, ch 9 (you will be working widthwise).

Rows 1–12: Ch 1 to turn, sc in next 9.

Fasten off. Make a circle with E as per Flag C and attach to the center.

FLAG J

With D, ch 12 (you will work height-wise).

Rows 1–3: Ch 1 to turn, sc in next 12. Fasten off after Row 3.

Rows 4–6 (A): Ch 1 to turn, sc in next 12. Fasten off after Row 6.

Rows 7–9 (D): Ch 1 to turn, sc in next 12. Fasten off.

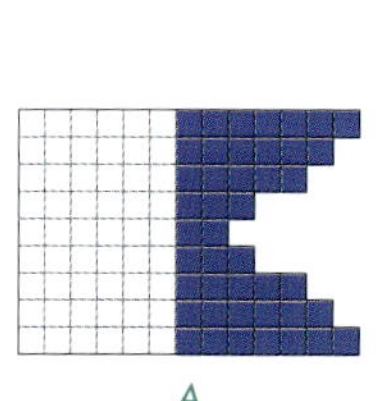
A

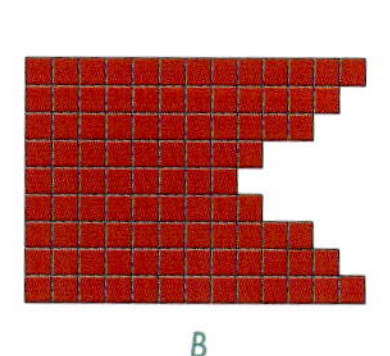
B

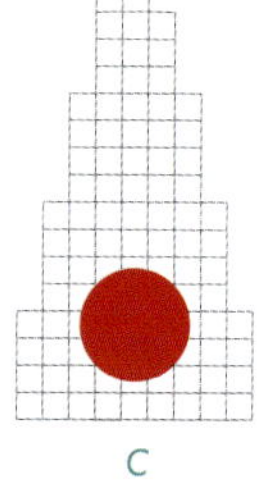
C

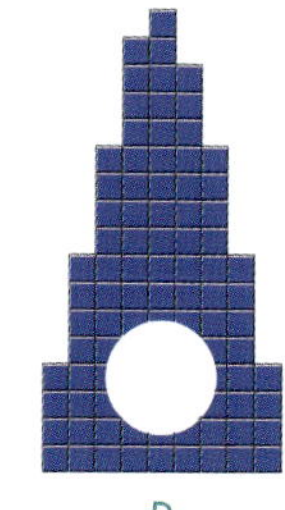
D

E

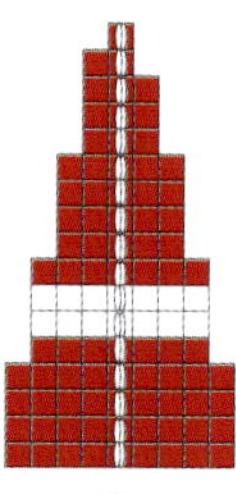
F

G

FLAG K

With B, ch 9 (you will be working widthwise).

Rows 1–6: Ch 1 to turn, sc in next 9. Fasten off after Row 6.

Rows 7–12 (D): Ch 1 to turn, sc in next 9. Fasten off.

FLAG L

Ch 12 with E for first 6 sts and B for next 6 sts (you will be working height-wise).

Work in jacquard: At col changes, cross threads behind work, leaving unused color on standby behind work; on return row, threads will be crossed in front and remain there.

Row 1: Ch 1 to turn, sc in next 6; with E, sc in next 6.

Row 2: Ch 1 to turn; with B, sc in next 6.

Rows 3–4: Repeat Rows 1–2

Row 5: Repeat Row 1. Fasten off.

Join E to first st and repeat Rows 1 to 5, reversing col.

FLAG M

With D, ch 9 (you will be working widthwise).

Rows 1–12: Ch 1 to turn, 9 sc. Fasten off.

Finish by creating the white diagonal lines of the flag. You can either embroider them with the chain stitch or crochet them. To crochet them, fold the motif just made on the diagonal and press on the fold to highlight the corresponding sts. Insert hook in corner st and pull up a loop. With A, crochet a row of sc inserting the hook in the top of the sc corresponding to the fold. Make 11 or 12 sc, depending on your tension. Fasten off. Fold on the other diagonal and working in the same manner, make 4 sc, remove hook from loop, bring loop under first diagonal, cut the length of thread needed to complete the row and pass it under the diagonal, put loop back on hook and make 5 or 6 sc depending on your tension. Fasten off.

FLAG N

Ch 12 with A for the first 10 and D for the next 2 (you will be working widthwise). Work in jacquard: Cross threads behind work, leaving unused color on standby behind work; on return row, threads will be crossed in front and remain there.

Row 1: Ch 1 to turn, sc in next 3; with A, sc in next 3; with D, sc in next 3; with A, sc in next 3.

CIRCLE APPLIQUÉ FOR FLAGS C, D, AND I

Row 2: Ch 1 to turn, with A, sc in next 3; with D, sc in next 3; with A, sc in next 3; with D, sc in next 3.

Row 3: Ch 1 to turn, with A, sc in next 3; with D, sc in next 3; with A, sc in next 3; with D, sc in next 3.

Row 4: Ch 1 to turn, with D, sc in next 3; with A, sc in next 3; with D, sc in next 3; with A, sc in next 3.

Rows 5–8: Repeat Rows 1–4. Fasten off.

FLAG O

Ch 12 with B for the first 11 and C for the last ch (you will be working height-wise). Work in jacquard: Cross threads behind work, leaving unused color on standby behind work; on return row, threads will be crossed in front and remain there.

Row 1: Ch 1 to turn, with C, sc in next; with B, sc in next 11.

Row 2: Ch 1 to turn, with B, sc in next 9; with C, sc in next 3.

Row 3: Ch 1 to turn, with C, sc in next 4; with B, sc in next 8.

Row 4: Ch 1 to turn, with B, sc in next 7; with C, sc in next 5.

Row 5: Ch 1 to turn, with C, sc in next 6; with B, sc in next 6.

Row 6: Ch 1 to turn, with B, sc in next 5; with C, sc in next 7.

Row 7: Ch 1 to turn, with C, sc in next 8; with B, sc in next 4.

Row 8: Ch 1 to turn, with B, sc in next 3; with C, sc in next 9.

Row 9: Ch 1 to turn, with C, sc in next 10; with B, sc in next 2.

Row 10: Ch 1 to turn, with B, sc in next; with C, sc in next 11. Fasten off.

FLAG P

With D, ch 9 (you will be working widthwise). From Rows 3–10, work in jacquard: Cross threads behind work, leaving unused color on standby behind work; on return row, threads will be crossed in front and remain there.

Rows 1–2: Ch 1 to turn, sc in next 9.

Rows 3–10: Ch 1 to turn, sc in next 2, with A, sc in next 5; with D, sc in next 2.

Rows 11–12: Repeat Rows 1–2. Fasten off.

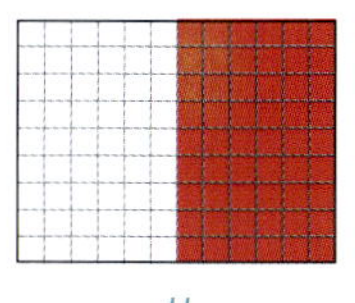

H

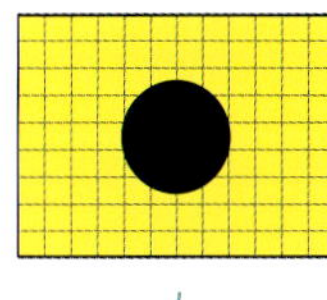

I

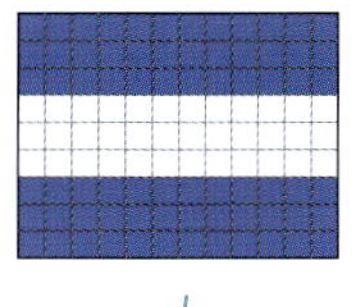

J

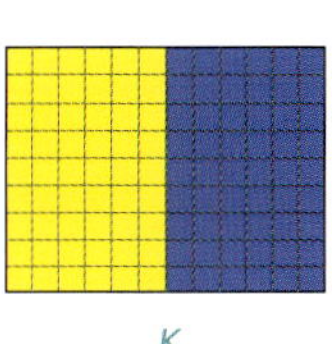

K

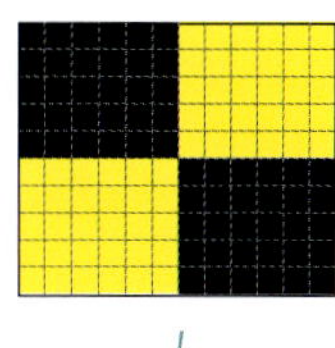

L

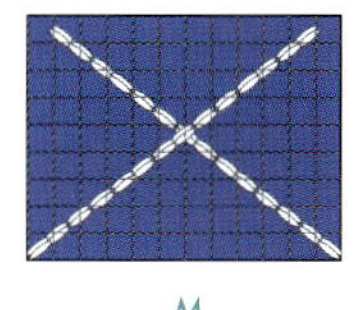

M

N

FLAG Q

With B, ch 9 (you will be working widthwise).

Row 1–12: Ch 1 to turn, sc in next 9. Fasten off.

FLAG R

With C, ch 12 (you will be working height-wise). From Rows 1–4 and 7–10, work in jacquard: Cross threads behind work, leaving unused color on standby behind work; on return row, threads will be crossed in front and remain there.

Rows 1–4 (B and C): Ch 1 to turn, with C, sc in next 5; with B, sc in next 2; with C, sc in next 5. Fasten off C after Row 4.

Rows 5–6 (B): Insert hook and pull up a loop, sc in next 12.

Rows 7–10 (B and C): Repeat Rows 1–4. Fasten off.

FLAG S

With A, ch 10 (you will be working widthwise). From Rows 4–9, work in jacquard: At col changes, cross threads behind work, leaving unused color on standby behind work; on return row, threads will be crossed in front and remain there.

Rows 1–3: Ch 1 to turn, sc in next 10.

Rows 4–10 (A and D): Ch 1 to turn; with A, sc in next 3; with D, sc in next 4; with A, sc in next 3.

Rows 11–13: Repeat Rows 1–3. Fasten off.

FLAG T

With C, ch 9 (you will be working widthwise).

Rows 1–4: Ch 1 to turn, sc in next 9. Fasten off after Row 4.

Rows 5–8 (A): Ch 1 to turn, sc in next 9. Fasten off after Row 8.

Rows 9–12 (D): Ch 1 to turn, sc in next 9. Fasten off.

FLAG U

Ch 12 with A for first 6, and C for next 6 (you will work height-wise). Work in jacquard: At col changes, cross threads behind work, leaving unused color on standby behind work; on return row, threads will be crossed in front and remain there.

Row 1: Ch 1 to turn, with C, sc in next 6; with A, sc in next 6.

Row 2: Ch 1 to turn, with A, sc in next 6; with C, sc in next 6.

Row 3: Repeat Row 1.

Row 4: Repeat Row 2.

Row 5: Repeat Row 1. Fasten off.

Row 6: With C, insert hook in first st and pull up a loop, sc in next 6; with A, sc in next 6.

Row 7: Ch 1 to turn, with A, sc in next 6; with C, sc in next 6.

Row 8: Repeat Row 6.

Row 9: Repeat Row 7.

Row 10: Repeat Row 6. Fasten off.

FLAG V

With A, ch 9 (you will be working widthwise).

Rows 1–12: Ch 1 to turn, sc in next 9. Fasten off.

Finish with the red diagonal lines of the flag. You can embroider them or crochet them. To crochet them, fold the motif just made on the diagonal and press on the fold to highlight the corresponding sts. Insert hook in corner st and pull up a loop. With C, crochet a row of sc inserting the hook in the top of the sc corresponding to the fold. Make 11 or 12 sc, depending on your tension. Fasten off. Fold on the other diagonal and working in the same manner, make 4 sc, remove hook from loop, bring loop under first diagonal, cut the length of thread needed to complete the row and pass it under the diagonal, put loop back on hook and make 5 or 6 sc depending on your tension. Fasten off.

FLAG W

With D, ch 12 (you will be working height-wise). From Rows 3–7, work in jacquard: At col changes, cross threads behind work, leaving unused color on standby behind work; on return row, threads will be crossed in front and remain there.

Rows 1–2: Ch 1 to turn, sc in next 12.

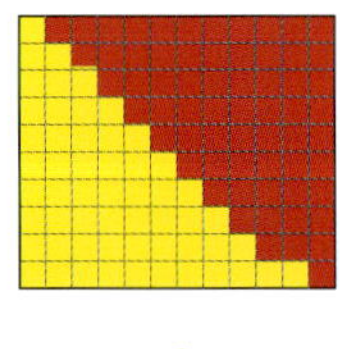
O

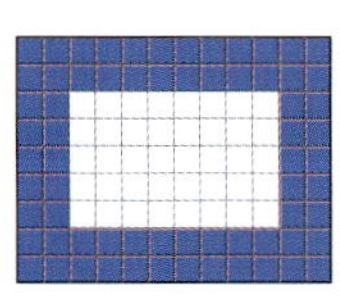
P

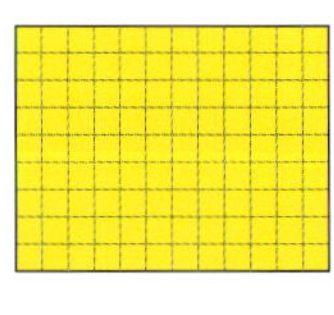
Q

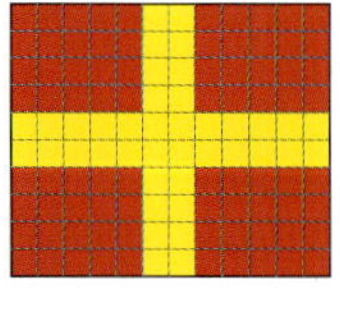
R

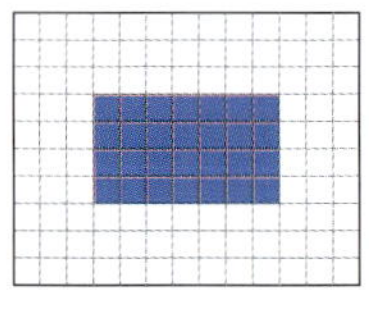
S

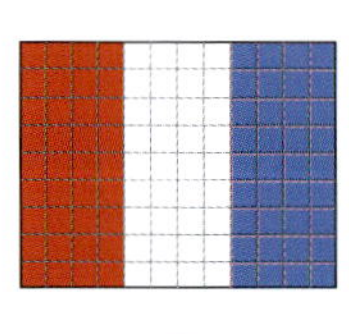
T

Row 3 (A and D): Ch 1 to turn, with D, sc in next 2; with A, sc in next 8; with D, sc in next 2.

Rows 4–6 (A, C and D): Ch 1 to turn, with D, sc in next 2; with A, sc in next; with C, sc in next 6; with A, sc in next; with D, sc in next 2.

Row 7: Repeat Row 3. Fasten off C.

Rows 8–9: Repeat Rows 1–2. Fasten off.

FLAG X

With A, ch 12 (you will be working height-wise). From Rows 1–4 and 7–10, work in jacquard: At col changes, cross threads behind work, leaving unused color on standby behind work; on return row, threads will be crossed in front and remain there.

Rows 1–4 (A and D): Ch 1 to turn, with A, sc in next 5; with D, sc in next 2; with A, sc in next 5. After Row 4, fasten off A.

Rows 5–6 (D): Insert hook and pull up a loop, sc in next 12.

Rows 7–10 (A and D): Repeat Rows 1–4. Fasten off.

FLAG Y

With B, ch 9 (you will be working widthwise).

Rows 1–12: Ch 1 to turn, 9 sc.

Fasten off. Embroider the stripes using the chain st. Fold motif on the diagonal and press on the fold to highlight the corresponding sts. With C, embroider chain sts on the fold. On either side of the diagonal, embroider 2 more evenly spaced parallel stripes.

FLAG Z

With C, ch 12 (you will be working height-wise). From Rows 2–10, work in jacquard: At col changes, cross threads behind work, leaving unused color on standby behind work; on return row, threads will be crossed in front and remain there.

Row 1: Ch 1 to turn, sc in next 12.

Row 2 (C, D, and E): Ch 1 to turn, with E, sc in next; with C, sc in next 10; with D, sc in next.

Row 3: Ch 1 to turn, with D, sc in next 3; with C, sc in next 6; with E, sc in next 3.

Row 4: Ch 1 to turn, with E, sc in next 4; with C, sc in next 4; with D, sc in next 4.

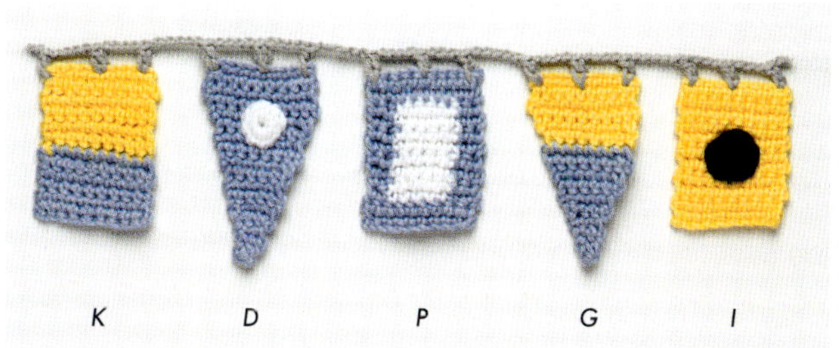

Row 5: Ch 1 to turn, with D, sc in next 5; with C, sc in next 2; with E, sc in next 5.

Row 6 (D and E): Ch 1 to turn, with E, sc in next 6; with D, sc in next 6.

Row 7 (B, D, and E): Ch 1 to turn, with D, sc in next 5; with B, sc in next 2; with E, sc in next 5.

Row 8: Ch 1 to turn, with E, sc in next 4; with B, sc in next 4; with D, sc in next 4.

Row 9: Ch 1 to turn, with D, sc in next 3; with B, sc in next 6; with E, sc in next 3.

Row 10: Ch 1 to turn, with E, sc in next; with B, sc in next 10; with D, sc in next. Fasten off.

Row 11 (B): Insert hook and pull up a loop, sc in next 12. Fasten off.

PILOT'S FLAG

With C, ch 10 (you will work widthwise). From Rows 3–10, work in jacquard: Cross threads behind work, leaving unused color on standby behind work; on return row, threads will be crossed in front and remain there.

Rows 1–2: Ch 1 to turn, sc in next 10.

Rows 3–4 (A and C): Ch 1 to turn, with C, sc in next 2; with A, sc in next 8; with C, sc in next 2.

Rows 5–8 (A, C, and D): Ch 1 to turn, with C, sc in next 2; with A, sc in next 2; with D, sc in next 4; with A, sc in next 2, with C, sc in next 2.

Rows 9–10: Repeat Rows 3–4.

Rows 11–12: Repeat Rows 1–2.

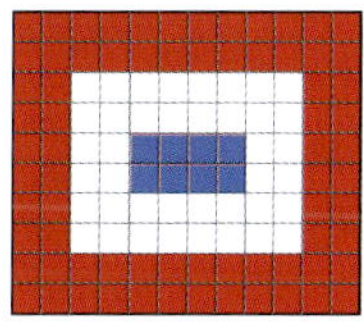

PILOT'S FLAG

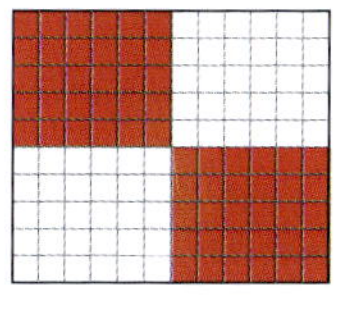

U

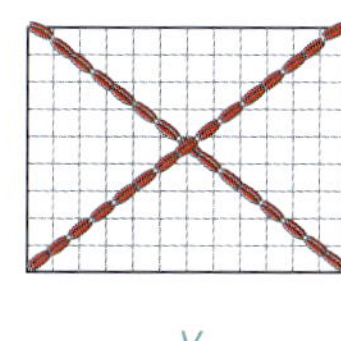

V

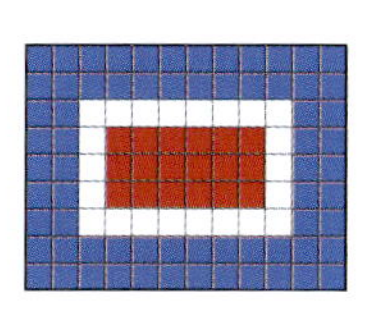

W

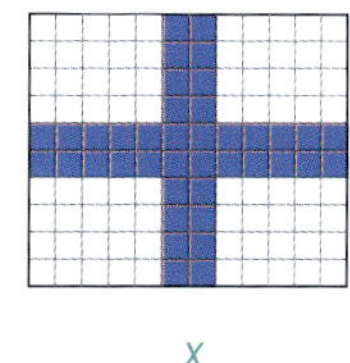

X

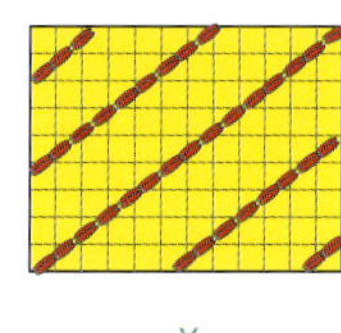

Y

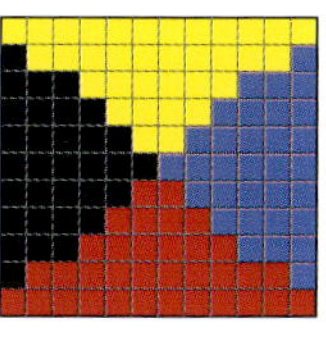

Z

CHART KEY

- Start
- Chain (ch)
- Slip stitch (sl st)
- Single crochet (sc)
- Single crochet behind the picot
- Crab stitch
- Half double crochet (hdc)
- Double crochet (dc)
- Treble crochet (tr)
- Front post treble crochet (FPtr)
- Double treble crochet (dtr)
- Chain-3 picot
- 2 single crochet together (2sctog)
- Elongated single crochet
- Crossed single crochet
- 2-half double crochet cluster
- 2-double crochet cluster
- 3-double crochet cluster
- 5-double crochet cluster